The Golden Bowl
Be Broken

PEASANT LIFE IN
FOUR CULTURES

Richard Critchfield

The Golden Bowl
Be Broken

PEASANT LIFE IN
FOUR CULTURES

Indiana University Press

BLOOMINGTON / LONDON

CONTENTS

PHOTOGRAPHS BY THE AUTHOR

ACKNOWLEDGMENTS

Tʜɪs ʙᴏᴏᴋ ʀᴇᴘʀᴇsᴇɴᴛs ᴀ ᴄᴏɴᴅᴇɴsᴀᴛɪᴏɴ of a 400,000-word report prepared for the Alicia Patterson Fund in New York, which sponsored the study. I wish to express my deepest appreciation to its executive secretary, Richard H. Nolte.

For their help, advice or analysis, I am also grateful to Dr. A. E. Boerma, Chester Bowles, Lester R. Brown, Samuel Bunker, Elizabeth Carter, Ralph Cummings, Jr., Gaetan de Chazal, Julian Fromer, Chadbourne Gilpatric, J. George Harrar, Eugene H. King, Wolf Ladijinsky, Robert S. McNamara, Daniel P. Moynihan, Diana Prior-Palmer, Jean Perrot, Odile Puesh, Seewoosagur Ramgoolam, M. S. Randhawa, Walt W. Rostow, Lt. Gen. Ali Sadikin, Hazaree Singh, Khushwant Singh, T. S. Sohal, Irene Taueber, Barbara Ward, Judy Bird Williams, and the many helpful officials of the governments of Iran, Mauritius, India, Pakistan and Indonesia, the Agency for International Development, the United States Information Service, the World Bank, the French Archeological Mission to Iran, the Indian Agricultural Research Institute, Punjab Agricultural University, and the United Nations Food and Agriculture Organization. I also wish to thank Newbold Noyes, the editor of my newspaper, *The Washington Star-News,* for generously granting me two years' leave to undertake this project.

As is evident, I owe a great debt of gratitude to my interpreters: Sherif Fawzli, Karim Kurd, Husein Parvini, Rafat, Dhanilall Thug, Krishanjit Singh, Bur Rasuanto, Bujung, Tjasidi and Widgna Tarma Husen. This book would not have been possible without their hard work, good humor, enthusiasm and forbearance. Nor without the kindness and hospitality of the people in all four rural settings.

Finally, it is to Jacob, Prem and Octave, Charan, Husen and Karniti that I owe more than I can put into words. It has been a great pleasure getting to know them and to share a few of their days on this good earth.

[vii

INTRODUCTION

Letters from Calcutta

...and the clouds return after the rain; in the day when the keepers of the house tremble and strong men are bent, and the grinders cease because they are few, and those that look through the windows are dimmed, and the doors on the street are shut; when the sound of the grinding is low, and one rises up at the voice of a bird, and all the daughters of song are brought low; and they are afraid also of what is high, and terrors are in the way; the almond tree blossoms, the grasshopper drags itself along and desire fails; because man goes to his eternal home and the mourners go about the streets; before the silver cord be snapped, or the golden bowl be broken, or the pitcher be broken at the fountain, or the wheel broken at the cistern, and the dust returns to the earth as it was....

—ECCLESIASTES

THIS BOOK WAS WRITTEN to try to shed a little more light on our changing human environment through true stories about the daily lives and present predicaments of four of its more representative inhabitants. These include a Bedouin on the Mesopotamian desert, whose way of life has endured ten thousand years but is now vanishing; an African Creole fisherman on the southern Indian Ocean island of Mauritius, where over-population has led to social breakdown and visions of the Apocalypse; a newly prosperous Sikh farmer in a Punjabi village in northern India, who is making the transition from subsistence agriculture to modern commercial farming; and a poor Javanese rice peasant, who must migrate to the city of Djakarta to survive. The stories are intended to touch on the historical background of agricultural society, the present population crisis, the transfer to Western farm technology to meet it, and the urbanization this helps to produce.

The four differ from each other and from us in their environmental settings, life-styles, aspirations and view of man's place in nature. Yet they are all centrally affected by the sudden, calamitous growth within their lifetimes of the world's population, which, freed by medical science, will soon reach four billion and could be increasing by a billion more every year by the time of Thomas Malthus' tercentenary. There has never before been anything like this increase in the number of human beings. Its greatest impact is upon the world's poor. We have considerable information today about the geography, history, economics, politics and customs of such people. Yet we know little about *them*. How they think and feel, what they worry about, argue over, anticipate and enjoy; the pain and suffering, the fun and laughter, the avid intense living of life in the unreported villages and urban slums all around us.

Under the pressures of population, the environment is changing

[3

so fast one writer has described the world of the 1970s as "a new political country, unexplored, ominous, planetary in scale, and conceivably, bordering on the end of time."

This book is based on a twenty-one-month journey, an exploration, really, into this new countryside of the world. During this period a series of interpreters and myself lived successively in a black-tented Arab desert encampment, a thatched tropical island fishing hut off the coast of Africa, a Punjabi cattlebarn, a Javanese bamboo cottage and the slum shantytowns of a great Asian city, sleeping on carpets, string cots or straw mats, eating mostly unleavened bread or rice washed down with tea, coffee, rum or homemade liquor, and losing our preconceived notions of Afro-Asian villages as dreary collections of huts, flies, grim fatalistic inhabitants, misery and no fun; none of the settings were sad at all; they were cheerful and possessed of an intensity of life beyond all my expectations. Illness proved no problem, and if the lack of sanitary facilities took some getting used to, this proved more of a cultural than a physical obstacle.

As will be self-evident, I owe a debt of gratitude to the late Oscar Lewis and his technique of portraying the daily life of ordinary people by drawing upon detailed observation, interviews and recorded conversation. Although used selectively, all of the dialogue in this book is taken verbatim from more than a million words written down by my interpreters or myself, as spoken or soon afterward. Some material, as in the flashbacks, or when it was necessary to clarify a point, was obtained through direct interviews, and I have taken the liberty of transposing some of this as thoughts. The complete dialogue, as recorded from day to day, is available at the Mass Communications History Center, the State Historical Society of Wisconsin in Madison.

In the introduction to *Five Families,* his Mexican case studies in the culture of poverty, Lewis wrote: "This book has grown out of my conviction that anthropologists have a new function in the modern world; to serve as students and reporters of the great mass of peasants and urban dwellers of the underdeveloped countries who constitute almost 80 percent of the world's population." I suppose, as a professional reporter, I have started from the opposite direction.

Yet while a journalist is not an anthropologist, the fundamental approach is the same: to understand people, whether in traditional village environments or uprooted into great city slums, it is necessary to live with them, share their good times and their bad, and eventually come to identify with them. Early on I discovered the value of engaging in the same daily physical labor as the men I was writing about, perhaps because hard work was the basic fact in all their lives; after I spent many days with them helping them to herd sheep, spear octopus, harvest wheat or whatever they were doing, a barrier of reserve was overcome, and in time the principal characters began to take our mutual enterprise very seriously and developed what might be called a strong sense of integrity. I suppose it was a kind of mutual commitment. Gradually, my interpreters and I developed a routine: they normally noted down the dialogue during the working day while I pitched in as a fairly silent co-laborer; and we relaxed with the principal characters in the evening, doing perhaps more drinking than one might have expected.

It is a fair question how much our presence influenced the subjects. My own feeling is that it was very little, partly because we spent several preliminary weeks or months with them, getting to know them and waiting for something to happen, before the stories which follow actually unfolded. Somehow they always did. For instance, we lived in the Punjab village almost three months before the harvest dispute of the story began. The Mauritian fishing expedition described took place on New Year's Eve, after we had been with them since September. Plenty of time and luck, shared physical labor and, in some cases, drinking together, were the essential ingredients of the effort. I do not appear in the stories, in hopes that you will see Jacob, Prem and Octave, Charan, Husen and all the others much as I did. All of them came to want their stories to be as natural and honestly true as I could make them; it is at their request that I departed from my original intention and have used real names, making no attempt to preserve anonymity.

A word about language: the first three stories posed no real problem, but I have left the dialogue of Husen, the Javanese peasant, largely in broken English. After years as a seasonal migrant to Djakarta, Husen spoke the peculiar argot of that city's poorer classes, which is as far from standard English as, say, the language of many young ghetto dwellers in this country. Husen possessed considerable knowledge of English and, for this reason, when possible, he serves here as his own interpreter, in my hope of capturing some of his flavor.

The idea of writing a book on peasants really goes back to an experience in Calcutta, during my first visit to Asia fifteen years ago. To quote from some letters I wrote at the time:

"Nothing prepares you for Calcutta. I am comfortably wearing a sweater in my frigidly air-conditioned room at the Great Eastern Hotel but outside it is as dank and steamy as any tropical rain forest. On top of blistering heat that melts the tar in the streets, there is almost 100 percent humidity. Yet on the sidewalk outside on Chowringhee Street, hundreds of half-naked, emaciated men, women and children are stretched out under the arcades, sleeping on threadbare cloths. A barefooted coolie passes, pulling a fat Chinese woman in his rickshaw; they say most of the rickshaw men are tubercular and only last a year or two. I can hear the ebb and flow of late evening traffic, the rattle of trams, the eerie jingle of rickshaw bells and haunting clomp-clomp of horses' hooves. I have just returned through Dharmatala Road, a frightening melange of thousands of naked light bulbs, surging people and beggars—blind, crippled, leprous; a whining woman with a naked baby clutched to her breast; a young girl with a lovely face and no feet or hands; she clumped upon wooden blocks strapped to her knees and elbows. . . . So many maimed children—they say made so deliberately at birth by criminals who collect their earnings each night. . . .

"I sought refuge in the air-conditioned splendor of a place called Firpo's; there was a burly Sikh, turbaned and whiskered, with a shotgun at the entrance. Dark inside. The lighting was so dim you could hardly see the women, elegant in gold-trimmed saris; the men all in white, their pale Bengali faces turned to watch a wan Anglo-Indian girl with hennaed hair sing "Blue Moon." Later chorus girls in g-strings macabrely pelted the audience with cotton snowballs while the band played "Winter Wonderland." When people walked to the street, swarms of beggars attacked them like flies, but the rich sent them away, without even looking at them, with an automatic sort of flick of the wrist. Friends drove me home in an old lemon-colored Armstrong-Sidley roadster; we sped through the streets the horn blasting away, just missing some pedestrians by inches. I was told that if you hit someone just keep going; otherwise a mob might gather and tear you to pieces. . . . There is real wealth here as well as poverty. Calcutta's jute industry is the mainstay of the Indian economy and 15 percent of the country's manufacturing industry is based here, as well as 40 percent of its import-export trade. The city produces a third of the nation's bank transactions and a third of its national tax revenue. And even the average annual income per head is the third highest in India, just behind Delhi and Bombay, although with so many destitute people a few must be very rich. . . .

"This morning I visited Kalighat, one of the most famous and gruesome of Hindu temples. Kali, the mother goddess of destruction who gives Calcutta its name, appears with fiendish eyes and a tongue dripping blood, with a garland of human skulls. Pilgrims drank and rubbed their hair and faces with a filthy mixture of Ganges water, crushed flower petals and goat's milk; it came out a drain below the temple after being poured over the idol of Kali. In the courtyard was a chopping block where rams and male buffaloes are sacrificed; the ground was covered with congealed blood. Women, said to be barren, rubbed the blood on their foreheads in hope that Kali would grant them children. The thuggees in central India used to murder pilgrims and travellers by the thousands as sacrifices to Kali; they befriended their victims on the trails then strangled them at night by the campsites, breaking their arms and legs before burying them; some say the practice still goes on. . . .

"This afternoon, not far from my hotel on Chowringhee Street, I met a shoeshine boy who spoke English. He said he had been adopted as a small child by American soldiers stationed here during the war. He no sooner invited me for tea in a kind of kiosk where he shines shoes, than a monsoon storm broke and I spent a couple of hours sitting under the roof talking with about twenty Hindus and Moslems. All were either shoeshine boys, beggars or pickpockets. A meal was served from a big tiffin can. It was rice and curry, mixed together, scraped off the plates at a nearby government canteen by some enterprising Bengali, garbage really. One portion costs two annas or about ten cents. It was dumped in a big pile on a newspaper and everyone squatted around in a circle avidly eating with his fingers. One man had two small children with him. His wife had died, and they played with a rag in the kiosk all day as he shined shoes. Another used to work on the docks along the Hooghly River until he was let off after a crate fell on his arm and crushed it. Now he begs. Each day is much the same. They bathe in the morning in a fish pond on the Maidan or big park, sit in the kiosk all day waiting for customers and sleep on some torn mats at night. They wear grimy *dhotis,* or cloths wrapped around like trousers, and torn, sleeveless singlets with holes where their glistening brown chests show through. No shoes, of course; each had what they call a *gom-cha,* a piece of faded red cheese-cloth which serves as towel, shawl, blanket or whatever and is always carried over one shoulder. These men of Chowringhee look alike: dark brown skins, for most of them are peasants from Orissa or Bihar who migrated here looking for work. Some have rags tied around their coarse black hair against the fierce sun or sudden monsoon rains. They are cheerful, remarkably so. They have shy, diffident manners and tend to grin when you speak to them, bobbing their heads to one side. A few are shaven-headed with a single long lock of hair at the crown; this is for Yama, the god of death, to seize when they die and he takes the spirit from the corpse. Well, tonight I am flying to Bangkok. I shall be relieved to get out of here. One feels a constant sense of apprehension in Calcutta. . . .

"Well, here I am, still in Calcutta. Wednesday afternoon a few hours before flight time the worst cyclone in sixteen years swept in from the Bay of Bengal. Today, though most of the cyclone has spent itself, squalls drench the city every few hours. The drainage system, said to be a century old, has backed up so that most streets are under a foot or two of water. Outside Calcutta, the surrounding countryside of West Bengal is inundated. Whole mud villages have collapsed, thousands are stranded and the official death toll is already in the hundreds. The fear is that Damodar Dam above the city will burst; government engineers are discharging water steadily and flooding the valley below. The town of Budwan, with 75,000 inhabitants, has been evacuated. In Calcutta itself, some twenty-thousand rickshaw men, running barefoot through water up to their knees and axles, are pulling passengers as best they can, the only means of transportation in the city. None of the trams and buses can run. There is serious damage to the rice crop. Nehru has personally given five thousand rupees to start an emergency food fund and there are already Communist-led rice riots. Several times I have seen howling mobs running down the streets. Sometimes I think I wasted these last two years studying German in Innsbruck and Vienna; Asia is so different from Europe. . . . I wonder how my friends on Chowringhee are faring in this rain. . . .

"Something has happened; let me see if I can explain it. I went to the airlines office but Dum Dum airport is still closed and it was anybody's guess when we can take off for Bangkok. Fighting down feelings of claustrophobia I started back to the hotel but got caught in a downpour, a torrent of solid shafts of water coming straight down; you could hardly see. There were no rickshaws in sight and by the time I reached the kiosk on Chowringhee, I was wading knee-deep in the filthiest water I ever saw. I was about at the end of my rope when I saw the men at the kiosk. They were huddling and shivering in a little group in the center as the rain whipped in and lashed at them from all sides. I thought, they must have been there all this time . . . I suppose they had absolutely no other place to go. The two babies, wet and naked, were sniffling and choking in their father's arms. Everyone looked wet through; they seemed hungry and their eyes were darkened as if feverish or very tired. With the streets awash they had no way to make money. The expressions of a few appeared baleful and I started to cross the road, fearing they might set upon me for money or out of sheer hate in their desperation. . . . But someone called out. . . .

"As soon as I turned back the others recognized me and they cried out in dismay that the "sahib" was wet; someone ran to fetch a dry box to sit upon. In a minute someone else came running, somehow producing a cup of hot tea. It was a trivial gesture perhaps, easily intended, but when I looked at their wet, hungry, trembling faces, half-numb and shivering with cold and lack of food and yet eager, cheerful, triumphantly alive, something snapped inside of me. It happened just like that, like a sharp pain, and I could not look at them but quickly turned away and went off into the rain. I never went back but wandered aimlessly, mindlessly through the streets of Calcutta for hours, afraid, really afraid for the first time in my life, as if in those men's faces I had seen the awful sufferance of grace."

[9

That was in 1959. Today Calcutta is a city gone mad. Since 1967 the city and West Bengal have undergone spasms of chaos sponsored by the Marxists. The purpose of the violence has been to increase Communist power, a strategy since helped by the breakup of Pakistan and the struggle for survival of Bangladesh. The possibility is raised of the two Bengals reuniting in some distant future in a new independent, revolutionary and possibly ungovernable republic.

Calcutta seems unlikely to reach fifteen million people as is sometimes predicted; it may be the first city of the industrial age to be dying. How the end may come, in a plague of disease, a reversion to savagery, a nightmare of knives and tearing claws against the rich, one can only imagine. In such poisoned air, the mindlessness and indifference of the rich is inescapably being answered by hate. The worst fear for the future, as the four stories—which in a way are only one story—try to show, springs from urbanization; one can only hope Calcutta remains just a place and not a generalized human condition.

It is in memory of an afternoon long ago in Calcutta that I should like to dedicate this book to the beggars of Chowringhee Street; and to my mother and father.

R.C.

Bannockburn Farm
Oakton, Virginia
AND
Djakarta, Java

I

Jacob

TCHOGHA ZANBIL

THE MESOPOTAMIAN PLAIN

Jacob

Sherif

Husein

I

No Arab shall pitch his tent there
No shepherd will make his flocks lie down there
But wild beasts will lie down there
And its houses will be full of howling creatures;
There ostriches will dwell
And there satyrs will dance
Hyenas will cry in its towers
And jackals in its pleasant palaces.

　　—*The Second Isaiah*

. . . while Jacob was a quiet man, dwelling in tents.

　　—*The Book of Genesis*

MORNING. THE SUN HAS RISEN. Concealed by wisps of cloud and desert dust, it strives to shed its light on earth; its beams radiate to all sides and flood a golden light on the horizon.

Sand dunes—grassless, poisonous and salty—fade into the distance; one cannot see the end of them. Wind whistles over the dunes, lifting sand from the crust. A spiral cloud of dust gets up from the sand and flees over the dunes, drawing after it bits of brush, dirt and feathers; in a darkening, twisting column it rises toward the sky. Alarmed by the whirlwind and not understanding the disturbance, a dusty hyena crawls out of the brush, looks about with his old murderous eyes, and trots across the wasteland. An eagle circles, watching him, flashing its wings in the sun's glare. In the sand, small black beetles stir, scuttling along, placid, heedless, leaving little scratches in the hard crust with their tiny claws. Little by little the sun rises higher; an invisible power fetters the wind and the air, lays the dust;

and once more, as if nothing has ever disturbed it, the stagnant stillness of eons settles over the great Mesopotamian Plain.

As the dust settles, visible to the north is a great pyramid of earth, a mountain inexplicably arising from the desert flatness. Only when the air clears can the many brick levels be perceived, the enormous archways, supporting walls and ceremonial staircases of a gigantic ruined temple. Up close, its eroded slopes are seen to be not of earth at all but of vast heaps of debris and rubbish: potsherds, broken bricks, fragments of statues, shards of sickles and spears and human teeth and bones.

Until it was discovered and unearthed in recent decades the temple's surface was buried beneath drifts of sand, and wandering Bedouin herdsmen called it simply Tchogha Zanbil, or "overturned basket of earth." Not completely excavated until the 1960s, it was identified by French archeologists from the Louvre as Dur Untashi, the royal temple of the Elamites, who together with the neighboring Sumerians, invented irrigation, writing, mathematics and astrology, founded the first cities and waged the first wars almost six thousand years ago. Today some twenty of these lofty, pyramid-like temple structures, called ziggurats, have been found on the Mesopotamian Plain; Dur Untashi is the largest and best preserved. Our first attempt at monumental architecture, a ziggurat was a great artificial mountain, dwarfing even the Egyptian pyramids, with many step-like levels crowned by a sky-blue temple housing the gods of storm and fertility, the forces the first settled cultivators would naturally worship. One, perhaps even Dur Untashi itself, is believed to have inspired the story of the Tower of Babel.

To the sheep-raising Semitic nomads who wrote the Old Testament, the ziggurats must have seemed like supreme symbols of human arrogance:

> And as men migrated in the east, they found a plain in the land of Shinar and settled there. . . . And they said to one another . . . 'Come, let us build ourselves a city, and a tower with its top in the heaven, and let us make a name for ourselves, lest we be scattered abroad upon the face of the whole earth.'

Today we know the plain was the Mesopotamian and that the land of Shinar was Sumer; recent archeological discoveries suggest that irrigation, which made an agricultural surplus and urban civilization possible, was probably first developed in Elam, just to the northeast of Sumer and the site of Dur Untashi. While there is some evidence that man used grain along the Nile as early as 13,000 B.C.—logical since it was in the African jungles he left the apes to walk erect on the plains, between one and two million years ago—the still most widely accepted theory is that he first became a shaper of the animal and vegetable life around him, rather than a mere predator upon it, around 11,000 to 9,000 B.C. on the Central Asian plateau. Here, north of the Zagros and Anatolia mountains, wild wheat, barley, sheep and goats still abound today.

What is firmly established is that with the retreat of the glaciers and the progressive drying up of the valleys of the plateau, animals gradually descended into newly formed grasslands and onto the Mesopotamian plain, and men followed them.

Once on the plain, the population diverged into two distinct life styles: hunters, who found field labor little to their liking and adopted instead the arts of the herdsman—of whom about fifteen million still survive in Central Asia, the Middle East and North Africa today—and mankind's first sedentary peasant farmers, whose food surpluses made possible the first towns and then the rise of urban civilization. As in the book of Genesis—"Abel was a keeper of sheep and Cain a tiller of the soil"—a perennial warfare developed between them that continues to this day. Only among the nomads has the traditional discipline of early man, the hunter, lived on: a system of patrilineal families, unity of kinship groups under the authority of a chieftain responsible for daily decisions as to where to seek pasture or pitch tents, with great importance attached to the courage and male prowess of the warrior.

This pastoralist bias is pronounced in the Book of Genesis: the Fall from the Garden of Eden after eating from the tree of knowledge; God's curse upon Adam, that his backbreaking toil will bring him no more than bare subsistence; the slaying of Abel by Cain.

One can easily imagine from the Tower of Babel story how the first cities, with the splendor of their palaces and temples, as well as their extraordinary cruelty, violence and vice, must have looked to the simple desert nomad tribes in their black tent encampments some distance from the city walls. At that time the landscape along the alluvial channels of the Tigris, Euphrates and Karun rivers was lush with fields of wheat and barley, vineyards and vegetable plots; here and there date palms rose out of tropical marshlands of reeds and rushes; there was an abundance of lotus trees and bamboo thickets, vivid orchards with glassy green fruit, and forests with gazelles, lions and hyenas. Few but the field slaves were aware of a gathering environmental crisis, the lack of salination and drainage, which would eventually lead to agricultural collapse.

To the nomads, the orgiastic religious processions to the ziggurats must have been especially an abomination. One can well imagine the panting, prancing bodies, dancing around the godhead and driving each other on: youths with elaborately curled beards and long hair, clasping the horns of sacrificial rams; young girls in transparent gowns uttering shrieks, with heads flung back and tambourines high in the air; the musicians with their blaring rams' horns, cymbals, flutes, lyres and drums, and the priests, shaven-headed and stark naked, bearing high the great green god of rain and storm, Enlil, "King of Heaven and Earth." Without Enlil, they chanted, "No cities would be built, no settlements founded, no stalls constructed, no sheepfolds erected, no king enthroned, no high priest born. . . . In field and meadow, the rice grain would not flower; the trees planted in the mountain forest would not yield fruit."

The destruction of these cities was a constant theme of the desert prophets, starting with Sodom and Gomorrah. Babylon was the prophets' supreme symbol of urban vice. But after it no kingdom's fall was more celebrated than Elam's. Jeremiah quotes the Lord, "Behold I will break the bow of Elam, the mainstay of their might, and I will bring upon Elam the four winds of the four quarters of heaven and I will scatter them to all those winds. . . ."

True to the prophecy, Elam, the most probable birthplace of settled village agriculture and the urbanization it made possible, was totally destroyed along with its entire population of several million by chariot-borne Assyrians in twenty-eight days in 640 B.C. Assurbanipal, the Assyrian ruler, vowed to wipe Elam off the face of the earth, and did.

The Assyrians razed Elam's three-thousand-year-old capital of Susa and fourteen other cities, and massacred or carried off all their people. Assurbanipal ordered salt to be poured on the plain, which by then had supported a settled agricultural society for almost eight thousand years, so that it would never again be fertile. He saved until last the destruction of the great ziggurat of Dur Untashi, and even ransacked its underground catacombs to unearth the bones of ancient Elamite heroes; these were taken to Nineveh where libations were offered to awaken the dead souls so they could taste the bitterness of defeat. Assurbanipal boasted to posterity: "The dust of the cities of Elam, I have taken it all away to the country of Assur. . . . I deprived the country of the presence of cattle and of sheep and of the sound of joyous music. I have allowed wild beasts, serpents, the animals of the desert and gazelles to occupy it."

So successful was he that for almost twenty-six centuries or until just a few years ago the greatest of man's first temples was lost beneath the desert sands, left, fulfilling Biblical prophecy, to hyenas and jackals and wandering Bedouin nomads. Our first narrative tells of a day in the life of such a nomad, an Arab shepherd who sets out to graze his sheep among the debris of man's oldest and, to this day, longest-enduring urban civilization.

I N HIS BLACK BEDOUIN TENT, Jacob had been the first to awake, rolling up his woolen quilt on the strip of carpeting where he slept. Buttoning the collar of his cross-stitched robe and wrapping a coarse wool homespun cloak around his shoulders against the biting cold, he took his rod and his staff and went to feed the lambs. Over the Karun River a mist was rolling high, and on the far bank the sands and marshy clumps of bullrushes and reeds seemed to shiver in the frozen dawn. Eastward stretched the plain, perfectly flat, grassless, sand-poisoned and sterile. The winter rains had been late and few. From the bramble bush enclosure that served as a sheepfold, the ewes were already bleating for their young. The hungry lambs, kept inside an earthen hut at night, answered back hungrily in a high-pitched chorus.

Jacob brought the lambs to the ewes, carrying many which could not find their mothers and tottered frantically about until he looked after them; soon the bleating died away in a hum of feeding and satisfaction. Deborah, Jacob's sister, ran past in her flapping black garments to milk the cows. Like all Bedouin women's faces hers was bare, disdaining Islam's veil.

Jacob wondered if there would be yogurt for breakfast; he turned back to the fold, gathered the flock together and moved it out on the open plain toward a sparse green pasture. This lay beyond some wheat fields sown by a few settled peasants who lived along the Karun. One of these, his head and body cloaked against the cold, called gruffly to Jacob as the herd passed him, "Watch your sheep today that they don't get into my wheat."

"Yes," Jacob called back in his clear, strong voice. "My brother, Husein, is also coming and we will take care."

The man became more civil. "Last night the dogs were barking, barking. Why?"

"I do not know. Perhaps men were coming, thieves, or maybe hyenas, or maybe dogs just barking for nothing. I do not know." Jacob ran ahead, shouting instructions to the sheep to keep closer together and rest in place; as for centuries, the Arab nomads talk to their animals and the animals understand and obey them, though why this is so no one knows. "Aooooeh, whssssss, whssss!" Jacob hissed and whistled and threw his staff high into the air, end over end, at some strays. "Brrrr-r-r-r-r! Br-r-r-r!"

Soon his brother Kazim came to relieve him so he could return to the tent for his morning tea. Jacob hurried back, running and breathing heavily. His eldest brother, Husein, and Sherif, a young cousin of his own age, who had come to buy a lamb, were crouched around a brushwood fire, breaking cold unleavened bread and washing it down with small glasses of boiling hot, sugary tea. Husein stirred the fire and ashes fell down, scattering sparks. An iron kettle sat in the red coals, and from time to time Husein would scald the small glasses and saucers with it, passing them from one to another. Each man poured the tea into his saucer to cool it, and drank it down quickly, the hot liquid reviving him.

"If it rains I'm happy," Husein said. He was a tall, large-boned man with fierce, hawk-like features and a perpetually dour attitude toward life; since the death of their father his word among the family was law. "If no rain, I'm miserable. This is a very dry year, Sherif. Usually the grass is a foot deep by now and covered with flowers."

Sherif told them he had passed two dead sheep on the desert the day before; since it was winter he had been able to bicycle over the sands from Shush-Daniel village, so-named because it lay on the ruins of the ancient city of Susa, for thousands of years the capital of the Elamites and, after an interval of desolation, the Achaemenians; Cyrus, Darius, Xerxes, his Queen Esther and Alexander had reigned there, and the Prophet Daniel was buried there. Sherif planned to stay a few days; he was only twenty-one but had left the tribe ten years before to become a peddler in the Shush bazar. Now he had been conscripted into the Persian army and wanted to buy a lamb to leave behind with his wife as a provision for hard days.

Jacob said one of their tribe had lost a ram two days before: it had dropped dead in the night from starvation. There was so little grass this year.

"You came across the desert by bicycle, Sherif?" Husein asked with a broad grin. "Many jackals, hyenas, wolves and leopards out there."

Sherif laughed. "I'll hit them with my bicycle. I'll take this knife and kill them." He produced a large flick-knife from his pocket. Its enamel handle was studded with multi-colored glass stones and one could fit one's fingers through brass knuckles decorated with heavy knobs. Husein and Jacob examined the wicked instrument with admiration. Husein handed it back with a laugh. "Don't go through the dunes by Tchogha Zanbil alone or all they'll find of you in the morning is your jacket. Many hyenas there. They howl at night. Some are as big as a donkey."

"I'm not afraid. I'd even go at night."

For a time the men discussed hyenas, the greatest menace on the desert. Husein told about one nomad who fell asleep, was bitten by a hyena, and went raving mad after some days. He said the hyena was not dangerous by day, but at night could attack and kill and devour even two or three men.

Jacob said no one in his tribe had yet been killed by a hyena. "Maybe if I was alone with the flock and two or three hyenas came, I'd just let them take one sheep and go."

Husein ordered Jacob to return to the flock, and the younger brother went off. Sherif was about to follow him when a querulous, frail but piercing voice called to him from the women's quarter.

"Sherif! Sheri-i-i-i-i-if! When is your father coming to see me?"

Husein led him into the other side of the long black tent; here two women, Deborah, and a comely, red-haired girl with kohl-blackened eyes, whom Kazin had purchased as a bride the year before, were spinning wool on a spindle. Near them, crouched in a corner on a pile of dirty carpets, was a woman of extreme age, the shepherds' mother. A tiny little creature, almost bent double, she was wrapped from head to foot in a grimy black shawl. From her face, weathered and wrinkled as a walnut and none too clean, stared two piercing blue eyes; although they were rheumy with cataracts, they were still good enough to recognize her nephew.

"Father's an old man now," he reminded her. "It's too cold for him to come in winter."

"Oh, Sherif, Sherif, come here," the old lady cried, in a plaintive wail. She snatched at his arm with trembling, claw-like fingers as he bent down to her. "I want to die," she hissed at him. "I am too old, too old. It is finished for me. You tell your father to come for a visit. I want to see my brother once more before it is time for me."

"I will tell him. Maybe he will come. Maybe not. *Inchallah.*"

"Mother, go give the horses water," Husein ordered her, disgusted by this show of age and infirmity. The old lady made no move and he went to do it himself.

"Oh, Sherif, Sherif," she started again. "I am almost dead. Today they give me bread. Tomorrow I don't know who will give me bread."

Deborah, busy at her spindle, snorted with exasperation. "She's getting really bad," the younger woman told Sherif, ignoring her mother as if she were a child or an imbecile. "You brought that dress for her from Shush last night and now all morning she's been saying you treat her better than her own sons. She sits there all day long and tells us to wash this and that. She can't even attend to herself any more. Last night she was really bad because Kazim and Husein hadn't come back from the gendarmerie."

"I heard them come in late," Sherif said; tired from his journey he had been asleep early. "What happened?"

Deborah explained that Kazim had been arrested. One of the peasants down by the river had complained to the Persian gendarmerie post that Kazim had let some sheep stray into his wheat field. Four policemen had come, eaten a full meal and demanded cigarettes, becoming abusive when the family could produce none. They took Kazim back to their post, beat him and locked him up in a cell. When Husein returned from grazing the flock, he went to fetch him, and the two brothers had not reached home until after midnight, coming across the dunes. The desert Arabs feared the Persian police and soldiers, who, resentful at having been posted away from the cooler, temperate Iranian plateau, often mistreated them.

There was a scream outside. A woman Sherif recognized as Husein's wife staggered into the tent, clutching her forehead where blood was flowing from an ugly gash. Husein had hit her, she cried; she asked Sherif for a bandage. He had none but volunteered to take her back to Shush on his bicycle. "That is a bad cut. Better I take you to a doctor."

"No, no," she protested. She hurriedly dried her eyes with a grimy cloth when Husein came into the tent. "I'll tie it with a rag."

Husein did not glance at his wife but told Sherif, "She forgot to tie up the donkey last night and he got into the wheat bin. He did not eat much but he could have died." He sat down and lit a cigarette, sullenly looking around as if defying anyone to say anything. The cut had been made by two heavy brass rings on the knuckles of his right fist. Sherif thought to himself that if he was going to hit someone it might well have been the other women for not washing the old lady; she looked as if she had not been bathed for weeks. He remembered his father telling him that when the shepherds' mother was young she had been very handsome and strong and had worked like a man, taking the sheep out to graze, carrying heavy loads—she had done everything. And now that the family had prospered with a herd of more than four hundred sheep they left the old lady to slowly die in a corner on a pile of rags. Maybe a hyena could come in some night and drag her off to its lair. Maybe that was what her children wanted.

As if reading his thoughts, Deborah said, "About seven in the morning two days ago a hyena menaced one of the shepherd boys. That boy waved his staff at the beast. It seized a two-year-old-lamb— about fifteen kilos—in its jaws and ran with it. One of the men jumped on a horse and rode after it and it dropped the lamb. When the man reached it, the lamb was already dead."

Husein said that the week before a hyena had come for him one morning and he had hit it with his staff. "Afterward a boy nearby was building a fire and that same hyena went for the boy. That hyena, he took one sheep by the throat and another by the stomach. Killed both. That boy just escaped. It came for me first." He added that a month before a hyena had actually broken into the sheepfold at night and got a lamb. He warned Sherif to be careful if they took the sheep into the dunes near Tchogha Zanbil.

Just then there was another commotion outside. Deborah went to see what it was and in a moment came running back, her black robes and shawls flying. "Husein! Sherif! Come!"

[25

The two men scrambled to their feet and hurried outside. Across the open fields to the west they could see the figures of two men fighting. Their long robes flew about and one was beating the other to the ground with his staff. Deborah shrieked, "My two brothers are fighting! Run, run!" Husein at once headed toward them, shouting at them to stop and waving his long arms in the air. As Sherif just stood and watched, Deborah roused him, crying, "Sherif, why do you just stand there and look? Go and stop it!"

When he reached the brothers, Kazim was roaring at Jacob, "Why didn't you come, goddamit?" A powerfully built man, taller and more muscular than the youth, he had knocked Jacob to the ground and now gave him a hard whack on the shoulders with his staff. Husein, who was almost as big but much older, tried to wrest it from him. *"Padar sag!* Son of a dog! I'll break your neck!" Kazim cursed Jacob.

"No, no, no, no! Your brother was coming!" Husein thundered. "Stop, brother, stop! This is not good like this!"

Jacob struggled to rise to his knees; he gasped for breath. "He's crazy," he spit out, his eyes on Kazim with fury. It took a moment more—as Jacob tried to rise to his feet, Kazim struck another blow and Husein tried to hold his arms, the three brothers locked in a great thrashing mass of robes and cloaks—before the two were separated.

"By the will of Allah, may you be torn to pieces by a hyena so I may draw comfort from it," Kazim cursed Jacob in a brutish voice. He turned his back on them and strode back to the tents.

"Why? Why should you beat me?" Jacob called angrily after him. "I was coming. I only went for tea and bread. Leave me alone or you'll pay for it!"

"Forget it, brother," Husein told him. "He is still angry because the gendarmes took him yesterday. Come, we must get to the flock."

"He passed some wheat fields before I returned. I think he was afraid he would be in bad trouble with the gendarmes if some of the sheep strayed and there was another complaint."

Husein ran ahead and Jacob and Sherif followed him. Jacob groaned, trying to keep up. "Too much my back is paining. Kazim is *palwan,* a wrestler and very strong. And as he is elder, I did not wish to hit him back. Maybe one day I will marry and go outside to work like you, Sherif. If every day we have trouble like this, I will take what sheep are mine and go. Not now. Now is not so bad. But if there is trouble every day with Kazim, I will take my sheep and my wife and go." Sherif said he had heard Kazim was the most powerful fighter in the tribe, that if he lost his temper he could knock a donkey over with his fist.

By the time they reached the herd they were a long way from the tents, and Husein was driving the sheep along in a dry canal bed between two wheat fields. Three ewes suddenly turned back and side by side began walking back toward the tents and their lambs; a shout and a wave of his staff from Jacob ended this independent course. A woman swathed in black riding a gray mare galloped past, covering her face from them. Jacob shouted to the sheep to slow down. Up ahead Husein could be heard cursing them aimlessly, "By the will of Allah, you will become lame and walk with one foot. . . . You will eat poison weeds so your belly will swell until you die and I will draw comfort from that."

On a distant knoll stood a woman, her hand raised to her eyes, watching them pass; Jacob said she was worrying about her patch of wheat. "Too much trouble for the sheep now," he told Sherif. "Not enough rain. They are hungry so they try to break away into the wheat fields."

By mid-morning the southern horizon began to grow steadily darker and a pale light started blinking as if a storm were approaching. "Over there it's raining," Jacob observed hopefully. He was getting more cheerful but his mind was still on the morning's beating. "Kazim almost killed me one time," he told Sherif. "It was in summer and I fell asleep and when I woke up the sheep had wandered off and eight were dead. The hyenas got them."

Far ahead Husein had stopped to sit and rest, and Jacob ran back and forth, trying to close up the herd, running from one side to another, shooing forward the laggards and strays. When they had been gathered in, he uttered a high-pitched cry, the signal for them to stop and graze in this place. Sherif laughed. "Ha! That's good. They understand you." A large white ram with curved horns came up to Jacob and nudged his arm with its nose. Jacob pulled from his robe a scrap of bread he had saved from breakfast and fed it to the ram. Then he drew a reed flute out of his garments. "One of the mouthpieces is missing," he apologized. "Kazim took it. He says I play the flute too much and will forget to watch the sheep. But they like music too much."

Sherif was glad for a chance to rest and he hopped around on one leg. "Too much walking, walking, these sheep! They want grass and they don't find it. Where are you taking them?"

Jacob pointed out across the flat plain. "Over there. If the weather clears up, we'll take them into the dunes this afternoon. There is some grass there in the draws which catch the moisture." He began to play his flute. To Sherif it sounded like music of long ago, perhaps thousands of years ago. Jacob said he had made the flute from a reed he had taken from the river bank. He played a song he said he had heard on Radio Araby Baghdad, which the shepherds preferred to nearer stations playing Persian music.

"How come Husein is barefoot today? He left his sandals at the tent."

"He thought it might rain."

A large ewe with long fleecy brown wool and a bell tied around its throat had fallen behind the herd and was resting on the ground beside them. Jacob said the ewe would deliver a lamb very soon. As they rested, he told Sherif how hard it was when Husein and Kazim went away and he was left to tend the sheep alone. "There was too much danger for me every day. The dunes are dangerous. The jungle by the river is dangerous. All the hyenas live in the dunes or the jungle. Also maybe a thief comes and I don't see him. Out here on the plain it is good. I can see a man, I can see a dog, I can see the sheep, I can see a hyena." He ran off to chase some strays back to the herd then returned. "Today maybe rain comes," he told Sherif, pointing to the southern sky.

A thunderstorm seemed to be gathering. A mass of heavy clouds lay over the tents, now more than a mile away. A few lotus trees on the otherwise bare plain whispered and crackled their dry leaves, stirred by sudden gusts of wind. As the two youths stood and watched, the sky flamed with dry lightning; occasional peals of thunder shook the plain. An eagle circled with outspread wings below the clouds and a covey of small birds arose to pursue him. Breathing out coldness a dark cloud passed up the Karun River from the south. Gradually all around them the sky blackened menacingly; the whole plain seemed to lie in expectant silence. Husein shouted that a storm was coming and they should move the flock back toward the tents. The herd was turned around and began moving quickly. But the large brown ewe now seemed to be in labor and could not keep up with them and Husein had to slow up the sheep in the front. As they advanced, the ewe seemed to be experiencing more and more difficulty; she would move a few paces, fall exhausted to the earth, rest a few moments and struggle to her feet and try to catch up. But she kept falling behind and they could not leave her.

"Maybe she'll deliver soon," Jacob called to Husein; his brother had his hands full as they were nearing the wheat fields again. "Watch that wheat over there," he called. "See they don't get into it."

Jacob and Sherif kept their eyes on the brown ewe, which now fell down again, rolled over on her side and shuddered with pain. A cold piercing wind rose on the plain. The ewe rolled over again and lifted one leg off the ground. She suddenly jerked her head upward to the sky and opened her jaw, baring her teeth. She did this three times but issued no sound.

"She's calling to Allah," Jacob said in a hushed voice. A white pillar of dust whirled over the earth, with such violence it tore at the shepherds' robes and head cloths.

"To the ditch! Run for the ditch!" Husein shouted and the three men ran and dove into a dry canal at the same time as thunder rolled back and forth across the sky. They were not a moment too soon for in the next instant the sky opened its mouth and breathed white fire; immediately the thunder roared again and there flamed such a brilliant flash of lightning that for a second they could see all the plain to its farthest ends, the black tents a mile away and the dunes and mounds of Tchogha Zanbil in sharp definition. At that same instant rain began falling heavily. "Look! The ewe!" Jacob exclaimed, just as a peal of thunder broke right over their heads and went rolling away across the desert. The ewe was giving birth; already they could see the head of a fleecy black lamb. Husein jumped up and ran to assist the delivery, gently pulling the lamb from the womb. This small creature, wet and bloody, at once shivered, wagged its little tail, jerked its head around with interest in the world it found itself in and kicked its legs. Jacob gave it to the ewe to lick clean, then he wrapped the lamb inside the folds of his cloak, tucking it carefully into the dry warmth to keep it from getting a chill.

As soon as Jacob moved, the ewe was on her feet, staying close to him; she did not leave his side until he gave the lamb to Husein to carry back to the tents, then she kept to Husein's heels, trailing the bloody placenta in the dust behind her. "Aaghh! Look, my robe is dirty," Jacob exclaimed. The lamb had wet on it. "I think when the rain stops I'll build a fire and dry it."

"I want a good lamb," said Sherif. "How about that one? The new one, it's mine."

"No, it will have to stay with its mother for some months. Better I take it to your wife in Shush then." The rain let up almost as soon as it began and the thunder rumbled off to the north.

"Not enough," Jacob said. "Maybe it will rain again. It is in Allah's hands." He sighed. "This new black lamb is very good. Last year we lost five sheep to hyenas and had to start growing our own wheat; we used to just buy what we needed in the bazar but nowadays it is very costly."

Far across the plain, the sun peeled out of a slash of broken cloud. The earth gleamed with moisture. Washed clean by the rain the air was crisp and clear. Jacob and Sherif built a brush fire to dry out their clothes. Once the flames caught, Jacob took out his flute and started playing, and Sherif hopped about on one foot, clapping his hands in the Arab manner and dancing to celebrate the lamb's birth. As Jacob played, Sherif sang:

> I am blowing on my flute of reed
> I have lost my camel
> And must seek a way to find it.

They laughed when they finished. The sun broke through the clouds now, and the sky was filled with large patches of transparent blue. "If a man has enough sheep, he is in need of nothing more," Jacob said with satisfaction. "A good flock brings you much wealth. Some Bedouins say we have too many sheep now, four hundred, and every year, if the rains are few, there is less and less grass. I say, 'Who gives the grass, you or Allah?'" Jacob jumped up and playfully seized Sherif from behind, flapping his robe and arms about his cousin to make it appear Sherif was attacking him. This roused the two mangy sheep dogs who accompanied the herd; they came running and barking and jumped around the two scuffling men, snarling and snapping their jaws. Jacob cried, "Bite him! Bite him! Help me!"

The dogs became so agitated and went into such fits of frenzied howling, the two youths fell to the ground laughing. In a burst of high spirits, they started to do handsprings, and Husein came running back—he did not like such horseplay when they were out with the herd and harshly told Jacob they would take the flock into the dunes now that the storm had passed.

Shortly after mid-day, the three men and their flock moved up into the hills. The sky was clearing to a perfect blue, and over the rolling pink dunes they could see the faint snow-capped ridges of the Zagros Mountains. To the east, the Karun River sparkled a deep blue; the wind had risen since the brief rain, sending white foaming breakers against the yellow-fringed banks. The tents, long, black and narrow, with their bramble bush enclosures and few earthen huts built for the lambs were distinct and sharply outlined on a sloping hill near the river; not far from the tents was a solitary yellow brick house, a school the Persian king had built for the wandering Arabs the previous year, hoping to educate at least some of them and tame them. To the west, perfectly flat and seemingly endless, stretching to the Tigris and Euphrates and on to the deserts of Arabia, was the vast, unchanging steppe.

Sherif laughed happily in the new warmth. "The sun is out now, no good," he joked to Jacob. "Rain and fog are better. Too many hyenas come for you then."

Somewhere, high in the sky, came the scream of a jet engine but they could not see the plane. Then Jacob, shielding his eyes with his hand, spotted it. "Look, Sherif, there it is. When the Karun flooded its banks two years ago, a helicopter came and dropped bread and sugar for us in boxes. One man was trying to catch a box of food. He was greedy and wanted it for himself alone. He pushed us all aside and shouted, 'Oh, for me!' and he ran out like this to catch a box in his arms. It came down with great speed and hit his chest and killed him."

Sherif laughed. Jacob said the plain had been flooded two meters deep and the family had been forced to take its sheep into the dunes. The Persian army had supplied them with tents, matches, sugar, tea and bread. Although their grazing lands lay within Iran's political boundaries, the Bedouins frequently crossed into Iraq, and as Arab nomads felt themselves to belong to the desert rather than to any particular nationality. Had Sherif stayed with the tribe and not gone to live in a settled village, he would not have been drafted into the army or, indeed, been subject to Iran's laws.

Husein, leading the herd far ahead of them, could be heard shouting to the sheep with a staccato cry like a machine-gun: "Hey-hey-hey-heh-heh-heh-heh-heh-heh! Whoooooo-oooo!" Sherif noticed that a passing black ewe breathed with a strange whistling sound; Jacob said a hyena had pierced its throat.

They climbed steadily into the dunes. Sometimes, where the grass and sand had been eroded by rains, they found the earth scattered with debris, washed down from the higher ground above. They would find potsherds, shards of glazed blue and green pottery, pieces of animal and human bones so old they crumbled in one's fingertips, bits of black obsidian and colored glass. The youths kept their eyes peeled for tiny green copper coins, for these could be sold in the Shush bazar, to be passed on to tourists in the cities. Mostly there were fragments of golden pottery, some burnished and of an almost eggshell thinness. Some of the bits of pottery showed painted decorations; Sherif and Jacob could make out reeds in a marsh, an aquatic bird, a turtle, part of a hunter's bow and the front of a date palm. Such findings were not rare; the dunes themselves seemed to be formed from great heaps of them as if a vast city, in size beyond their imagination, had once been in this place. But where had such wondrous people come from and where had they gone? The crude implements and pottery the Bedouins knew were primitive by comparison.

"Look, look!" Jacob cried, kneeling on the ground to smooth his hand over a calcite and alabaster surface exposed on the side of a slope. He found a shard of flint from a broken sickle. "There was a a house here before; maybe a village." The youths soon lost interest in hunting coins and Jacob drew out his flute from his robes and began to play notes of the strangest sweetness; the sound was deep and beguiling and sounded very old, as the first music on earth must have sounded. "What's that?" Sherif asked. Jacob shrugged. "I don't know. I just made it up." The dunes, perhaps two or three hundred heaps of sand and rubble in all, extended along the river for half a mile, and westward almost half that distance. Despite the sun a chilly wind whistled about them as they climbed; something about the

strange landscape made Sherif uncomfortable; he was glad he was
not in the dunes alone.

Husein, up ahead, shouted angrily, "The sheep are moving too
close to those wheat patches in the draws. Go, brother, and bring
them!" Jacob, his robes flapping behind him, went running around
the edge of the flock, back and forth, up and down one dune after
the other, until he was only a small black silhouette; he ran about
like this all day long and never seemed to tire. Sherif, who made no
attempt to keep up with his cousin, climbed a dune to where Husein
had sat to rest on the crest, a vantage point from which he could
see all the flock. Sherif spotted a green expanse on the plain to the
west. "There's grass over there; why not go there?"

"They have many flocks in that tribe. If I took mine, there would
be trouble." Husein pointed to the edge of the dunes where another
herd was following in their footsteps. "See, that man has brought
his sheep here because he saw mine were eating well."

"You bring your sheep first ahead of him. Let's go that way and
cut him off."

"No, never mind," Hussein told him. "We'll go as we are." The
older man squinted as he surveyed the dunes ahead. "This grass is
as if it's been burnt. We must take the flock closer to Tchogha
Zanbil." He rose and shouted to Jacob. "Bring the dogs. Keep them
close at hand as we go deeper. There may be danger." At a signal
from Jacob the sheep grazing placidly below began to move forward
again. Husein joined his brother who was running about chasing
strays back to the flock, sometimes flinging his staff high into the
air and shouting curses, "Goddam, what people like to be a shepherd! *Menhoobah!* May thieves take you all! *Ma soobah!* You bloody
sheep. . . . May you fall to ruins. . . . May you sink into the
earth!"

When Husein had moved far away, Sherif joined Jacob and in
no time they were wrestling again, grabbing each other around the
neck and shoulders with oaths and hoots of laughter. They started
playing another game: one stood and held the other upside down,
they flipped backward and the other was standing. They flipped
backward again and up was the other one. Then Sherif took off his
sandals, clasped his bare feet and rolled down the slope doing somer-
saults. Jacob tried to do a handstand but flopped over on his back,

laughing. Husein roared at them to quit such foolish antics, and the two raced to the top of the next dune, then stopped, struck speechless.

There it was, visible at last above the dunes, its great mass pink in the bright sunshine against the green-streaked pastures at its base and the yellow ochre dunes: Tchogha Zanbil. The great temple struck awe in the two young Bedouins just as it did in everyone who beheld it for the first time, even in its ruined state, a great tower seemingly with its top in the heavens; it seemed incredible that it could have been built by men like themselves.

Closer, Sherif could see a dark eroded gorge; its cliff-like sides were pocked with black recesses; Jacob said these were shallow caves, lairs of hyenas. Some said they were piled with skulls and bones of sheep, dragged back alive for the kill. It was believed there were human skeletons inside the caves also. This precipitous valley was still in deep shadow; it reminded Sherif of death. He looked away to the tops of the ridges; they were brushed with faint streaks of pink lichen and sparse gray heather which seemed to sparkle in the sunshine.

In a draw just below them a man from the river settlement was plowing a patch of wheat; he had no draft animal and had to strain, bent over to push the iron blade into the earth. "Like a donkey," Jacob said contemptuously. The wheat seed, if sufficient rain fell, would grow into small green, spike-leaved plants within a month; it was simply scattered on the earth, and where it would grow thick and heavy a lamb could stray inside and not be seen. Once the wheat grew tall, the peasants would stand on the ridges above it all day long and keep watch against the shepherds and their flocks. They always seemed to find some sign that sheep had trodden the grain to earth or eaten of the stalks. Near the harvest time, if they found crushed or eaten wheat, they would become angry and savage; and there were sometimes bitter struggles with the shepherds, and killings. To Jacob, these cultivators were his natural enemies, planting the ever-scarcer grasslands with their crops, even though now, for the second year, his own family had sown some wheat among the dunes. Every ten days his brothers' wives and their children would come to the dunes to pull weeds from their wheat patch. While it was true the Bedouins sold milk, wool and manure to the settled cultivators and, in turn, were allowed to feed their flocks on their grain stubble, Jacob had always looked down on them. But life was changing on the desert.

The shepherd who had brought his flock behind them now caught up with Husein, calling *"Hoi! Salaam Aleikum!"* "Hoi!" Husein greeted him. "Where are you bringing your sheep?" The man, who called to a boy with him, telling him to keep the flocks separate, sat down with Husein on a ridge to smoke cigarettes, and Jacob and Sherif joined them.

The newcomer was a kinsman from a neighboring encampment; he complained that the herds of Abdul Khan, a local sheikh whose grazing lands had been taken over by the Persian government for an irrigation project, were now moving into his tribe's land. "Those sheep of Abdul Khan will take all our grass and that of your tribe too," he predicted gloomily. "They have guns and men, and are eating us up. I see you have good, fat sheep. Do you find enough grass?"

"Since the rains."

"This grass here is not good yet. It should be left to grow." The man scratched his head. "Your cow is good? You feed it good?"

'Yes, my sister gives it two bales of hay a day." Husein turned to Jacob. "You go, go, brother, watch the sheep." Jacob ran off without protest, whistling and shouting to the herd.

"Did any men among you find work at Tchogha Zanbil?" Husein asked the other shepherd. "I heard they were hiring several hundred men there. Since they dug out those old ruins eight years ago, the rain has started to wash them away and they are going to build some brick retention walls. I heard they were hiring."

"Yes. Some men found work. They are rebuilding the walls of that old place." The man scratched the earth with a stick. "Those men of Sheikh Abdul Khan brought six herds today. There is not enough grass this year because the rains are few and now shepherds are fighting shepherds. They trespass into our grasslands. We want to keep them out, else how shall we live? Everyone races to reach what little grass there is in the mornings."

Husein suggested that to prevent a fight, boundaries be set up for the flocks of both sides. "Maybe at the new canal line. Beyond that neither side should graze its sheep on the other's land."

The small shepherd boy, whose robe and cloak were in tatters, torn by brambles and thorns as he ran about, came up and respectfully kissed Husein on both cheeks. Husein remonstrated with the youngster's father, "You ought to buy him good sandals, a good robe. Why like this? You don't give him wife, no good food, just everyday he herds sheep for you—shoes broken, his robe all torn and ragged. You should look for a job outside, boy." The youth grinned and told him, "I don't know any other job. Just sheep herding."

"Maybe after I have money," the other shepherd said. "When I shear the sheep this spring maybe. If I have enough."

Both men interrupted their conversation to shout orders to their sheep and for a moment the air was full of shouts, "Br-r-r-r! Whoooo! Yeoooowoooow! Yeeelllellleoleow!"

"Your dress it too white," his friend told Husein, when they returned to their conversation. "That's for a young man. Not for you is good."

Husein laughed. "You want my dress to be old dirty rags the same as you, eh? You're an old man. I'm still young."

Jacob came running up and the older shepherd asked him his age. Jacob shrugged good naturedly, "I don't know. Nobody kept a record. Maybe twenty-one. Maybe thirty-one."

The man rose and heaved a deep sigh. "Today where can we take our sheep? Over there is a flock and over here is a flock; where shall we go? My sheep don't eat much. Those of Sheikh Abdul Khan are big and strong. His eat twice as much as one of mine."

"You tell Abdul Khan's men they can come so far and no farther," Husein told him.

"When they come again, I may trouble them. We don't want these new people bringing their flocks to our pasture." He and his son moved on with their sheep.

"Oh, I'm hungry!" Jacob exclaimed. "You take my sheep, you take my dogs, Sherif. I'm finished. I'm so hungry." Sherif, holding Jacob's staff between his legs, joked, "Here, eat this." Something in the far distance by the river caught Jacob's eye. "A gazelle! Over on that last ridge. Ah, it saw the sheep and now it's gone." Scanning the horizon with his sharp eyes, he pointed out an ostrich and two jackals to Sherif, who never would have spotted them himself.

"Too much noise you're making," grumbled Husein, who resented his younger brother's vitality and exuberance. "Maybe a viper is coming."

"Why a viper?" Jacob scoffed.

"If you always talk so much I'll strike you myself. It's not good."

Jacob shrugged and ran off after the herd. Husein called after him, " Leave them, leave them, brother! Why do you stir them up so much. Here the pasture is green. Make them lie here." Jacob, already on another ridgeline, called to Sherif, "Hey, come and play!"

"Look at him," growled Husein in a disgusted tone.

"Let's run to the far hills! Catch the gazelle!" Jacob called, defiantly, then he froze. "Hey brother! Sherif! Come here, quick! Hyenas!"

In no time they had reached him and Husein spotted two of them on a dune toward the river; they were moving about what appeared to be a carcass. "Maybe they found a sheep," Husein said. "Sick or dead. They're eating him." He ordered Jacob to send the dogs after them to chase them away. Jacob raced up and down the dunes, shouting to the dogs, who barking and running, took up the pursuit. The two hyenas raised their heads and stared toward them, transfixed, then they turned and bolted toward the river; as they ran, they would be visible on the ridgelines, then disappear on the downward slopes. The dogs followed them for some distance, then stopped, apparently giving up the chase and waiting for Jacob to call them back. When he did they came quickly, wagging their tails with relief, their tongues hanging out. Husein wanted to get the herd out of the dunes when there were hyenas so close; they moved the sheep rapidly down toward a flat green pasture near the base of the ruined temple. He said they would have to return onto the lowland that evening, taking the long way around the dunes.

When they drew near Tchogha Zanbil, Husein refused to let Jacob and Sherif climb the temple, but sullenly agreed to watch the herd while they explored some of the ruins at its massive base. So it was that in mid-afternoon, howling and punching each other as they ran toward the ziggurat, the two young Arabs stumbled into the ruins of ancient Elam's royal catacombs preserved in the dry desert air almost as they were that day almost 3000 years before, when the chariot-borne Assyrians came to loot and massacre.

They were still five hundred yards or so from the ziggurat itself when they came upon what must once have been a large palace; the walls of the foundations still stood, some rising ten and twenty feet in the air, and the stone floors were still intact. On one tiled staircase

Sherif spotted the footprint of a dog, and he imagined some work-man like himself cursing it for straying on the still-wet brick. The two youths picked up shards of broken pottery as they went, hastily examining them for something of value and then casually tossing them aside as so much rubbish. "Look for coins," Sherif said. "You can sell them for two, three hundred riyals in the bazar." Grass and desert weeds sprouted from some of the ruined walls, and as they entered one long narrow chamber a covey of birds rose into the air, startling them. Crawling across the tiles were small black, crab-like beetles, outsize repulsive insects which scuttled back into the crevices of the crumbling brick as they drew near. Jacob warned Sherif to watch out for vipers and scorpions.

They wandered from one ruined chamber to the next, all the time the massive pyramidal height of the ziggurat seeming to get higher and higher until it fairly towered over their heads; it rose more than one-hundred-sixty feet into the sky. In sheer size, the zig-gurat dwarfed any man-made structure the two shepherds had ever seen or even imagined. A hundred or so Arab laborers were scattered along its sides; some were repairing the temple's gigantic entrance gates while others were working on a great steep staircase rising under a series of ceremonial archways. High above in the dazzling sunlight, the ziggurat was crowned with what resembled a jumble of ruined altars, heaps of earth and rampart-like ruined temples.

Jacob told Sherif he had once climbed to the top; it had taken him almost half an hour, and when he returned some Persian gen-darmes from a small desert outpost near the temple's base had seized his flock; he was arrested and held for an hour, but then, when the gendarmes told him to go, he could hear one ewe bleating from inside the post. "They wanted to kill and eat it," he told Sherif.

Sherif gazed up at the ziggurat. "This place is very old. Before the Prophet Daniel. I don't know how many years ago."

"These rooms are all broken," said Jacob, equally awed. "Every-thing has fallen down." He gave a cry of delight, finding a fragment of pottery that had been decorated with human finger imprints around the rim. Each of the Arabs put his fingers over the prints but found they were from a much larger man. "These people were very big," Jacob guessed. "Bigger than us." He began poking the ruined walls, breaking off old bricks and imbedded pieces of human teeth and bones. The only sign of life around them was an old

woman, wrapped in a black shroud, who went by on a worn pathway
through the ruins, leading a camel. The youths moved deeper into
the palace entering a section where thirty-foot walls still stood and
the rooms were very long and narrow. The afternoon was still warm
but Sherif shivered; he did not like this place. Jacob also felt uneasy;
he was about to suggest they return to the herd when Sherif exclaimed in surprise and hurried ahead of him into the next room.
It was very long and narrow, like a corridor and there were three
rectangular openings in the tiled floor. Within each was a steep
stone staircase leading deep underground into some kind of cellar.

"Let's go see!"

"No. I don't go down there. Too dangerous."

"Why?" Sherif wanted to explore what lay below.

"Maybe danger. Maybe wolves, hyenas."

Sherif laughed, curiosity now stronger than fear. He gathered
some sage brush into a torch, found his matches and crept down one
of the steep stairways, slowly descending about thirty feet. Reluc-
tantly, Jacob followed him. Once below the desert's surface, it became
very cold. The walls of the staircase were plastered white; Sherif
touched them and the gypsum crumbled in his fingers. At the bottom of the stairs was a low black entrance way; the opening was
only about two feet wide and four feet high and was partly filled
with broken masonry, debris and rocks. The place had a foul and
loathsome smell, sickly sweet and rotten—as of wounds, uncleanli-
ness and decay. Jacob suggested they go; he wanted to get back to
the fresh desert air. But Sherif picked up a piece of rock and threw
it into the black recess. It landed with a hollow ring far within;
whatever the space was, it was large and sounded as though it had
a tiled floor. "C'mon," he said, grabbing Jacob by the arm, and they
scrambled over the debris; as Sherif had guessed, once they were
inside, the floor beneath their sandals was smooth and tiled. Sherif
lit his improvised torch and they found themselves in a great caver-
nous hall, with high, arched ceilings and an arched doorway at the
far end. Here, too, the walls were plastered with white gypsum; it
came off at the touch. Awed speechless, the two Arabs, fearful the
torch would not last, hurried down the great hall; the archway at
the end led to a short tunnel, then they passed into a second, even
larger chamber. The torch burned low and they had to scramble
back outside. Held by the mystery of the place now, they quickly

made new torches of sage brush and went down the other two stair-wells. They soon discovered the first two chambers led into four more, all linked together by the low tunnels and archways, and each boy was as cold as a man suffering a chill. In one, there was an enormous slab of white marble, in another three pits with ashes and what looked like human bones. This subterranean palace was built on a grander scale than anything they had seen before; in the flickering torchlight it seemed to possess a demonic quality—if horned and hairy monsters had suddenly appeared before them in an explosion of flames, the two Bedouins would not have been surprised.

As their last torch scattered a trail of sparks, they reached the innermost chamber. Jacob gasped. Just visible in the torchlit gloom at the far end was a great marble table; what he later swore were human skeletons were seated about it in large, throne-like chairs. Below them on the ground were pools of a dried, caked and cracked substance of yellowish hue; the stench was so rotten and overpowering they had to hold their breaths as if even a whiff of this foul air would be deadly poisonous. Sherif yelled and dropped the torch; scared witless they ran for the light at the opening, bumping and pushing each other through and up the stairway to the ground as if all the furies of hell were after them.

"Aaghh, Sherif!" Jacob gasped, as they hurried to find their way out of these accursed ruins, "Why did you drop the torch like that?" Despite the fresh air and sunlight, both of them still felt a nameless dread, and when they reached the open ground, they again broke into a run. It was not until they rejoined Husein and told him what they had seen that they began to speculate that perhaps the underground chambers had been meant for keeping cool in summer, but neither really believed in anything so harmless.

It was almost dark when they reached their encampment. They had stopped at the still waters of a swamp near the river so the flock could drink, and as they drew near the tents they saw Deborah come out and release five little lambs. The lambs came running and bleating toward the herd, which, hearing their cries, itself began to run, all the ewes bleating at once. This rose to a great chorus as the rest of the lambs were released and came running and the ewes searched out their own by scent, nudging stray lambs away from them. In a few moments the bleating died away and the scene became one of quiet contentment as the lambs fed, their tails wagging and their noses pushing and nudging their mothers.

Once the feeding was over and the lambs and ewes had been gathered in for the night, the smallest to their warm earthen stall, Jacob built a brush fire in the shallow pit on the men's side of the family tent. He spread long strips of homespun carpeting on both sides of the blazing hearth for himself and Sherif to lie upon, and the two young Arabs held their shoes in the fire to dry, and scraped the mud of the day away, putting their bare feet right into the flames.

After some scalding hot tea, Husein carried a fleecy little white lamb into the tent and gave it to Jacob to hold. The older brother took a knife and began to sharpen it on the iron poker used to stir the fire. Then he knelt down before Sherif, took the lamb from Jacob and bent over it. The lamb made no sound, and it was not until the blood began to flow into a pool on the earth that Sherif realized Husein had cut its throat. It was the Bedouin tradition in honoring guests. They would have lamb stew to eat that night.

In the excitement of their adventure in the ruins, the morning's fight seemed forgotten, and big, muscular Kazim listened as fascinated as the rest of the family while Jacob described the underground chambers at Tchogha Zanbil. "I saw it and it's some old thing," Jacob told them. "Sherif saw it and I saw it. No dead bodies, but their bones, dried oil on the ground and a bad smell."

After feasting on the lamb and gravy, with bread and onions washed down with fermented milk and tea, Kazim left to join his wife, and Husein to stand watch over the sheep. Each of the brothers stood guard in turn during the night, protecting the herd and family against hyenas, wolves, thieves and bands of desert marauders. Jacob brought a pile of heavy wool quilts and pillows and spread them out on the carpets on either side of the fire, for himself and Sherif. Sherif, tired from the day's journey and feeling the frigid air of the desert night, and the cold coming up from the ground, hastened to wash his face and teeth from a pitcher of cold water, then rolled up in his quilt, burying his head under the covers to gain the added warmth of his breath, as Bedouins always did.

He soon got up, cursing, "This bloody food. Plenty of salt in the meat—I drank too much water and now I'll have to go outside all night." In the darkness beyond the brush enclosure, Sherif heard a dog whimpering as if it were hurt, and called to Jacob. Jacob fetched a kerosene lamp from the women's quarter and they went back to investigate. About halfway to the tent of the next family, they found a large, deep and freshly dug pit. Jacob held the lamp over it. At the bottom was a thin, miserable dog curled up on its back. Its bones stood out on its rib cage and it was whimpering and trying to bark.

Sherif thought it had fallen in. Jacob said no and waved the light toward the other side of the pit where there was the bleached white skull and skeleton of a sheep. "He must have attacked and killed it." He said that this was the fate of any sheep dog who turned against his charges, that the dog would stay alive only as long as it survived on the flesh of the sheep.

Sherif laughed nervously, but back in the tent, once more cosily wrapped in his warm quilt, he thought about the harsh discipline of desert life and was glad he had escaped it and would soon return to the village. "The life of the Bedouin is no good," he told Jacob as they lay there in the flickering fire light. "No good tea, no good coffee, no good biscuit, your clothes smell of smoke all the time, it's too dark at night. Bedouin, Bedouin, it's not good, the life of a Bedouin. You can't see at night. You go outside and don't see. There's no electricity." He could still hear the dog's whimpers and guessed its punishment might be intended as a warning to humans in the encampment too. How brutal life was here he had forgotten.

"Yes," Jacob agreed, but not for Sherif's reasons. "Nowadays there is not enough grass for the sheep so we must scatter some seeds for wheat for our food." He found the need for a Bedouin to cultivate the earth shameful and degrading.

"Before," Sherif went on, sensing his cousin's feelings, "before, all the Arabs were hunters, warriors and bandits, all crafty, brave men. No digging in the ground, no planting, just riding up and taking what they wanted. Maybe thirty years ago. My father told me." He yawned sleepily. "My legs are aching. Those sheep are like little boys. They enjoy running up and down the hills too much."

Jacob drew something out of the folds of his quilt.

"What's that?"

Jacob gave him a sly grin. "Last year the King sent a teacher out to show the children how to read. But men could go and learn at night. Sometimes when there was no work to do and I could slip away from Husein and Kazim, I went over there. You been to school, Sherif?"

Sherif was ashamed of his illiteracy, since most of the settled, village Arabs could read and write. "No," he mumbled and rolled over, shutting his eyes. It was quiet now and Jacob put the book close to the kerosene lamp, shielding it from view from the tent's entrance with his quilt, and leaning so close to it his face almost touched the pages. Slowly, with painful concentration, he began to pronounce the words, letter by letter. The book was not written in his native Arabic, but Farsi, the national language of Persia, so it was very difficult for him.

"*N . . . a . . . n. Nan,*" he muttered slowly, saying the word for "bread."

"*C . . . h . . . o . . . u . . . p . . . a . . . n. Choupan.*" He lingered over the sound with pleasure. "Shepherd. I . . . am . . . a . . . shepherd." Jacob repeated the phrase several times. A shrill voice called from outside the tent. It was Deborah.

"Jacob! Bring the lamp. The sheep were running all directions a moment ago and I don't know where Husein has gone."

He called back, telling her they had been roused by a cat fight; he had heard it and it was all over now. He added, "I need the lamp." She must have gone away for he heard nothing more. Jacob continued to read aloud from his book:

"Water. . . . Rain. . . . The rain brings water. . . ."

"You can read." Sherif had raised his head out of his quilt and stared at Jacob with admiration.

"Yes."

"Why are you learning?"

Jacob thought and could give no answer. After a long time he said, "We go out to the pastures each morning and come back at night. We graze our sheep, we must slave for our food, there is no end to our troubles. Nothing is left for us but thorns and berries of the lotus tree. . . ."

Sherif raised himself on an arm, watching his cousin, whom he had never before heard speak so, nor with such quiet intensity.

"Like the son of a dog, the shepherd has no sabbath day, there is no day of rest but he must always be with his sheep. There is no reward but suffering and the hope of Allah's generosity in the next life. We are as bones that have been cast aside. There is no bread and nothing to gnaw on. We cannot read and write. Allah alone comforts us in this suffering. And we are told to be happy in this country, that our life is good, that if there is rain and green pasture, we should ask no more of Him. And so we feast on those days that we can. And I bring my flute so we can dance and sing and make some happy shoutings. And it is as if all the shepherds from now on will be happy by the will of Allah and there shall be no more fighting and trouble between men. . . . But, Sherif, it is not a full life for a man. . . ." And Jacob groped for words but could not find them; how could he explain the unrest and the yearning, soaring in his mind like the temple in the desert, for great and hidden things he did not yet know nor could even imagine?

I I

Octave and Pren

GRAND GAUBE VILLAC

MAURITIUS

Octave and George

Prem

George

Octave

I I

THIS STORY TAKES PLACE on the remote tropical island of Mauritius.
This tiny, twenty-nine-mile-wide island is one of a scattered group
known as the Mascareignes, situated just north of the Tropic of Capricorn
in twenty degrees of southern latitude, some one-thousand-two-hundred
miles out into the Indian Ocean from the east coast of the lower African
continent. An isolated remnant of a vast geological unheaval of uncertain
antiquity, the island itself is the exposed tip of a volcanic colossus jutting
up from the floor of the ocean abyss two-thousand fathoms below. Green
and mountainous, celebrated for its waterfalls, shooting stars and rainbows,
the island is almost entirely ringed with coral reefs enclosing lagoons of
brilliant clear blue-green water.

Our second story spans only a few hours and is the account of a
morning's journey into the lagoon near Cap Malheureux on the northern-
most extremity of the island.

It is perhaps fitting that our setting bears the name Cape of Unhappiness, that the characters are all very young, and that the island is single,
beautiful and vulnerable. For this story, like that of Jacob, the Arab shepherd, while it is true, has elements in it of the allegory.

To envisage the island now is to see it much as the astronauts saw
the earth when they first circled the moon on Christmas Eve, 1968, and
quoted the opening passages of Genesis: "In the beginning God created the
heavens and the earth . . ." Since then a profoundly different way of con-
ceiving the earth has entered many minds.

It is small. It is finite. It is fragile. Its airs and climates, its oceans
and waters, the great swirls of white, thin atmosphere over its bright blue
surfaces bring home the planet's inescapable unity, and the common dangers of over-population, over-use of resources and over-pollution. It is
only one earth. And before long one moves on to the realization that its

most critical problem in survival is the deepening poverty of two-thirds of its ever-increasingly interdependent people.

In many ways, Mauritius is a microcosm of this earth, and what it may become in the future. The island is already so over-populated and so depleted of resources it is fast approaching breakdown.

Its inhabitants, soon to number a million, are drawn from all the major races and religions: Chinese, Indian, African, Arab and European; Confucian, Buddhist, Hindu, animist, Moslem, Christian, Jew and agnostic. There are the same gaps in wealth and power and ideology as divide the planet; the island's hope of survival is rooted in the same need to curb births, reshape the economic processes, remedy the grosser inequalities and build common institutions, policies and beliefs. The island has felt the impact of modern technology; there are an Apollo tracking station and a Russian naval base. The rich white minority have their golf, theatre, cars and Western culture; the poor—black, brown and yellow—exist on bare subsistence, and some, in their dingy wooden or mudhut hovels, have starving children. Yet all the island's people share the same radio broadcasts, television and newspapers, the same network of modern highways, the same jet-age airport and the economic interdependence that has made the earth itself so intimate and vulnerable a place to live.

The island is so small and isolated it seems like a sea bird or cloud resting on the waves. Southern trade winds breathe over the waters, drawing up their moisture, to hover in thick mists about its volcanos. Along the white sandy beaches, casuarina and coconut trees waft in the breezes, and below the craggy volcanic peaks on the fertile central plateau there are a lake and sparkling rivers. Until the age of discovery the island was unpeopled; it was so cut off that its ecosystem developed separately, and fascinating species of birds, insects and reptiles lived there. For long, silent milleniums the plateau's ebony forests swarmed with bats, gigantic tortoises, snakes, lizards and strange gaudy birds like the dodo, that plump innocent creature with twisted beak and round bottom, which danced the quadrille with Alice.

In the long mists of time, the island was visited by Phoenicians, and by golden-skinned Malays crossing in their wooden craft to Madagaskar, and by Vasco de Gama when he rounded the Cape of Good Hope. It is said that rats swarmed ashore from the sailing ships of the Dutch and Portuguese, that the sailors killed and ate the dodo because it could not fly and the species became extinct with the arrival of man. But the rats multiplied, unchecked by their natural enemies, and drove the first explorers

off the island. For over a century there were few human visitors except
from a rare pirate ship or a sloop of Arab slave traders interested only in
provisions or in refreshing their crews after the strain of a long voyage.

It was not until the development of sugar plantations in the Carib-
bean, based upon African slavery, that Europeans sought to settle Mauritius. The French came first, named it *Ile de France* and by the revolution
of 1789 had established a prosperous colony of some ten thousand French-
men and thirty thousand African slaves. A refuge for fleeing noblemen
from Louix XVI's court, the island declared itself independent. This
proved to tempt the British, who landed troops and seized the island as a
crown colony in the early nineteenth century. As in so much of the world,
the French brought their language, culture, slavery and miscegenation and
the British their ideas of human rights and liberal government, racial prej-
udice and the color bar. They brought other things as well: mongeese to
destroy the rats, Javanese deer and gray-faced Macaque monkeys from
Malaya, black-naped Indian hares, and—besides sugar—coffee, manioc,
corn, fruit, vegetables, indigo and cloves. In time the island's unique birds
and reptiles shrank back into the forests, and as the forests were cleared to
make way for cane fields followed the dodo into extinction.

The British ruled the island but did not settle it, leaving it to the
French and their black slaves to transform the rocky plateau into great
sugar plantations, which, despite rats, fires, hurricanes and epidemics of
smallpox, cholera, influenza, bubonic plague, enteritis and dysentery, somehow prospered. The British got their share of the profits and the French
kept their language, laws, customs and lands. Slavery, under pressure from
liberal London, was soon abolished; the freed slaves, mostly Creoles of
mixed African and French blood, deserted the plantations forever, seeking free lives as fishermen, dockers or artisans in the towns. The French
were forced to import indentured laborers from Bombay; by the mid-
nineteenth-century the population reached 160,000 and Chinese and Arab
traders swarmed in to cater to its needs.

In time, agriculture became so specialized all food but sugar had to
be imported, most of it rice and flour. With the opening of the Suez Canal,
the island's single port declined, its repair docks fell into disuse and the
economy became wholly dependent on sugar. After World War I, sugar
prices quadrupled and the French plantation owners grew very rich. The
British built a network of modern roads, installed a purified water system
and introduced free compulsory education for former slave and master
alike. After World War II, the British eradicated with DDT all malaria;

[53

it had been the major cause of death. The death rate fell in five years from 36 to 14 per 1,000, the birth rate rose from 38 to 50 per 1,000. At the same time the price of sugar began its slow, steady descent on world markets. In London, a postwar British government, threatened with bankruptcy, announced a planned pullback East of Suez.

Stocktaking began. Two distinguished British scholars, an economist and a demographer, arrived and soon announced that the island's population had risen from 160,000 in the mid-nineteenth-century, to 420,000 by 1944, 500,000 by 1952 and 800,000 by 1970. And unless something was done, they predicted it would reach 2,000,000 by 1982 and 3,000,000 by the year 2000. One concluded Mauritius had become one of "the most densely populated agricultural areas in the world" and spoke of "a catastrophic situation soon." The other warned the island's population could quadruple in another generation.

In Washington, the World Bank said the island was facing "the first true Malthusian breakdown." In London, a Whitehall spokesman told a relieved Parliament that it had been decided that Mauritius "should be independent and take her place among the sovereign nations of the world." The *Economist* complacently commented that "free from London's restraining influence, Mauritius will be able to tackle efficiently its problems of overpopulation, unemployment and over-dependence on sugar."

The island's first general election was held. The Indian caneworkers, who by now had multiplied to 420,000, won 40 percent of the votes and control of the government. A Hindu journalist, who had spent fourteen years in London and had spoken out against "British colonialism and imperialism," was knighted by the Queen and became the island's first prime minister. A referendum to elect a legislative assembly to decide the question of independence was won by the Hindus, with almost twice as many votes as the other islanders. Riots immediately broke out and thirty persons were hacked to death. British troops flew in from Singapore to restore order. Half the population boycotted independence celebrations even though Britain agreed to buy two-thirds of the sugar crop at a subsidized price 150 percent above that of the world market.

The island joined the United Nations as its fifth smallest member. Soon experts arrived from the UNDP, EPTA, ILO, FAO, IRBD, IDA and WHO to survey the island's resources, advise on family planning, suggest economic policies, study schemes for tourism, emigration, industry and diversification of agriculture, open a new university and found a John F. Kennedy vocational high school.

By now, official employment figures account for only 67,000 cane workers, 5,000 industrial workers and 33,000 on government payrolls. In alarm, the government hires 15,000 more men as public relief workers at 80 cents a day three days a week, despite the island's already swollen $50 million a year budget. There is talk of making the entire island another tax-free Hongkong, luring foreign capital with tax concessions, and of developing tourism. Several luxury hotels are built along the best beaches, and eight international flights land on the island each week. Emigration rises to three thousand a year but most of it is from the educated white minority; few of the island's black, brown and yellow citizens are welcome anywhere.

A birth control program is started, the Catholics urging the rhythm method and the Hindus distributing the pill and IUD. Schools continue to throw 24,000 literate youths into the labor market each year; almost no one finds a job. Half of the population is below the age of fifteen and there are 900 people per square mile.

Riots begin between the island's 420,000 Hindus, 230,000 Creoles, 134,000 Moslems, 25,000 Chinese and 10,000 white Europeans. In an atmosphere of demoralization any government decision seems horribly dangerous. Acts of sabotage begin: water pipes are dynamited, setting off an epidemic of enteritus; mysterious fires break out in the cane fields, destroying 5 percent of the crop. A newspaper charges the prime minister offers the people only circuses, not bread, declaring, "We are the men in the Colosseum, enfeebled gladiators, against whom have been unleashed the four horsemen of the Apocalypse, Pestilence, Death, Hunger and War, while a mildly interested emperor looks on." Forced to swallow such humiliations, the government has to face its problem squarely: race, language, wealth, power and culture hold the island's peoples apart. If it is to survive, the government must discover what unites, not divides them. But how?

In his chateau atop the plateau, in an all-white enclave of mists and deer parks, high bamboo hedges and an air of seige, a proud aristocrat of French descent talks of dispensing charity to the poor. "Five years ago there was a gulf between us," he says. "I hated them and they hated me. But when we came down from our castles into the streets we found they were just like us. Better than us in some respects." His wife, pouring tea, says sadly, "My children are strange; they do not want to grow up." When her husband observes the whites could only muster a small strike force, if it came to that, she shudders. "I know. I think about that. Every minute of the day I think about that."

In the shantytowns, a brown-skinned revolutionary speaks: "Now there is talk in the villages of rising up and killing all the whites. But our men say, 'The moment is not yet.' We will revenge years of slavery by the capitalists and wipe out this corrupt government which betrays the people. I know it will destroy the island and I do not wish it but when the night comes I will join."

One walks through the streets of Port Louis, the harbor and only town of any size, and wonders. The faces show that wanderers from all the earth have been here: Dutch explorers, exiles from Versailles, legionnaires from North Africa, bourgeois French colonists from the provinces, bearded Arab traders, paunchy Chinese hoteliers, slaves from Madagaskar, Abyssinia, Mozambique and Zanzibar, indentured Hindus from Bombay, Calcutta and Madras, prime English civil servants and all the human flotsam that gets washed up with the driftwood from the seven seas.

Above the port rise the sooty ramparts of an English fortress; there is a staid Anglican cathedral, and a statue of Queen Victoria, glaring stonily from her pedestal in front of the old Government House at coolies loading cargo in the harbor. The back streets are tortuous and twisting; along the narrow lanes, the forbidden mosques and tottering houses of the Moslem medina cling to the hills like fungus; the Evil Eye is still potent, and a hundred taboos and incantations restrict the course of daily life. In front of a cheap cinema, curly-haired Arabs in skull caps smoke hashish; and in a Chinese street, a no-man's land of pagodas, Mao posters and watchful neutrality, there is a cold dead look in the eye of merchants who will sell you anything. Near the harbor the African dockworkers' quarter throbs with the sound of jazz, the beat of calypso drums, laughter, oaths and curses.

There is an almost eerie sense of spacelessness and timelessness about the place, with its fog and mists swirling slowly about the green volcanos. Charles Darwin was struck by this and noted in his Beagle diary that "masses of white clouds were collected around these pinnacles, as if merely for the sake of pleasing a stranger's eyes." And Mark Twain wrote of a native telling him, "Mauritius was made first and then heaven; and heaven was copied after it."

Riders on the earth together, brothers in that bright
loveliness in the eternal cold . . . .

> —*Archibald MacLeish, inspired by man's first*
> *televised view of the earth from the moon,*
> *Christmas Eve, 1968.*

Guidé par ton odeur vers de charmants climats,
Je vois un port rempli de voiles et de mâts
Encore tout fatigués par la vague marine,
Pendant que le parfum des verts tamariniers
Qui circule dans l'air et m'enfle la narine,
Se mêle dans mon âme aux chants des mariniers.

> —*From* Parfum Exotique, *a poem*
> *about Mauritius by Baudelaire*

Ah! Mon Village, comme tu es beau
Quand le ciel es sans nuage
Et avec tous ces chants mélodieux des corbeaux . . .

> —*From* Mon Village, *an unpublished poem*
> *by George Stephen Fanfan, a fisherman of*
> *Grand Gaube*

ALWAYS, WHEN THE DAY BEGAN, Octave rose from his bed and went to the open door of his family's thatched hut to look at the sky. This morning the air was cool and fresh, swept by a slight southeasterly trade wind, perhaps moving up from Antartica. The morning mists had not yet rolled away from the mountains, the sky was just beginning to gray over the stars, and a pale, late, quarter-moon looked insubstantial and thin.

The village was already awake even though only the sky showed the approach of dawn. Some of the pirogues in the cove were already going out to the reef, and Octave could hear the dip and push of the oars. Sometimes one of the fishermen would swear and call out gruffly to another boat. But most of the pirogues left the cove silently except for the whisper of their oars. Octave quickly pulled on a pair of faded short pants and hurried to a neighboring stone and thatched hut. His sharp call of "George!" was answered by a muffled groan from inside, and he returned home where his mother was preparing his tea. He was waking now, although it was hard for him to leave

[57

his sleep; he sat on a rock in the yard drowsily sipping the sweet hot tea and listening to the wind voices in the wind-bent filao trees. An old man, his Uncle Robert, came up the path from the cove, carrying a mast with its furled sail on his shoulder. Robert fished alone at night with bamboo cages and now he was coming home.

"Mofine, mofine," the old man complained. "Bad luck, bad luck." He said he had only three pounds of fish to show for his night's work. *"Ena trop boucoup pechere, zotla rode poisson partout —et poisson misere,"* he said, in the patois of the island. "Too many fishermen now, they hunt fish everywhere in the lagoon—the catch is miserable. It makes for unhappiness—bad luck, bad luck."

Octave's voice was harsh. "Don't say *mofine*. Don't speak of bad luck, my uncle. It is the will of God."

Octave drank a second mug of tea. It was all he would have until noon and he knew how thirsty he would become in the water. He gathered up his diving gear, his harpoon gun and spear, and lifted his mast with its furled canvas sail to his shoulder. "I'll put the gear in the boat and wait for the others there," he told his mother. He walked down to the cove, his bare feet moving gingerly on the coral rock and then easily when he reached the pebbled sand, and he lifted the pirogue and slid her gently into the water.

The village of Grand Gaube, founded by freed slaves a century before, lay quiet and serene around its small cove. Spreading inward from the shore toward the cane fields were five small communities, Grand Gaube itself, Callasse, Roche Terre, Melville and Batie, each a cluster of no more than thirty houses. Two paved roads, one following the shore to Cap Malheureux, where the rich whites had their weekend bungalows, and the other twisting inland toward Port Louis, the port and capital city, met in the center of the village, so there was little through traffic. Here were the police station, post office, dispensary, "family planning" clinic, a few stores run by the Chinese, and wine shops and a gracious park along the beach with its grove of filao trees, where, in the afternoons, the Creole fishermen sat mending their nets, repairing their wooden pirogues, weighing their catches, haggling with the Hindu fish mongers and, for much of the time, just sitting, gossiping, playing rummy or gambling and waiting for another day to pass. Extending in a semi-circle around the cove and up and down the two main roads and numerous small cobbled lanes were small one-story stone or wooden huts with small yards, a few trees or tropical plants and sometimes a garden set behind low stone walls.

In the little settlement of Roche Terre where the Hindu cane workers lived, stood the house of Octave's friend, Dhanilall Thug or Prem as his friends called him. Prem was not a fisherman but a Hindu student who lacked money to finish his studies. Nor could he find a job, even cutting cane on the big white-owned plantations like his father. Almost hidden by some leafy leela and mango trees, Prem's home was a tin-roofed shanty of cheap lumber; its three small rooms were almost bare except for two beds, a crude table, two chairs and the cooking utensils in the large shed where his mother cooked on an open floor hearth with charcoal. On the pink-painted walls of Octave's hut there were a picture in color of the Sacred Heart of Jesus and tinted photographs, torn from magazines, of European film actresses. The walls of Prem's hut were bare, plastered with yellowed newspapers against the night winds. As the only one of his father's seven children to be educated, Prem was allowed a small cubicle of his own, with a cot, a desk and one chair. Here he kept his stamp collection and seashells, his Boy Scout uniform, his Junior Lifesaving Certificate and his library: *Romeo and Juliet, Macbeth, Julius Caesar, As You Like It, Henry the Fifth,* a New Testament, *Saint Joan, Tom Sawyer, Huckleberry Finn, Coral Island, The 39 Steps,* a Milton anthology, Joseph Conrad's *Rover,* the action of which took place partly on Mauritius, and Bernardin de St. Pierre's *Paul et Virginie,* the most famous literary work about the island. The cheap editions were yellowed and mildewed; rats had nibbled away some of the edges.

This morning Prem's mother was away. She had fainted while peddling fried *samosas* and little cakes in the schoolyard; the hospital said she was suffering from severe malnutrition, having given what food there was to the children and going without, herself. Prem's father, a worn, sad-faced little Hindu with yellow, rotting teeth, was near a caneworker's retirement age; after working in the fields all day he took his bicycle to peddle peanuts in the cove to the fishermen. A brother, Dutt, a tailor's apprentice, who would not receive pay during five years while learning the trade, had already left the house when Prem awoke. It had been a restless night. His father, who slept beneath the table in the next room and suffered a respiratory ailment, had snored loudly, and Dutt had awakened him, grumbling, *"Pas faire tapze la hein!* Don't make noise, eh!" Ashamed, the father had turned on his side without saying a word, and Prem had called to Dutt from his bed, *"Do, mi, do!* Sleep you!" In the evening there had been an argument; Dutt had declared to the family, "In the very near future, there will be a revolution."

Prem had seldom seen his father so angry. "Why do you put such ideas in your head?" he had asked Dutt. "Only cowards do so." Later Dutt had told Prem, "He's an old man. He doesn't know anything. He doesn't understand the younger generation. All his life he spent in the cane fields; that's all he knows." Dutt, a ruggedly handsome, brown-skinned youth with coarse, long black hair, spent whatever money he could earn weekends as a laborer on clothes, girls and the cinema. *"Manger, boire, donne jazz,"* he would tell Prem, quoting a popular Creole adage. "Eat, drink and amuse yourself. Why do you always think and worry so much, Prem? Tomorrow we die." Dutt read only cheap *romans d'amour* with gaudy covers and titles like *She Will Come Tomorrow, Only You Know the Secret,* and *You Lack the Dignity to Be a Mother.* His taste in films was the same, the most recent favorite called *Primitive London,* which he told Prem was about "how hippies act, how prostitutes are being strangled and how a doctor tried to save a woman in childbirth." Unlike Prem, Dutt went to the village community center in the Creole section of the village each night to watch American television shows such as "Combat" and "Mission Impossible" on the community set. Dutt wished he could become a secret agent; he hated the drudgery in the tailor's shop.

For some weeks now Prem had been going fishing each morning with Octave. They had met two months before when Prem, despondent about his family's future and his own, after four years of unemployment, had gone to sit and watch the sunset every evening under the filao trees by the cove. One evening Octave approached him and said two tourists from South Africa had hired his pirogue for a week's skindiving in the lagoon. He wanted Prem to come along as an interpreter since the tourists knew no Creole and Octave spoke but little English. The week had been a grand adventure to Prem. One of the South Africans had hit a shark with his harpoon gun, and Prem helped to pull its thrashing body into the boat. Then the tourists had left, giving Prem one of their sets of fins and a mask as a tip, and he had continued to go fishing with Octave each day. If the catch was not good, Octave would give him one or two fish to take his mother to cook, but sometimes, if they speared as much as twenty or thirty pounds of fish and octopus, Prem might make two or three rupees, a rupee being twenty cents.

Prem's future was bleak. His father was fifty-six; in four more years he would face mandatory retirement as a cane worker and the family's income would fall from 31 rupees a week to a mere 20 rupees (or four dollars) a month. Prem, now twenty-two, had spent two years writing to seventy-six hospitals in England applying for training as an orderly, as many Mauritian youths did. He thought if only he could get to England he could save enough money to send some home so that his three youngest brothers could go back to school. As time wore on, his applications became more desperate and the rejections more perfunctory. It was a race against time in another way also. Not only was his father aging but there were already fifteen thousand other high school graduates on the island without jobs, and each year the number was growing by four or five thousand more. All were trying to go abroad. A happily-ever-after, in Prem's mind, came to take the form of acceptance by such imagined havens as St. Matthew's Hospital in London, the Royal West Sussex Hospital of Chichester, Southend-on-Sea Hospital or Pontefrant General Infirmary. But month by month, the negative replies came in. "I have my full quota of overseas applicants for some time ahead . . . I am sorry, so many Mauritian students have applied. . . . I regret . . . unable to help you. . . . your application has been unsuccessful. . . . cannot consider. . . . no vacancy. . . . no vacancy. . . . no vacancy."

Finally, a different letter came. Seeming to Prem like a guardian angel, a Miss H. K. Ware, Principal Nursing Officer of Churchill Hospital in Oxford, wrote that he could be admitted for training as soon as the hospital secured a worker's immigration permit for him. She warned that this might take as long as three years. Many more months passed and the island's government tightened up its qualifications so that Prem was no longer eligible to emigrate. Dismayed, Prem went to the labor ministry and was told that in his case the new requirements might be waived if the hospital matron in England agreed. A letter to this effect was forwarded by the ministry to the island's diplomatic representative in London. For some reason, it was never sent on to the hospital. After a year Prem wrote Miss Ware in desperation, trying to explain what had happened. Her reply had just been received. "I am deeply sorry, but as you have been turned down by your Government, I am unable to help you in any way."

Unable to help you in any way. What would become of them, Prem asked himself, his family, the fishermen, the cane workers, the children, the multitudes of children, everyone on the island? Sometimes he felt an angry, wild defiance rising up within him and he thought of violence and revolution and Lucifer's words in *Paradise Lost:*

> The mind is its own place, and in itself
> Can make a Heaven of Hell, a Hell of Heaven.
>
> . . . .
>
> Better to reign in Hell than serve in Heaven.

Although Prem's mother prayed each morning before a small shrine of the Hindu monkey god, Hanuman, Prem from his Christian education in the British schools of the island believed in the Biblical account of creation and in Adam and Eve. He half-believed that there would be a Day of Judgment. One of his friends, André, a wild-eyed Creole fisherman so fair he could be taken for a Frenchman, claimed the island's predicament fulfilled the prophecies of Daniel and Revelation. "The Apocalypse is drawing near," he would tell Prem as they sat in the filao grove and André mended his fishing nets. "Day after day, we see people are becoming more evil. There is a place in the Book of Daniel where it says that in the last days and the last times before the ending of the world, God will fill all the people with intelligence. 'And there shall be a time of trouble, such as never has been since there was a nation till that time. . . . And many of those who sleep in the dust of the earth shall awake, some to everlasting life, and some to shame and everlasting contempt. . . . the wicked shall do wickedly; and none of the wicked shall understand; but those who are wise shall understand. . . .' Before and after Daniel's time until now this was not true, Prem, but we see it in this generation, in this time we live in. We are living at the point of time, Prem."

Prem thought André a little mad and yet he too felt a sense of apocalypse. In the village, the old men like Robert, Octave's uncle, spoke of it and said starvation was coming. Even three years ago a fisherman might take home a catch from the lagoon worth five rupees a day; now he was lucky if he got two. And what would happen a year, two years, five years from now? There was much Prem did not understand. Only a few days before, Malcolm de Chazal, the island's painter, had told him while sketching a landscape on the beach, "It is not going to the moon that is important; it is the astronaut. I believe this will be shown in future history. When the astronaut went beyond the gravitation of the earth, he was a dead man. He turned around and for the first time in history a human being saw the earth as a whole, beyond himself, and he said, why do the people on earth fight one another? They belong to one earth. Why do the members of the same family, living in one house, fight one another, from room to room? When man reaches the moon, the moon has disappeared. There is only here, only the earth, before him and he sees the earth which has become the moon. We are here, no more in this physical world but in a magical world; we are in the trinitary and dialectic concept of the earth. The physical world of Isaac Newton, Copernicus and Einstein is dead. The feat of the astronauts is not only a spectacular thing but the entry into a new world. Our planet has become one and a whole, with no possibility of division without destruction of the whole. We are coming to a new form of thought which is totally revolutionized, like the thought of Christ, but it is prolonged, it is applied in the cosmic sense."

Prem did not know what to make of such talk; he thought André wise from reading but the old artist wise from thinking. He did understand why both the fisherman and the artist felt things were reaching a climax; everyone on the island sensed that. He felt the same way himself; things could not long continue as they were. Only a week before one of his Hindu school friends had committed suicide. His parents, illiterate caneworkers like Prem's own, could not understand why their son could not find a job after they had sacrificed and saved, penny by penny, for years for his education. One evening Prem's classmate had gone out behind his hut in Roche Terre and hanged himself.

If the old spoke of apocalypse, the young, like Dutt, talked of revolution. Many of Prem's school friends had joined the new *Movement Militant Mauricien,* which vowed to overthrow the island's government. Its leader was the son of a rich white island family, educated in England and a veteran of student riots in Paris; yet he was only two or three years older than Prem himself. At public rallies he accused the government of "allowing famine, disease, prostitution, humiliation and exploitation among the people" and called for violence to "sweep all the capitalists aside." Prem silently agreed with much of what the revolutionary said but he did not understand how the *M.M.M.* could do any better than the present government in getting jobs for the poor. An explosion of violence would only ruin what there was of an economy and force everyone back to subsistence poverty and probably starvation since the island had to sell its sugar abroad to pay for the rice and wheat it needed to keep everyone fed. Prem felt there had to be an alternative to violence and revolution.

Yet the speeches which disturbed him most at the *M.M.M.*'s village rallies were those made by a young Hindu schoolteacher who had once declared that "the present educational system with its heavy emphasis on parrot learning produces masses of expensive literates who have been psychologically raped. . . . There are those who argue that the present system prepares Mauritians for emigration. But anyone who has given the emigration question some attention will understand how facile and unrealistic, not to say tragic, such a stand is. Our educational system should prepare Mauritians to live decently in Mauritius."

Listening to him, Prem thought, "I was a fool to think everything would be solved if I could only get to England. . . ." The Hindu had declared that "Latin and Greek, Shakespeare and Milton, are still taught in many schools while the knowledge of modern technology and agriculture and Mauritian history is practically nonexistent; Mauritian students burn the midnight oil to learn by heart the date of the Battle of Hastings." "September 29, 1066, at Semlac," Prem had automatically recalled while hearing the speech. . . . But should there be only training in technology at the expense of the rest? Prem thought not, for in truth he loved English literature and found the poems and stories and dramas a great solace in life, even though he misquoted a number of his favorite passages. Often, sitting in the filao grove and watching the waves break against the reef in the evenings, he would repeat over and over such passages as Juliet calling from her balcony, "It is the dark of night. How come you here?" and Romeo's reply, "For stony limits cannot hold love out." In Prem's somewhat faulty memory, even Milton's sonorous passages were domesticated and homey, with Adam telling Eve, "With thee conversing I forget *all* the time. . . . God has assigned us, nor shalt we pass and praise for nothing lovelier can be found in woman than to study household duties." Prem compared the island's pudgy Hindu prime minister to Julius Caesar, "Why does he bestride the narrow world like a colossus? We petty men under his huge legs peep about to find ourselves dishonorable graves." Watching the sun set he would think, "Oh, for a muse of fire that would ascend the brightest heaven of invention," or, thinking of his friend, Octave: "Goodness was so mixed in him that all nature might stand up and say, 'This was a man.'" Sometimes he had memorized the passages in French, as with Milton's *Samson Agonistes: "Oh! Femme tu es la racine de tous les moeux mais ta beauté est une piège."* Like most educated Mauritians, Prem spoke both Hindi and Creole at home and had learned English, the official language, and French, the language of the island's cultural heritage, in school; like most of his friends he had ended up with a smattering of four languages and a mastery of none. Although Hindu marriages on the island were arranged by parents, and the bride and groom sometimes met for the first time on their wedding day, Prem's ideas on romance, as on so many things, came from books. His favorite of all was *Paul et Virginie,* the tragic love story of a dark-skinned Creole and a French girl. Virginie, forced to leave for France to marry one of her own countrymen after an idyllic childhood romance with the family's servant, Paul, returns to Mauritius only to be shipwrecked and washed ashore, drowned, at Paul's feet. Prem never tired of quoting Virginie's final farewell to Paul upon her departure for France: *"Maintenant je reste, je pars, je vis, je meurs; fais de moi ce que tu veux. Fille sans vertu! J'ai peur resister à tes caresses, et je ne puis soutenir ta doleur."*

The quick flutter of morning birds brought Prem out of his reverie. The cane scurried with waking life as he walked toward the cove. The quiet thudding of his sandals in the dust, the squeak of mice and the chirping of feeding birds sounded against the other secret noises of the dawn. In the village, too, one heard talk of revolution. Not from the fishermen or the cane cutters but in the gangs of relief laborers the government had hired to repair roads and reduce the frighteningly high unemployment statistics. The Hindu foreman of the gang, a great strapping bearded man, often cursed the government's leaders as "Vampires" and "Ali Baba and his forty thieves." He warned of the day when the people "will walk on blood," and one time he had told Prem, "Our blood has not yet become hot, but when it does there will be a revolution. Our children cry for bread but the ministers and their deputies and relations are eating gold and diamonds." Sometimes Prem would stop and listen to the laborers speak as they worked.

"They must start factories."

"Four rupees a day: do you think it is enough?"

"We are walking naked on this relief work."

"I have six children and only four rupees a day. Even with one child it is not enough."

"You yourself are guilty, having so many children."

"Day by day, the population is getting bigger."

"Day by day, we are growing poorer. A minister gets three thousand rupees. Sent by the assembly to England and France they amuse themselves at our expense. We are eating rocks and dust."

"*Pe ena plasir.* There is no pleasure."

"If they discharge us, there would be a revolution very soon."

"Ha! If you riot, they will just throw tear gas at you and kill you. And they will cable the English troops to come again."

"The ministers are burying the people; they are digging our tombs."

"The New Year is coming but we don't know what to eat. Better to take poison and die. But who has money for poison also?"

"If you have such a hot temper you will surely kill someone. And for that you'll hang yourself."

"*Misere. La misere.*"

"We must have a revolution."

"*Hein!* Some of you will say I must go see my family, some will say I must go to fish; no one will come. Words mean nothing. You must have a strong, fierce wind. It takes a cyclone to blow down a banyan tree."

Prem saw that few of the villagers blamed the island's problems on the begetting of too many children; everyone seemed to prefer to curse the government instead. Once he had accompanied a foreign woman doctor who was studying birth control for the World Bank; he had helped her interview fishermen mending their nets under the filao trees. Always the response was the same.

The doctor would ask, "How many children do you have?"

The answer would be, "Five," or "Seven," or even "Ten."

"There are methods to limit the number of children and space them. Do you approve of them?"

"*Non.*"

"Do you go to church?"

"*Oui.* Every Sunday."

"If the church tells you to use one method, would you agree?"

"*Non.*" A pause. "Unless my Master says."

"Where will you meet God where he can tell you this?"

"*La volonte,* faith will tell me. If God gives one, two, three, six, or even twenty, we must take."

"What do you do for a living?"

A shrug. "*Mo alle la peche.* I go to fish."

"Do you get enough fish?"

"*Non.*"

"Why?"

"Because there are no fish."

"Are there no fish or are there too many fishermen?"

"The fish are too few. We have no fish. Long ago God gave but now he doesn't."

"God has given us intelligence. Why not use it?"

"In the days to come I'll go one day to sleep for good. We can't say how many children we will have. God gives and it is not up to us. You must take what is given. God gives and when it is time he takes you to heaven and you must go."

"Do your children have good clothes and a good house?"

"*Non. Misere, misere. Misere pe vini.* Misery is coming."

Always the answers were the same. The day after the foreign doctor left in exasperation, Prem watched the same fishermen passing in a procession from the village church. A Creole priest in a long white cassock led them, chanting through a cardboard megaphone, "Blessed are the poor in spirit, for theirs is the kingdom of heaven. Blessed are those who mourn, for they shall be comforted. Blessed are the meek, for they shall inherit the earth . . . Ye are the salt of the earth; but if the salt has lost its savor, how shall its saltness be restored. . . ." Prem watched and wondered and went home and anxiously wrote more letters to England.

Now he hurried his pace. He could see George, a young Creole who served as Octave's boatman, already pushing the pirogue through the shallow darkness of the cove. Octave and Karl, another fisherman, were wading toward it with their diving gear, the mast, sail, harpoon guns, spears and a gaff. Prem felt the pebbled sand under his feet and then the water. As he slid off his sandals he felt, as he always did, as if he were entering another world. He heard the fishermen laughing and thought to himself, "Octave welcomes life as it comes." The young Creole fisherman, a mason by profession, had turned to the sea only two years before, when most construction on the island stopped as the economy began its steep slide downhill. Now, unable to earn more than a rupee or two a day fishing with the nets, lines or cages the other fishermen used, Octave had struck out for himself in the more dangerous occupation of underwater fishing, using spears for octopus and a harpoon gun for large fish just outside the reef where the coral fell precipitously toward the ocean floor. Since large sharks and giant barracuda sometimes rose from these black depths, at times coming into the lagoon itself, few of the fishermen in Grand Gaube cared to swim underwater, and very few would dive beneath the surface. Many had never learned to swim, and each winter in the stormy waters of June and July when hurricanes swept the island a few of the fishermen always drowned. Their boats were too small, for one thing. The fathers or grandfathers of all the men in Grand Gaube had been slaves, descended from Africans, who, when emancipated by the British, had fled the plantations to try to gain, in freedom from their former white masters, a meager living from the sea. Fishing techniques were crude and rudimentary, and because of the island's isolation, had remained so.

Octave and Karl greeted Prem with nods while he stowed his diving gear in the bow; together they put the gaffs and spears across the wooden seat slats. Octave fitted the rope lashing of the oars into the thole pins and Karl laid the mast and rigging to one side of the pirogue; leaning forward against the thrust of the blades in the water, he began to row as the others waded alongside in the shallow water. The pirogue was made of local *bois noire* wooden beams and planks imported from Singapore; it had been built in the village by one of the families of marine carpenters. Heavy rocks had been put in the hull for ballast, and a large rock tied to a rope served as a makeshift anchor. The water of the cove was very low now that the tide was out. Karl began humming a tune; he was a small but muscular Creole with skin blackened almost purple by the sun, and was considered the toughest fighter in the village. He always got into fights when he drank too much rum, turning violently aggressive, and had been jailed for two months for knifing another fisherman. Without nerves, and strong, he was one of the ablest underwater divers on the island and, unlike Octave, usually doubled his earnings by gambling each afternoon and evening. The fishermen and Hindu fishmongers all said Karl knew all the tricks, but no one had ever caught him cheating. Still he usually won at cards.

In the darkness Prem and Karl climbed into the boat as Octave gave directions to George and pointed out into the lagoon. "We'll be at Ile d'Amber by sunrise," he said, lifting the heavy mast into its fitting. He put a worn stick into the rudder's slot as a tiller and stepped the mast. With its boom rigged, the gray, patched sail drew, and the pirogue began to move. George laid down the gaff, Karl stopped rowing, and the sail after flapping wildly a few seconds caught the trade wind; the boat skimmed over the water, the waves slapping gently at the bow. The eastern sky grew lighter and they could see other boats, low in the water and well out toward the reef. It was possible to see the church steeple now and the huts along the shore; a flock of pigeons started up from somewhere and flew around the cove and settled again, white pigeons with iridescent wings. Near some rocks as they moved into the lagoon two Hindu boys were wading, hunting for crayfish in the rocks. One caught a small octopus and beat it against an outcropping rock.

"Look, I'll scare them," Octave said. He shouted, "Hey, over there! What's that *couyonade?* Will you let that baby octopus go? You will have trouble! Will you leave it alone?"

One of the Hindus turned upon the other. It was illegal to kill a young octopus in the lagoon. "You are silly. You are hitting a tiny one. Let it alone!" He started wading for the shore. "I'll wait for you at the church! Hurry!" The two Hindus scrambled out of the water. Karl and Octave laughed.

"These coolies from Malabar," Karl said, "we make them go away."

"That's not good," Prem told him, feeling a stab of loyalty toward his fellow Hindus. "They were frightened."

"Shut up your *liki*," Karl cursed him with a grin, using the Creole word for the female sex organ. "You have not the right to be angry. You are not a coolie from Malabar any more. You are a Creole."

"Look at the light coming," George called from the bow, "like silver." A little color came into the eastern sky and almost at once the lonely dawn line crept toward the sea turning it from leaden gray to a misty dark green. Green appeared in the treeline on the shore and the open patches of earth were gray brown. In the pirogue, the faces lost their grayish shine. Octave's face, half-hidden under a shapeless slouch hat with a torn brim which he always wore fishing, seemed to darken with the growing light.

"This is a good time of the day," Octave murmured, feeling wide awake now that they were under sail. "Will I get some fish with you, George? Will we catch fifty pounds today?"

"Non," coughed George, in a drowsy voice.

"I must have twenty rupees for the New Year," Octave said. "Now I have not one cent to buy my sweetheart a present." Octave was hoping to marry a girl in the nearby village of Poudre d'Or, but, as the others were aware, he lacked enough money to pay for a wedding. A church wedding was expensive since Creole custom decreed the groom had to hire a hall and jazz band in Port Louis for *bals* that lasted all night; then there was the cost of furniture. Octave planned to live in his father's house in Grand Gaube, adding a room or two of stone and thatch which he could build himself.

"Not even one cent for the New Year, I have not," grumbled Karl.

"We must fish hard to have twenty rupees," said Octave.

"Fishing? You make so much fishing?" growled Karl. *"Non."* He twisted his face into a sardonic grin. Lately they had been bringing home catches of twenty to thirty pounds. This meant about twelve rupees in all, with two going to pay the rent of the boat and the rest being split among the four of them. Karl called to Prem, "Hey, Prem, you are no Malabar coolie. You look like a Creole. You eat chicken, beef and pork. You can ask for the hand of Octave's sister."

Prem was embarrassed. Hindus did not joke about their sisters. He had danced several times at Creole *bals* with young Lydia, who was only eighteen, pretty and very fair, not a dark brown like Octave. "I don't eat pork," he told Karl.

Octave agreed. "No, he doesn't eat pork. . . . But if you ask for the hand of my sister, Prem, you must eat pork and rats. And if you come to court on Sunday you can stay all night if it rains. And on Monday you and I shall go fishing together. You can sleep with my. . . ." Karl began to guffaw at Prem's embarrassment. "You know, Prem," he joined in, "the girls here don't like fishermen. You must tell them you only go fishing for fun."

Octave stood up, holding on to the mast and began to sing, in the manner of a French *chanteur, "La coeur guérira la blessure, parlez-moi d'amour. . . ."* Warming up, he switched to the tune of *"Oh, Capri, c'est fini,"* improvising the lyrics:

> Dance with me
> Don't hold me tight
> We will fall down
> And the others will laugh
>
> She is called Gabriel
> She is beautiful
> She doesn't give her love for free. . . .

"There is a woman in Beau Bassin," began Karl, "who is called Belinda. She has a beautiful *liki*. I met her at the *bal* last Saturday in Tamarin. I got into a fight. There's some bad ones there in Tamarin. All because I boasted of Grand Gaube."

"Is she a little woman, this one you flirted with?" Octave asked.

Karl leered and gave a little laugh. "I made her younger sister too. At the dance itself. But I had no taste to sleep with them, these city girls from Beau Bassin. The older one got mad. I was a little drunk."

"If I had been with you, we could have passed along that road together."

"Her little sister sat on my lap and I squeezed her breasts. I told her, 'I must sleep with you.' I asked her, 'What do you want? A necklace? A Coca Cola? But I must have you.' "

Octave laughed. "If she was hot enough, who could have stopped her?" He called back to George, who was now holding the rudder. "Hey, *gogot*," he said, using the Creole slang for penis, "put the rudder to the outside." Octave looked around at the water. "Little

[71

Arnaud said he saw a barracuda around here." Octave leaned back on the seat and began to sing again, this time in a noisy parody of Edith Piaf:

> *Non rien de rien*
> *Je ne regrette rien*
> *Non rien de rien*
> *Je ne regrette rien....*

"When you go to Tamarin," Karl went on, "you must have a firm friend with you. Those people are tough and proud."

"Like me," Octave joked.

Karl laughed. "Four times truth, forty times lies," he said, quoting a village saying. "No, Octave, she was much older than me, that woman from Beau Bassin."

Octave gave a hoot. "Not much! Only forty-five! Two old ladies and Karl!" He laughed again and said, "Perhaps the two of them were whores." He sang,

> Little woman
> The gallants promise you, then run away
> Don't hold me too tight.
> I'm fragile; you'll make me afraid.

"Buffoon," snarled Karl. "*Liki* of your mama." He yawned and stared out at the sea. After a time he said indifferently, "That woman of Beau Bassin wrote me a letter." Octave became interested and asked seriously, "Will you go again?" Karl shrugged. "To hell with her. There is not one taste to them, the women of Beau Bassin." Octave laughed and began another mocking chorus of *"Je ne regrette rien."* A redness grew up out of the eastern horizon, catching with pink and silver light the small patches of broken white on the choppy water's surface. Smoke rose from the chimney of a sugar factory. They could now see the green slopes rising to the high plateau and beyond, blue hazy hills all still, and far, far distant the strange volcanic peaks with the names the French and Dutch had given them: the Moka range, Corps de Garde and, pointing like a rocky finger into the sky, Pieter Both, after a Dutch sailor who scaled the peak and then, like Icarus, centuries before, fell to his death. Octave took off his shapeless hat and mopped his face with it. His shorts and tricot were in rags, eaten away by salt and one could see the hard muscles through the holes. His face was weathered a deep brown and his eyes, as they searched the water, were a startling bright blue and piercing, and the skin was wrinkled in the corners from the sun. Thick black curly hair framed a face that was both Gallic and African and yet neither; savage, humorous, gentle, wise, the face of the Mauritian Creole. There were strong deep lines cut from his cheeks in curves beside the mouth, and it was only when he laughed, as he did often, showing his fine white teeth, that you saw how young he was. His hands were hard, with broad fingers and nails as thick and ridged as clam shells, and the hams were shiny with callus. His feet bore small cuts from the coral, as did Karl's and Prem's, because of the long hours spent each day in the salt water; they took a long time to heal. Prem asked Karl what to put on the sores; his were festering.

"The only good thing is to masturbate and rub the sperm in. Rub it well. It's a good medicine." Karl hooted with laughter and Prem, as often, could not tell if he were serious or not. Octave was singing again, this time to the melody of "Island in the Sun."

Oh mon Ile au soleil
Paradie entre terre ciel
Ou le flot le long du jour
Change au sable fin chanson d'amour....

Oh, island in the sun
Paradise between earth and sky
Where the boats set sail all the day
And we sing by the white sand soft songs of love

"George was masturbating this morning," Karl announced with his habitual leer. "I saw him waiting on the road and the headlights of a car came behind him and the light caught his hand. I saw something shining and I said, 'George, do you wear such a big ring?' '*Non,*' says George. 'I don't wear any ring.' 'Then why is your finger glittering?' George wiped his hand on his shirt but I saw it in the headlights of that car." Karl laughed. "The hell with you, George. The hell with you. You were masturbating."

George protested. "*Non, non,* I was not." He looked chagrined and embarrassed.

"Shut up your *liki*, Karl!" Octave called. "George, spit!" George leaned over the side of the boat and tried to spit but nothing came; his mouth was dry. Octave and Karl hooted with laughter. "George

[73

don't lie," Octave said. "You masturbated." To Prem's surprise, George lowered his head and mumbled, "Well, only men do it," causing the two fishermen to carry on like lunatics. Octave was in high spirits now. Filling his lungs with air, he sang "Never on a Sunday."

> *On voit des gris sous le ciel bleu*
> *Un bateau, deux bateaux, trois bateaux*
> *S'ent vont chantant*
> *Dans le réal ou coup de siècle*
> *Un oiseau, deux oiseaux, trois oiseaux*
> *Font du beau temp. . . .*

> We see some gray in the blue sky
> One boat, two boats, three boats
> Go singing
> In the real the blow of the century
> One bird, two birds, three birds
> Make the weather good. . . .

"O, *Bon Dieu*, oh, *mo mama*, will I get fish with you today, George?" Octave teased the boy. "Will I have to tell you everything, always?"

They were nearing the reef now and there were outcroppings of niggerheads and meadows of sea grass and the watery roar of the sea beating against the reef masses of broken coral and sand. They passed over the deeper channel of the lagoon and entered the shallower waters of a shoal. As they drew nearer and nearer the crashing surf, and as the blinding sun came over the horizon and fell on the pirogue, they sailed alongside a little fleet of five pirogues moving into the tossing waves; the fishermen aboard them were splashing their gaffs on the water's surface, hissing and beating *batage* sticks against the seats and hulls to frighten the fish underwater into their large nets, which flashed with beaded light in the spray. The sun fell on their own sail. The gray weathered canvas was gold and bright, and they felt the sudden warmth of the sun. The white foam of the surf, crashing and spraying and roaring and foaming, glittered and sparkled with reflected light.

"*Alle degage!*" the *patron* shouted and the two net boats began moving together, the rowers straining all their muscles, and in the sterns of the *batage* boats men with gaffs pushed faster and faster and the drums went out over the water, bum bum te dum, bum bum te dum dum dum dum dum dum dum dum dum. . . . A roar of shouts and oaths went up as all five pirogues collided and bumped together and the drumming stopped and their voices came over the water as all hands began to slowly haul the heavy dripping net in.

"Pull hard!"

"Swing around!"

"Draw it in. Faster, faster!"

"Turn, turn!"

"Let the plomb go! Take the oars! Hold it fast!"

"Change your wine, Francois! That Bordeaux is too strong for you."

"Quickly, Pa, quickly! Pull it in!"

"No, not that way, Herve. I'll kill you! You are good for nothing but whoring and stealing!"

"*Liki to mama,* go fix the net."

"Pull your boat in line, Pa."

"Rolland, you *gogot!* Barricade them with the net!"

"Hurry! Hurry!"

"Ah, mo mama, ah, Bon Dieu, ah, mo mama!"

They all loved to watch the excitement of the spectacle when the boats crashed together and the men pulled the great net in. Before striking out on his own, Octave had worked for some months with them and he had felt the thrill of maneuvering the boats to catch the shoals of fish and tossing the nets in the heavy surf. But there had been too many days of sharing a catch of twenty pounds among fifteen or sixteen men and boys. A man could starve on that.

Octave watched intently, squinting his eyes, as the boats moved apart and the separate boats unfurled their sails again. In each a lone man stood in the bow or stern with a gaff, turning the pirogues into the wind. He was silhouetted black against the sunrise and as the gaffman lifted his long wooden staff and splashed the water, the boats seemed to have wings of glittering golden spray. Octave looked past them to where, outside the reef, three large double-sailed craft had gone far out to sea. Each was thirty-two feet long, twice the length of the ordinary pirogues inside the lagoon, and with motors and ten-man crews they could take the heavy waves of the open sea and go to the three offshore islands, L'Ile Platte, L'Ile Ronde and the fortress-shaped Coin de Mire, and even fifteen or twenty miles beyond the reef where the currents were enough to carry a regular pirogue helplessly out to sea. Such a larger boat, called a *peniche,* brought home an abundant haul of fish every day. All three were owned by prosperous proprietors in the village who hired men to do their fishing for them.

Grand Gaube was the largest village in Mauritius. Its six hundred fishermen accounted for about one-sixth of all those on the entire island; aside from these, who were registered, there were several thousand more men who fished at least part of the day in the lagoon to help feed their families until they found work. The fishermen in Grand Gaube had long sought their government's help in getting large enough boats to get outside the depleted reef, but in several years of trying they had not been successful. Two months before, relief had seemed to be in sight when the United Nations sent an American fisheries expert to the island. But his assignment, requested by the island's Hindu-led government, had turned out to be to conduct a five-million-rupee investigation of deep sea fishing, which, if it benefited anyone at all, would help a few rich Hindus and the big, largely white-owned commercial fishing operations in Port Louis. The Grand Gaube village council had still gone ahead and invited the foreign expert to come and hear their problems and advise them. One day he drove up in a shiny American car and spent an hour talking with the fishermen in the Roman Catholic primary school, the only large hall in the village. The schoolroom was packed; some two hundred fishermen came. Prem acted as interpreter and he saw that the American, not understanding Creole and not familiar with the fishermen's rough appearance and manners, was ill at ease. Prem himself became alarmed when several Creoles shouted that they had been bluffed too many times by the government in the past and no longer trusted it. When the American said hotly that any assistance would have to be channeled through the government, about twenty men stomped out, swearing under their breaths and muttering oaths, and did not return. The others were more reasonable. The American said the important thing was to get the fishermen offshore and out of the depleted and over-fished lagoon. He said if they would choose leaders among themselves and form an association of at least one hundred men, he would see what he could do about helping them get bigger boats. The meeting ended on a promising note and the American pledged to return in about two weeks. When two months passed and he did not come, Prem and Octave went along with three of the older fishermen, all *patrons* of the village's net fishing cooperatives, to see the American in his office. They learned he could be found in the agricultural ministry some twenty miles away on the other side of the island, so they hired an old taxi and assembled in suits and ties and slicked down hair as if they were going to Sunday mass.

When they reached his office, the American was friendly, if surprised, to see the fishermen suddenly appear at the ministry. He had not neglected the matter, he told them, but had discussed the possibility of getting bigger boats with the minister himself, and had been informed a fishing association already existed in Grand Gaube, as in other villages along the coast. Octave told Prem to explain that this had been formed by Catholic priests anxious to get the fishermen to inform on anyone who used illegal dynamite or mosquito nets in the lagoon at night. While the practice was illegal it had proved difficult to enforce laws against it since the fishermen refused to inform on each other. In Grand Gaube, this association had been headed by a rich carpenter; he had charged a rupee's membership fee and twenty-five cents a month. Less than thirty fishermen joined. The others objected to the fee, asking what was the money to be used for, except to line the pockets of the rich carpenter? Prem tried to explain and then Octave whispered in his ear with some agitation, "It is just to make fishermen catch fishermen. To create hostility among friends. We are only poor fishermen. . . ." Prem translated and the American said curtly, "All fishermen are poor the world over."

After hearing their case once more, the American told them, "If you do not like the existing organization, it is up to you to change its character. It is already legally registered and the government wants us to work through it. Now I have also contacted the American Embassy for assistance. I think I have a fairly firm promise of help. They have agreed to give the necessary materials. But the boats must be built in the villages by the fishermen themselves. We call this 'self-help.' The fishermen must contribute the labor."

Prem translated this to the fishermen, knowing already what the answer would be. In the villages the boat builders or marine carpenters were not fishermen. By tradition, boat building was a completely separate occupation. And how could the fishermen on one or two rupees a day pay the marine carpenters to build boats for them? Hadn't the American spent any time in the island's fishing villages to see how it all worked? What did he do with his time, Prem wondered with irritation.

The American was adamant. "It has to be self-help," he said. "The fishermen must contribute something. Otherwise they will not take care of the new boats. We have a lot of experience in this in Africa. They must contribute something."

Prem translated. The fishermen wanted him to tell the American that the boats they needed cost 20,000 rupees each and that ten would be enough for Grand Gaube. As the American took this in, Prem thought to himself, multiply 200,000 by 6 and with 1,200,000 rupees or $240,000, you could change the island's whole fishing economy and help a substantial proportion of its people. Fishing, aside from coolie labor on the docks in Port Louis, was the main occupation of the island's 230,000 Creole men, women and children. And yet the government and United Nations were spending almost that much just for an investigation of commercial deep sea fishing that would not benefit anyone for years and then would only enrich a few whites and Hindu political leaders, even if it did increase the island's food supplies.

Prem tried to put this into words and discovered how angry he was getting. The American too was getting testy.

"Tell them there are just too many fishermen," he told Prem. "There are not enough fish in the lagoon. I know fishermen have many problems. I am familiar with them and I sympathize with them. But frankly speaking, there are too many fishermen and there aren't enough fish in the lagoon. Also, I should remind you that I am here on a project requested by this government. The government has not asked the United Nations for assistance to the lagoon fishermen. There are simply too many of them. They have got to find something else to do."

But what? Prem was reminded of Miss Ware. . . . I am deeply sorry but as you have been turned down by your Government, I am unable to help you in any way. The American's voice went on, "There are too many fishermen. There are not enough fish in the lagoon. . . ." He kept repeating himself, as if he suspected Prem were not translating him or had not gotten the point across. Prem wondered if he should keep repeating this same thing. The fishermen knew that before they came. That was why they came. For help. Did all these people, the American and the Miss Ware's of the world, want a revolution, Prem asked himself with rising bitterness. He was about to put this into words when a big American car drove up outside and a woman got out and approached the office; she looked inside, saw there was a meeting, and mouthed some words to her husband. The American rose, said he was sorry but he was already late for another engagement. He shook hands with all the fishermen and Prem. He said nothing about meeting again.

The fishermen stayed glumly silent on the return trip until they entered the outskirts of Port Louis; when they passed the harbor Octave finally spoke up. "You had a hot discussion, Prem," he said. He suggested they stop for a drink at one of the open-air taverns along the waterfront. "We are exhausted," he said. "To be relieved, we must have a bit of rum." Prem took only a glass of beer, but the fishermen, after a double peg of rum, became more cheerful and ordered another round. Walking back to the taxi, Octave put his arm around Prem's shoulder. "You are like a brother to me, Prem. I am very, very unhappy when I look to the future. Who will help us? I'm saving every rupee now to get married but I don't know what will happen when winter comes. Sometimes it is so cold in the water I want to cry out." He stumbled on the curb, feeling the rum, then straightened up and said, "I do not live for money, Prem. I live for dignity."

Now for many weeks there had been no more talk of getting bigger boats. Prem saw only a bleak future for the village. If the fishermen could have big enough boats, he thought, and training, they could have a good life. If they could only organize, he thought; if they could not, they would never have anything. Sometimes he felt there was no hope for them. Somehow they seemed to lack the spirit to unite and fight for what they must have to live. In the next two, three, four years what would happen to them? There would be more fishermen, fewer fish; perhaps some would starve. It was a hard life already. At sea they could get drowned at any time. Some days they caught almost nothing. And as poor as they were, they were extravagant. At a *bal,* Prem had seen a barefoot Creole woman pay three rupees for a ticket to go and dance all night. A Hindu, he knew, would have bought a pair of sandals instead. The fishermen frequently got into drunken brawls and knife fights, and yet they always went meekly to church the next morning.

"Hey, Cokol!" Karl shouted at a passing boat, bringing Prem back to the present. "Cokol is the premier buffoon of Grand Gaube. One day he told his wife he was ill. She was pregnant and he took one of her pills. He was sick for a week."

Octave joined in. "One time his wife bought a milk can. He used it for a *sega* drum and cracked the side."

"Once he spent ten rupees on rum and then started to weep about it, the *liki* of his mother."

"Once he was cutting his hair and he drew a plastic comb across it and split the comb three ways."

"Cokol stepped on a poison fish but when he took his foot away that *laif* was dead. You and I would have gone to sleep in the hospital." Octave shifted the sail into the wind and they all ducked their heads as it swung around and the boat changed direction, moving closer along the reef. Octave was impatient to start fishing. He said, "The boat is as slow today as a *morpion* at the funeral of a *femme petain*" [a crab and a prostitute]. He sighed, "Will you give me a heart attack, George?.... The roughness of the water is determined by the size of the waves. Oh, George, you are a pubic hair. You are like a *gogot*. Rest a moment. The current itself is moving the pirogue."

George sat down on the wooden edge and watched Octave rethread the line of his harpoon gun. Shafts of sunlight pierced the shallow green water beside them and the light made prisms above the pink, green, yellow and lavender coral. The boat entered deeper water, the green and brown and white of the deep shoal. "Karl, pull down the rigging," Octave called. Below, sand stretched emptily in the mist between little islands of coral and there was not a living thing in sight. They were close to l'Ile d'Ambre now, a deserted sandy mound of tall grasses and filao trees. "Push, push, George, take the gaff!"

"Where are we going?" George asked.

"On your mother," Octave replied. He turned the tiller to the side, pointing the pirogue's bow directly into Barracuda Pass, a turbulent break in the reef leading into the open sea. The milky green water became rougher and it turned blue-black where the rampart fell thousands of fathoms to the ocean depths. The boat started to toss gently in the slow swells and choppy waves. Octave stood in the bow, watching the sea. Dark gray clouds were beginning to form on the northern horizon. But toward the island the billowing white cumulus looked friendly and only the thin feathers of cirrus clouds were overhead. Octave stripped down to his swimming trunks and settled against the boat's wooden edge. He squinted judiciously at the water, dipping in his fins to make them wet and slippery. "Wake up, Prem. Hand me the speargun. You kill me, George. Can you reach the bottom with the gaff here? If not, use the oar."

Prem rubbed spit on the inside of his visor to prevent it from clouding up underwater. Octave and Karl donned their fins and masks and without losing a second flipped backward into the water with a splash. Once the two fishermen were swimming away from the boat and then disappeared under the surface of the water, George told Prem, "Octave takes me to be stupid. He believes that I don't know how to hold the boat. But how would he manage if I had not come?" Prem knew this to be true. Octave was dependent on the skill of the seventeen-year-old George, whom he had taught to use the gaff and sail. He also knew George trusted Octave's knowledge of the sea completely.

George, after his silence in front of Octave and Karl, now grew talkative and he told Prem about an experience he had had the evening before. There was a girl in the village who had no boyfriend, or *gallant* as George put it, and he had approached her and said, "Where are you going, *ma jolie*? You will get lost in the wind." But instead of replying in the same vein as the girls did in George's *romans d'amour* the girl swore at him, *"Liki to mama,"* and flounced away. Prem stifled a smile. George said he wanted to tell Prem about a troubling dream he had in the night. "You know what it was about? I have loved a girl. Her father caught us when we were together. He dragged the girl away from me. The girl slipped away and said to me, 'I'll stay with you.' When I told her I had nine younger brothers and could not keep a woman like her in my house, she didn't care. But my father also finds out and he wants to push me out of the house. My mother speaks to my father and he finally agrees to our marriage. This time my wife gets a job in the house of a *blanc*. We have got some rooms to live in the same house of this white man. I have left my mother and father and gone to live there. Then one day I find the *blanc* sleeping with my wife. I was so afraid and mad I woke up then and was shaking."

"Do you really know the girl?"

"Yes, I met her but she doesn't live in Grand Gaube."

Karl swam up and dropped a red parrot fish into the pirogue. He held onto the side for a second, catching his breath and called to them, "There's a lot of old women sitting around the boat today."

Prem hurriedly dipped his fins over the side of the boat, spat again on the inside of his visor, strapped on the mask and dropped backward into the water, going slowly to avoid splashing George. He swam away from the boat toward Octave, moving slowly forward, his fins pulsing softly just below the surface so as to make no sound. He looked around him through the glass visor, trying to pierce the misty horizons of Barracuda Pass. To his left, the coral reef fell sharply and perhaps fifteen or twenty feet below there was a flat shelf, scattered with black rocks, open stretches of white sand and clumps of posidonia, the common seaweed of all oceans. Unlike the choppy surface of the pass, the sea was calm below, almost sluggish. The great coral reef of l'Ile d'Ambre, which reached out into the sea past Grand Gaube like a giant wall, was varied; each pass had its distinct character: Kalodin was light and shallow; Ramzan full of caves and tunnels; Basmaurice like a small sunken island under the sea. Prem liked Troualbert best. It was named after Albert Hall in London and was a deep break in the coral, shaped underwater like a giant cathedral or amphitheater. Everything was a deep green color and Prem always half-expected to hear a ghostly chorale of sea spirits rising from its silent, misty depths. But the surface waves at Troualbert were too turbulent for the small pirogue on most days; George could not hold the boat in deep water with his gaff or the oars and there was a danger it would smash into the reef rocks. Several times it had almost been carried against them and Octave and Karl had had to come quickly swimming back and help row into calmer waters.

Prem saw Octave's blue fins ahead and the luminescent air bubbles they left in their wake. Octave was suspended, floating on the surface, pausing a moment to look below, and then he dove to the floor of the sandy shelf, investigating a few promising rocks thick with weed. Prem watched his friend tense as he spotted a spiny-backed Cordonier fish; it must have weighed two pounds and, as a fish in the premier class, would fetch two rupees a pound. It was nibbling algae from a lump of coral. Octave held his heavy blue *Champion* harpoon gun before him and moved slowly toward the fish, lowering his body flat in the water like an infantryman edging himself toward an enemy position. The harpoon was tipped with a needle-sharp trident—a short-range weapon of perhaps ten to twelve feet of killing power but best for reef fishing. In the air, it was said, the harpoon could pierce the bodies of three men. Prem swam to just above Octave; he never dove down beside him until Octave pulled the trigger. When he heard the sharp ping as the harpoon was released and no longer feared disturbing the fish, Prem dove below. As he glided down he remembered to cast a glance around him to see if there was any big lurking shape. There was always a danger, once Octave and Karl began to bring in fish, that a shark or barracuda, drifting up from the depths, might witness the kill, or the blood of the harpoon's wound would bring scavengers in from the deep water. But there was nothing in sight. Prem saw a pink parrot fish, watching without fear but curious, as the Cordonier lashed its tail in reflex aggression. Prem broke the surface to beckon to George, who had drifted more than fifty yards away, to bring the pirogue closer. Octave swam quickly toward it, holding the fish in his hand to show George and then dropping it into the boat. Octave held on to the boat for a moment's rest, then swam back again. He beckoned to Prem to follow him closely.

As they dove deep into the water together, exploring the caves and hiding places along the face of the rampart, a dense mass of silvery *brette* fish, glinting blue and yellow in the shafts of sunlight, showed up ahead. Below, near the sandy greenish floor of the shelf, was another shoal of larger black fish. As they dove after them, the mass divided sharply leaving a wide channel, and then closed behind them in a single black cloud. Prem and Octave swam softly forward. A carpet of sea grass began, waving back and forth like wheat in a rainstorm, and then came a patch of broken coral and a large niggerhead. They stopped and floated, their eyes scanning the brilliant jungle. A blue green form materialized through the far mist and came toward them, a beautiful Cato Verte. It circled closely beneath them as if displaying itself, and its dark blue eyes examined them closely. The large fish began nibbling on some algae on the underside of a coral rock, and Octave moved toward it slowly raising his speargun. Just as he aimed and pulled the trigger the fish made a dart at a speck of something suspended in the water and Octave missed; he had to hurriedly reload the gun, paddling almost vertically in the water. But not long after he had his harpoon restrung the Cato Verte circled back once more, and Octave fired a second time, piercing the fish in the head with his harpoon. Once he heard it fire, Prem looked around in preparation to dive. The rampart, he observed, fell very steeply toward the black depths in this place and it was very hard to see any distance in the green mist. Then his body tensed and his head swivelled sharply to the side. Some secret sense had warned him of danger and now he saw the lurking black shadow, probably attracted by the thrashing of the Cato Verte.

At first Prem thought it was a shark. One had once come to within a few feet of him, and his stomach had crawled with fear until Octave beckoned to him, and together they slowly swam back to the boat, being careful not to make any darting movement or sudden splash. Prem had had only one good look at the shark's wide, flattened, shovel-pointed head and the white-tipped pectoral fins. It looked evil and obscene, the hateful scavenger of the sea, and for a long time afterward he shuddered to think how close he had been to it. It had seemed almost seven or eight feet long, although of course everything looked bigger in the water.

But this was not a shark. Its back was as blue as a swordfish and the belly was silver. It was longer than the shark but narrow, and Prem found he was watching it with as much awe as fear. It was slowly slicing its giant erect tail through the water but otherwise did not move. To Prem, it seemed majestic and dignified. This fierce fish was very beautiful. Prem's skin tightened, but he kept swimming toward Octave in the same gentle rhythm. Then he saw the fish was moving on, ignoring them for some other prey somewhere beyond in the misty, moving seagrass. Octave had also seen the big fish now and was swimming slowly and carefully toward the boat, dragging the Cato Verte the full distance of the harpoon line. When the fish was safely inside the pirogue, Octave called excitedly across the waves to Prem, pulling off his mask, "Barracuda! There's a barracuda here. Follow me, Prem. Stay with me when I shoot a fish. Perhaps he'll go away." He told George to try to keep the boat very close to them, not less than thirty feet, and pulled his visor back on.

Soon, on the third dive, Octave harpooned a parrot fish and swam for the boat. Prem, swimming a few yards behind, again saw the big barracuda first. He took two quick but steady strokes and touched Octave's shoulder. The big fish was moving in behind Octave. Octave spun around and froze in the water for a second, then he slowly pivoted his body until he was face to face with the barracuda, separated by only twenty or so feet of water. Slowly, slowly, Octave pushed the parrot fish off the spear and began to restring the harpoon. Prem stayed as close as possible to Octave's side, just treading the water as slowly as he could and still stay in place. The barracuda seemed to drift forward until he was about six feet away. Octave kept his visor pointed right at it; he didn't look away or move a muscle. For some seconds, the three of them, the two men and the big fish, hung suspended in the water. Then Karl's blue fins came into view out of the mist; he had been alerted by George from the boat and held his harpoon gun poised, pointed at the barracuda. Karl drifted close to them, and with painful slowness, with Karl behind never turning his back to the big fish, Octave and Prem swam the few yards back to the boat. They lifted themselves over the edge and kept the boat in place directly beside Karl who stayed in the water for some moments, waiting for the barracuda to vanish once more in the mist, before he climbed in too.

"Let's go, Karl," Octave said breathlessly. He was taking his fins off. "We can't fish here with a barracuda around." He told George to step up the mast. Water dripped from his body and he sat hunched, quivering with the cold and a delayed nervous reaction.

"George, give me my tricot and my cigarettes." From the pocket of his ragged shorts, Octave brought out a rumpled packet of cheap Embassy cigarettes. He passed one along to Karl and another to George, then bent to light his own, putting it between his shaking knees so the wind could not get at the match. Inhaling and wrapping the tricot around his shoulders, Octave felt instantly better, and the pinched, ashen look left his face. He laughed. "Shall we have curry tonight? Shall we? If you don't eat fish, you shall eat greens." He stared at the shimmering sea and air for the first time. The clouds along the northern horizon were getting darker, almost dark blue in the center of the mass. "George," Octave said, "set sail, we will go to

Roche Blanch to hunt octopus closer to the cove. I don't like that sky. Maybe a storm is coming."

Prem, who could still hear his heart thumping, looked anxiously at the sky, but Karl laughed and said, "Thunder is good for octopus. They look out from their rocks. The most beautiful sea is today when it's rough."

George stepped the mast, struggling under its weight to put it in place. He lost his balance for a second when the boat rolled and a tip of the canvas sail dipped in the water.

"George, *to pena ene la vie?*" Octave called. "Have you no life in you?"

"George masturbates too much," Karl said.

"George is very slack today," Octave went on, teasingly. "Eh, George, how can you make your living as a net fisherman? And you want me to take you outside the reef!"

Flustered, George forgot to pull up the rock which served as an anchor before stepping the sail. He had dropped it into the water during the excitement over the barracuda when he was trying to stay close to the men in the water. Now Karl and Octave hooted with laughter and Karl pulled it in, teasing him, "What kind of fisherman puts up sail without pulling up anchor?"

With the boom rigged, the patched old sail drew and the pirogue moved swiftly in the water now that the wind was rising, tipping far to one side. Octave told George about the barracuda. "Six feet long, it was a *lichien tazar,* a dog barracuda. Its mouth was very big. When it sees you it follows you, moving its tail right and left. It came and looked at me right in my mask and opened its jaws twice. Now why did it do that?" Octave involuntarily shuddered. Then he laughed and imitated the fish snapping its jaws. "When you shoot a fish the blood gets scattered in the water. A barracuda comes. If you have a fish on your harpoon it can hurt you, the *liki*-of-its-mother beast. It was only six, seven feet away, opening and shutting its mouth, maybe only five feet away from Karl. As you move toward it, it moves back. Very, very clever and treacherous. If you shoot a shark with the harpoon it will go away. A barracuda has a grudge. He will always try and fight you. A big head, the *liki* of its mother. When you get cut by coral and the blood is coming out, it will attack."

"Barracuda," Karl said, relishing every syllable of the word and then puffing on his cigarette. "Ha!" The pirogue passed another boat now, at anchor with its sails furled. A lone fisherman was casting lines into the water.

"Hey, Nicole!" Octave shouted. "I don't waste my time with little fish like you do."

The man called, "I fish little by little."

"I fish once and in great quantity," Octave shouted back, holding up the Cordonier for the man to see.

"Watch out or I'll shove it up your *liki*," the man threatened with a grin. When the other boat was out of earshot, George held up the harpoon gun and pointed it at the man; "I'll shoot you like a dog," said George with mock fierceness.

"George, you are a savage," Octave laughed. "You are a black comic. Now where are you going? Roche Blanch is not outside the reef; it is inside. We'll go outside the reef on a calm day. With those dark clouds spreading every way it is dangerous."

The northern sky was a very deep blue over the three off-shore islands and the wind seemed cold on their bare wet skins. "It's good to fish in the early morning," George ventured conversationally. "One has the appetite to work." They were closer to the reef again and the roar of crashing waves came nearer.

"Where are you going, George?"

"To the shallow place for octopus." George leaned forward, examining a callus on the bottom of his left foot.

"George stepped on a sea urchin yesterday," Karl said.

"You are lucky, George," Octave said. "But you take me for a buffoon when you say this is Roche Blanch. I think you will never succeed in bringing me to Roche Blanch. But we can fish here. At any time there is plenty of octopus in this place. Put down the sail."

The water was very choppy now and Prem looked at the gathering clouds with apprehension. Spray splashed into the boat and suddenly an unexpected wave came over the side, drenching them and causing all four to burst into laughter.

"The octopuses come in from outside the reef here, not one by one but three or four hundred at once. *En bloc*. In a single mass that spills over the reef and then separates."

"Did you ever see it happen, Octave?"

"No, but I heard about it."

"Once I was net fishing with Bally when an octopus grabbed me around the chest," said George. "I was wading on the reef. We were pulling in the net and the octopus came and walked on me. I was afraid. Bally shouted to dive into the water so the octopus could relax and then I should bite its head. I was afraid but I bit it and it let go."

"George, you are a *couyon,*" laughed Karl. "George is the premier buffoon of Grand Gaube."

"The octopus is very, very clever," Octave said. "If it has seen an eel, it will send out one tentacle and when the eel tries to eat it, it will send another to hook it and pull the eel back into its hole." Octave started to sing again as he prepared to dive back into the water, this time with a *larfine,* or wooden spear with a barbed steel hook at the tip, rather than his harpoon gun. He stood up in the bow with his back to the others, moving to the very edge.

> Her husband is a fisherman
> Catching small fish
> And when the sea rises
> And the line breaks
> She will find another husband. . . .

"You piss in the sea, you, Octave?" George scolded.

"Where do you want me to go?"

"Is this the bank here, Octave?" George pointed to a steep fall of rocks under the water.

"*Oui.* Pull the boat forward. Can you hold the boat?" The waves were heavier now.

"*Oui.*" Octave, Karl and Prem slipped into their gear. "George, follow us with the boat," said Octave and the three of them dropped into the cold water. Although the world above the surface was dark and gloomy, the floor of the lagoon was brilliant here with open stretches of sand and yellow seaweed, like a desert landscape. Here and there were little islands of coral, with the blue and green feelers of langoustes waving from their crevices. There were schools of tiny little golden fish and the beautiful splayed fingers of a Venus harp. The water was a very pale green, almost clear and only about seven feet deep; one could see much farther in the distance than at the reef, and Prem marveled at the beauty of the place; no wonder it was called "white rocks." But the lagoon was commonplace to the fishermen and they paddled their fins steadily on, interested in the coral formations only as cover through which they could catch a glimpse of octopus head and eyes. Octave did not have long to wait. A small octopus under a flat rock, feeling the men's shockwaves, turned from dark brown into a pale gray and squeezed itself softly into the dark crevice of the rocks that were its home. But too late. Octave's barbed *larfine* cut through the water and pinned the octopus to the coral. Octave plunged the point in and out as a cloud of brown ink spread across the water. Still the creature lived on, its three-foot tentacles clutching at Octave's arm as he ripped it off the *larfine* and, holding it away from himself as best he could, carried it back to the boat with one hand. There he again had to rip the tentacles off his arm before handling it to George, who beat the squirming head with the tiller stick until the octopus was dead and the tentacles stopped clutching and relaxed.

For almost an hour George held the boat steady, pushing it toward the swimmers whenever he saw their heads rise above the surface, the bottom of the hull filling up with the oozing, sometimes still squirming bodies. The wind became stronger and rumbles of thunder could be heard from the north, but Octave and Karl were anxious to work as long as possible, and they kept on. Prem, too, speared a few of the slimy creatures but he couldn't keep up with the pace of the two fishermen, and twice he climbed aboard to rest in the pirogue. Now the whole northern horizon above the white foam at the reef was a dark purple, although it was still midmorning. George confided to Prem he felt afraid, even though the sight of a dozen or so Pirogues still scattered around the lagoon offered some reassurance. He had to work hard now, struggling with the gaff and trying to hold the boat in place, but the waves kept beating it closer and closer to the reef and farther away from the swimmers. Once Octave's head broke the surface and he ripped off his mask to shout angrily at George, "Don't go on that bank. Drop the anchor if you can't hold it. Stay out in the deeper water. It's dangerous that close to the reef."

George threw in the anchor. But the waves still seemed to be dragging the boat; he thought of tying a heavier rock to the anchor rope but he was afraid to put down the gaff. Octave swam up to the boat, dropped another octopus over the side and vanished into the water without a word. Karl brought two more, Prem one, and then, finally, when Octave threw in what must have been his twentieth octopus, he climbed into the boat, shivering with cold. "That should make twenty pounds, with the fish," he told George. "Not much for the morning." Octave wrapped the wet sail around his shoulders and squatted in the bottom of the boat, shivering. Prem and Karl were still in the water, and when they surfaced he shouted to them to return. But they didn't hear; the next time he saw them they were quite far away, so he told George to pull up the anchor and row over to them.

"You can get knocked over by the waves today. . . ." Octave pulled out his crumpled pack of cigarettes and studied it. "George, to hold a boat, you cannot." He took out the last remaining cigarette, lighted it and threw the burning match into the sea. "A scarcity of cigarettes," he mumbled. He went back to the stern and sat by the tiller while George rowed toward the swimmers. "Later you are going to die, George." Octave stared north at the black sky and the waves toward the reef, which were turning a deep green color. "The darkness is spreading everywhere, *mo mama*. This eastern wind makes the sea agitated. No, the wind has changed. It's blowing from the north now. That's bad. If it was really bad, though, all those other boats would turn back to the cove." Octave's blue eyes rested heavily on the sky and then on the pile of octopus on the bottom of the boat. He reached down and ripped away the tentacle of an octopus from the beautiful blue-green scales of the dead Cato Verte, whose blue eye was staring reproachfully up at him. Octave sighed deeply. "So the hour demands we go home."

Karl's voice rose from the water. "Octave, come! The gaff! Bring the gaff! A big octopus!"

Octave sprang to life. "Don't touch it, *frere!*" In excitement he grabbed his fins and visor, pulling them on and yelling before biting on the mouthpiece, "Don't disturb it, *frere!*" George watched as Octave dove in and swam swiftly toward Karl and Prem; together they fought the octopus underwater, the tips of their spears and the heavy gaff breaking the surface as they thrashed around below, stabbing the creature over and over. The water churned and splashed, a great cloud of brown ink spread out on the waves and then Octave was swimming back to the boat, holding the gaff ahead of him with the octopus impaled on it. George guessed it was at least five pounds. It was too heavy to bring live into the boat and Octave told George to beat it with his stick over the side. "*Attention!* It might escape! Hit it, George! Hit it!" Climbing aboard Octave joined George and taking hold of the octopus by the eye sockets, he slammed it again and again against the side of the pirogue. Then he tossed it into the bottom of the hull. "Beat it again!" George yelled. "It's still walking." But it seemed to have given up the fight and slithered under a seat, its tentacles still flexing and twitching.

In the excitement, the boat had moved much closer to the reef and was tossing violently as Octave and George both grabbed gaffs to push it away from the rocks and into deeper water. "Stop it!" shouted Octave. "Stop it, George! Push it away, push it away!" But George caught his gaff in the rocks. "Let go of it! You'll break it! What are you doing?" George had it loose again and the two of them pushed the pirogue back. "Push straight, George, push straight!"

"Where shall we go?" George asked, when they were again a safe distance from the reef.

"We shall go home, we shall go to eat, drink tea and sleep." Prem and Karl, who had stayed out in the deeper waters, swam up to rejoin them; they were shivering with the cold. Octave started to sing as they climbed aboard:

> My father is holding your mother fast
> My mother is holding your father fast. . . .

"When you have octopus," he told Karl, "you have a taste for fishing. But I lose my taste for it today when the sky is so black. This north wind brings heavy rains, terrible. Once it was winter, I could not work as a mason, and when I got in the boat in the morning I cursed and trembled. When you wake up in the morning in winter, you must calculate the cold and rain." The boat lurched and George tripped into Karl. "What kind of a *gogot* are you, eh?" Karl cursed. He, too, was watching the sky. "Now the darkness is spread everywhere."

Prem stared at the water itself. It had turned an intense pale green. He had never seen the sea such a vivid color before.

"This is in the day. In the night it is more dangerous," Octave reassured them. The other pirogues in the lagoon were rigging their booms and setting sail. "See the fishermen are rushing in every way.

I am afraid when we have a north wind." He shivered. "I am feeling cold. C'mon, George, we'll step up the mast; the pirogues are rushing about."

"They have all set sail for home," Prem observed nervously. "We are the last." There was more wind every minute and he hoped it would not take them long to reach the shore. The northern sky had turned a midnight blue and the sea was an unnatural bright green.

George was openly afraid. "It's growing worse," he said, as he rigged the boom and the sail caught the wind.

Octave told them not to fear anything. "It's nothing. The winter is harsher."

Karl hunched over, unconcerned about the storm. He was shivering and put his chin on his bare knees. "This weather is only good for playing rummy."

"See, all the fishermen are going back to the shore," Octave said. He, too, was shivering now. "Have three women, have intercourse, it may be that you can't because it is too cold. Let's go walk to the Majestic Cinema. Let's go to Tardieu Forge." He named the two centers of prostitution in Port Louis.

"Karl is the *macro* of the Majestic," said Prem, using the Creole word for "pimp" for the first time.

"Watch out," Karl joked, shaking his fist at Prem. "You must experience a storm like this to become a real fisherman, Prem. You must have trouble like this. The weather is bad."

"Look, look," cried George, pointing to the reef. They all turned to see the roaring breakers; they had risen to a boiling wall of churning white foam. "The wind is bringing cyclone-like waves to the reef," Octave said. "Like smoke!" exclaimed George. "It's becoming bad, Karl. Look, look at those waves, coming over the reef."

"Our pirogue is last," laughed Octave. "Oh, Karl, Karl, Karl, *macro* of the Majestic."

"We shall not have a storm tomorrow for the New Year," said Karl. "We shall put the boat up to dry."

The sail whipped in the wind as a sudden gust hit them; the pirogue was moving hard for the shore now. It was as dark as at dusk and all they could see was a flat tree line; the island was hidden by the rain clouds. To the north there were distant flashes of lightning; the deep blue of the sky, just as if it were overweighted, seemed to be bending over the boat. The lurid green water was extremely choppy; waves broke over the side drenching them but now no one laughed. A large cold drop fell on Prem's knee, another on his hand. He glanced around for his shirt, saw it was a sodden mass in the bow and thought of asking George to hand it to him; but at that moment there was a pelting across the water, on the sail, and the boat. The squall had hit them. Suddenly, with a fearful deafening din, the skies smashed just above their heads; Prem crouched and held his breath, and saw a blinding bright light that seemed to burst all around them, and then the rain was coming down in a torrent, solid straight shafts of rain, blotting out all sight of shore and the reef as well. Not far away, across the water, a fisherman in another boat pulled in his sail and crawled under it, dropping his anchor to sit out the storm.

"That pimp is putting his sail down to hide himself," Octave said. "He will die if he stays out here. Winter is always like this."

The rain pelted down harder, settling in. Then the noise stilled. The wet, sodden sail stopped flapping, and all at once the green waters lost their vivid hue, the waves went away, and they could see the cove, much closer now. Octave and George huddled down in the hull as deep as they could, feeling a chilling wetness; water was trickling down their hair; they pulled their wet tricots over their heads and hunched over, clasping their legs, as if they had decided to do nothing but sit still and wait out the rain. Karl and Prem sat up on the edge of the stern, bare chested and wet, their glistening faces turned upward. Pelted by the heavy rain, the sea turned almost perfectly still.

"If we had a bigger sail it would be good," said Octave, shaking himself off and snatching up his sodden old hat and wringing it out. "Tomorrow it will be calm. Or maybe as soon as we get home we will hear the radio saying, 'A cyclone is coming.' " He stood up and began to sing gustily.

> O, Capri! C'est fini
> Et dire que je quitte la ville
> Mon premier amour
> Je ne sait pas que je retournerai

"This rain will last," said Karl.

"This rain will be here till evening," George echoed.

Karl shuddered with cold. "You must have a woman to get warm after this." He shouted violently at a passing boat, *"Attention! La Mort! Attention!* Beware! Death!"

Octave kept singing:

> *Coca Cola tire du feu*
> *Quand mademoiselle ine soif*
> *Li pour demande Coca Cola*
>
> Coca Cola puts out the fire
> When young ladies are thirsty
> They ask for Coca Cola

Karl leered menacingly at George. "You *gogot,* just now I will break your *liki.*" He, too, began to sing in a loud, hoarse voice:

> My priest has raped me, so I yelled to my husband,
> To my husband, oh. . . .

Octave laughed. "Have you husband? From where you have this husband, Karl?"

"Go to hell. Octave is like a *gogot* in Paradise."

"Karl is like a *gogot* in torn pants. When he fights, many go to prison and must pay bail and some sleep in the hospital."

George scanned the shore; one could see the cove clearly now. "By luck, Benny the Fish Monger will still be there. He will say only forty cents a pound because we are so late." The wind stopped entirely and the boat moved slowly through the heavy rain.

"It's like a broken Johnson motor," Octave said.

"Can you see Benny on the shore, Octave?" George was anxious to get paid so he could spend the rainy afternoon at a secret agent film in town. Octave was still singing loudly. "Twist again, like we did last summer; oh, twist again, like we did last year. . . ." He let go of the mast and started to dance on the bow. A fisherman called from another pirogue, "Hey, Octave, you might get killed!"

"Little by little we are going to die," Karl muttered, trembling with cold now as if he had a fever. He heaved a deep sigh and said hoarsely, *"Liki to mama,* I am a tired body."

Through the pouring rain they could see a teenage boy standing on the beach in front of a large bungalow near the cove. He was blond, a Mauritian of pure French descent, and he cupped his hands around his mouth and shouted, "Where are you coming from?"

"Barracuda Pass!" Octave shouted back.

"You can have my *gogot!*" George, for no reason, yelled at the boy. He explained to Prem, "I don't like *blancs.* Everywhere I meet them I ill-treat them."

Octave agreed. "A bunch of *blancs* are a bunch of *gogots. Liki* of their mothers. A bad bunch. White-skinned Mauritians I don't like." The pirogue's hull bumped against a rock. George called from the bow, "Who has the tiller? Oh, Karl, he doesn't look where we are going in the sea. He looks at women on the shore, the *gogot.* Go into Port Louis and have a *femme petain,* Karl."

"*Couyon,*" the other cursed him absently; he watched some girls with umbrellas walking near the schoolhouse, then turned back, "I'll hit you with the *larfine.* You are dead, George. I'll break your *liki.*"

The pirogue entered the cove now and Octave began to sing a *sega,* the Creole's own fast, throbbing, calypso-like music. He began beating out the rhythm on the side of the boat with the tiller stick. Karl picked up the *batage* sticks and joined in, beating them on a crosspiece and making a thundering racket. George took the gaff and began pushing them across the shallow water.

> Happy New Year, Happy New Year, Grandpapa
> Happy New Year, Happy New Year, Little Children

Octave's strong, young voice rose above the rain, "If I win a lottery, I shall sell my pirogue to buy a big *bateau.* . . ."

Karl raucously sang out a few lines at the top of his lungs:

> *Mo mama,* give me a gun
> And I'll go fight in Malagas
> And when I die don't weep. . . .

Octave roared back, "*Hou, hou, ou, ou, la bas, la bas, la bas!*"

Then Karl: On Chamaral Mountain
             The Condin bird flies

Octave: The Heavens have chosen my island
             To make Paradise

Karl: Happy New Year, Happy New Year, Grandpapa
        Happy New Year, Happy New Year, Little Children

[95

Octave: A house that has no mother
       Is like a house without a door

Karl: *Limonade! Frappe!*

Then the two of them broke into a loud but plaintive Creole ballad:

    The River Tanier if it could speak
    Would ask how many clothes I washed today
    Tell my wife I can stand it no longer
    Give me my packet of clothes
    I go back to the house of my mother
    Where I sit I think
    How well I lived in the house of my mother
    I want to go back
    I want to go back
    But my feet don't move
    Where I sit I think
    How well I lived in the house of my mother
    Now that I'm married
    All the days I get nothing but onions and greens. . . .

"Hou, hou, ou ou, la bas, la bas, la bas!" roared Karl, picking up the fast *sega* beat again. The two fishermen sang back and forth, shouting out their improvised words, until the songs turned into a cursing match.

Octave: Farewell, the sun forever
       Farewell, old my old friends

Karl: Dance with me
    Don't hold me tight
    We will fall down
    And the others will laugh

Octave: Farewell, my island home
       Farewell, the clouds and birds

Karl: If you don't let me sing, Octave
    You will have trouble

Octave: You are lying
       I'll hit you with a bottle

Karl: You are dead
     I'll break your *liķi* and bury you

Octave: *Macro* of the Majestic!

Karl: You make *couyanade*,
     I'll break your *liķi* like a bottle!

Octave: *Gogot, liķi to mama!*

The shore was very close now, and some little boys, running about naked in the rain and excited by their roaring songs, came running from the sand and splashed into the water, swimming toward them. Trembling with cold, water dripping from his hair, Prem suddenly did not want the journey to end. Grand Gaube looked huddled, cramped and lifeless in the rain and he gazed at the road leading inland from the cove, listening to the songs and shouts, his eyes following the road until it disappeared into the wet gray dreariness, the road that led to an England that did not want him. He did not want to go down that road and leave the fishermen behind, yet he knew he would.

Now every second left seemed precious. A feeling of happiness possessed him and he wished a wall would suddenly rise from the water and prevent them from going any further; then he would remain only with a past and the glory of this morning's journey into the lagoon. He wanted to stay as he was forever, rain and all, and he took a deep breath, filling his lungs, and felt an almost painful sense of joy, and he too joined loudly in the singing.

> Happy New Year, Happy New Year, Grandpapa!
> Happy New Year, Happy New Year, Little Children!

Then Octave leaned across to him, his face wet and glistening with rain, and his voice breathless from the shouting; when he spoke Prem saw he had become serious.

"You come fishing with me as long as you like, Prem," Octave said. "If you come with me in the water, you know, I am not afraid when I see something. I can shoot it and I can chase it. When you see a barracuda or a shark, don't go away. Stay beside me and we'll break his *liķi*. When a friend is with you, you have the courage to dive."

Charan

III

Charan

GHUNGRALI-RAJPUTAN VILLAGE

THE PUNJAB PLAIN

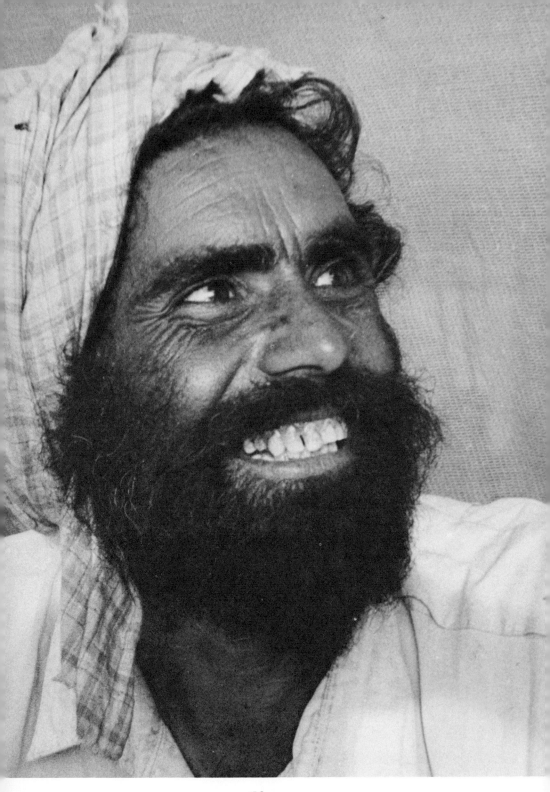

Charan

The Mazhbis

OLD CHANAN

BENARSI

KAPUR

BAWA

Surjit

Pritam Singh

III

O UR THIRD STORY IS ABOUT the human impact of the so-called Green
Revolution on one farmer and his northern Indian village. As
governments in most of the poor two-thirds of the world now realize,
growing enough food is the basis of everything else. But it can also cause
as many problems as it solves.

The time frame of the story is the harvest season, a month-long period
from early April to early May. The setting is the great Punjab Plain, the
broad, fat and fertile expanse of land extending from the headwaters of
the Ganges north of Delhi up to the foothills of the Himalayas and the
Hindu Kush near Peshawar. "Punjab" means "land of five rivers," and
the area it designates extends across the five waters which come together
to form the Indus Valley, one of the cradles of civilization. The Punjab is
dry; it receives only five to fifteen inches of rainfall a year, and it was
not until the British rulers of India began to irrigate what was a near-
desert in the 1930s that the land became fully settled, and the Punjab
became known, as it is today, as the breadbasket of India.

Even so, by 1950 population growth ate up its agricultural surplus and,
as elsewhere in the densely-populated areas of Asia and the arid lands of
the Middle East, the Punjab's future looked disastrously unpromising.
Between 1960 and 1965, it appeared the Malthusian prophecy would be
fulfilled in some poor countries such as India, for population, increasing
by 11.5 percent, threatened to outstrip food supplies, increasing by only 6.9
percent. Throughout Asia, Africa and Latin America, an average farming
family of between five and six people had about six-and-a-half acres on
which to feed themselves and just over two-and-a-half other people in the
towns and cities. By 1985, it seemed, the average acreage would be down
to five, and the city folk dependent on it would rise to four. In the great
power capitals of the West, there were predictions of global famine in the
late 1970s, and the American government for the first time tied its food
assistance to greater local investment in agricultural production.

Then in 1967 came the great breakthrough in agriculture. Thirty years of research—in Japan, the American Pacific Northwest, Mexico and the Philippines—went into producing new, carefully selected strains of wheat and rice which could safely absorb up to 120 pounds of nitrogen per acre. Traditional tropical strains could do this, but the resulting heads of grain were simply too heavy for the thin stems and they fell over or lodged if more than forty pounds of fertilizer was applied to the acre. This increased tolerance for fertilizer, combined with a quicker period for maturing— only 120 days compared with 150 to 180 with older species—made the new seeds two or three times more productive, provided they received enough fresh water as well as the fertilizer. Once more the poor countries were able, except in times of drought as in the winter of 1972–73, to keep the growth rate of food production slightly ahead of population. In the early 1970s countries like India regained their self-sufficiency in food for the first time in two or three generations.

But the Green Revolution was based on a purely scientific phenomenon. Such a rapid transfer of Western farm technology, without social leveling, creating more food but more unemployed farmers as well, could be expected, like the first use of the irrigation ditch or the traction plow, to produce new styles of life, new systems of human relationships.

Man's first known agricultural settlements on the Mesopotamian plain were extremely stable social units, surviving pretty much for the span of four thousand years between about 8,000 to 4,000 B.C. A technological breakthrough—the invention of irrigation—quickly shattered this stability, leading, in a relatively short space of time, to a surplus food supply, the development of towns and cities, a rapid expansion of population and a decline in the absolute number of villages. Intercity warfare began almost with the first Mesopotamian temple communities, along with the construction of defensive walls, the abandonment of outlying villages, migration to ever-larger urban centers and the rise of soldiers, organized armies and generals and then kings and sovereign states. Gradually, small, family-sized farms of free men living in peaceful anarchy were replaced by larger estates, farmed with the economies of scale, by serfs and, later, slaves captured in war. Like the first temple communities, some of history's greatest urban civilizations—Pharonic Egypt, China and Japan under the seventh-century T'ang dynasty and Fujiwara clan, Mexico under the Mayas and Aztecs—practiced something close to state socialism, with heavy taxation of the food-producing peasant population.

In Europe, the disintegration of traditional peasant society began with the introduction of heavy mold-board plows and the manorial system of farming these made possible, starting about 1000 A.D. It was hastened when calculations of price and profit in the medieval cities began to introduce modifications in crop rotation and methods of cultivation. The death blow to traditional agriculture came in the eighteenth and nineteenth centuries with the gradual introduction of modern farm technology and the treatment of lands, rent and labor as commercially negotiable properties. As mounting debt blanketed the villages of Europe, fifty million peasants migrated to North America in the century after 1820.

Another agricultural revolution followed in the United States from 1890 to the 1950s. The creation of land grant colleges and a countrywide agricultural service led to a great accumulation of basic research. A tremendous upsurge in American farm production resulted, at first due to farming virgin lands on the Great Plains, but starting in the 1930s, due to newly developed seeds, irrigation, mechanization and the massive application of fertilizer.

Man's great agricultural breakthroughs have been instrumental in creating the first civilized urban society in Mesopotamia, the eventual rise of the West and, in modern times, the imposition of Western culture and technology on the great cities of the world, in poor and rich countries alike.

Historically left almost untouched were most of the villages of the poor two-thirds of the world, at least until the late 1960s, when the great transfer of American farm technology to their rice and wheat lands really got underway. In most of Asia, Africa and Latin America, as in the very first Mesopotamian rural settlements, there were basic cultural traits: the village was the fixed point by which a peasant knew his own position in the world and his relationship with all humanity. Considerations of kinship and blood ties had heavy weight. The head of the family had to provide food, shelter and clothing for all, and each member in turn was obligated to work for his food and shelter. There were also communal rights and obligations such as the right to graze cattle, cut fodder and gather wood anywhere in the village. Services had to be provided one's neighbors, such as loans without interest and hospitality without cost. Age was respected, tradition and custom binding. Delicate balances of this sort are what have held together peasant society in most of the world for some ten thousand years. The introduction of modern medicine and the resulting population explosion gave village culture a rude shock and weakened the aged foundations. What will happen, now that it has been subjected to a rate of technological advance that has telescoped hundreds of years of advance into five?

The Punjab Plain has historically borne the brunt of all foreign invasions into southern Asia, from the Aryans to Alexander, from the Mongol hordes to the Moghul emperors, who traditionally followed a path along what became known as the Grand Trunk Road. Now, with the march of tube wells, irrigation canals, electricity, deisel power, tractors, the solving of salination problems and, above all, the new American-developed dwarf grain, the Green Revolution has taken this same path to produce the most rapid change in agriculture and rural life in man's history.

In the Punjab, this change has fundamentally challenged the caste system, the foundation of the Sikh as well as the Hindu village social structure and one of the oldest forms of human social organization. It has produced a confrontation between the traditionally interdependent Jats, or farmer-landlords, and the Harijans or untouchables, most of them landless agricultural laborers, who today are gradually being faced with the choice of becoming a rural proletariat or urban migrants.

As a team of oxen are we driven
By the ploughman, our teacher;
By the furrows made are thus writ
Our actions—on the earth, our paper.
The sweat of labor is as beads
Falling by the ploughman as seeds sown.
We reap according to our measure—
Some for ourselves to keep, some to others give.
O Nanak, this is the way to truly live.
    —From The Granth Sahib, *the sacred*
    scripture of the Sikh religion

EARLY ONE APRIL MORNING a springless, creaking bullock cart rumbled out of Ghungrali-Rajputan, a prosperous Jat farming village just a few miles southwest of the Grand Trunk Road, that celebrated thoroughfare that stretches from the Khyber Pass across the Indus Valley to Delhi and on down the Ganges to Calcutta. The villagers have only to go to the road to see the life of all India passing by. This is nowhere more true than where it crosses the vast, flat expanse of green wheatlands of the Punjab Plain.

The cart groaned and uttered a loud creak at the slightest movement; a copper drinking vessel, hanging from a pole fixed to the cart's side, chimed in, like a bell. By these sounds, apart from its pathetically worn wooden flanks, you might have concluded as to the cart's age and readiness to fall to pieces. In the cart sat two inhabitants of Ghungrali: Gurcharan Singh, a Jat farmer known as Charan to his friends, and his hired laborer, Mukhtar. As they moved, Charan crouched on his haunches on the cart's wide tongue, holding the reins and coaxing on the bullocks in that strange falsetto mixture of praise and curses Punjabis use to address their cattle: *"Tat-tat-tat-tat-tat-tat. Ta-hah, ta-hah!"* The bullocks, grave and dignified, kept to the accustomed ruts they had followed to the fields in the morning and back at night these many years. The flat, dusty road was as much their daily lot as the cool shade at Charan's well where they munched grass all day long, or slept, rolling over on their sides.

Charan himself was in a sullen temper. That morning his father, Sadhu Singh, the old patriarch, showing nothing above his quilt but a white beard and a towel-wrapped head, had called to Charan from his *charpoy,* testily complaining the buffaloes looked thin; the old man had fretted to his wife in a grumpy voice, "They don't feed the cattle properly." The old lady, busy churning milk, shouted to Charan's oldest son, Suka, in the fierce-sounding screech she habitually used, "You! Go help Peloo feed the cattle!" The boy had replied in a low defiant voice, "I'm not used to it," and he had stayed where he was, sipping tea in the warmth of the fire.

Taking in the old man's pot-bellied figure comfortably bundled in its quilt, Charan had lost his temper. "Why don't you go and feed the cattle, Father? You won't lift your finger, but you criticize those who really do the work all day. It's very easy to find fault."

The old lady, alarmed by Charan's surly tone, snapped to her husband, "He's responsible for the wheat crop. Why should you talk aloud? Let him do whatever he likes. We'll see when the wheat is harvested."

"He acts as if I'm going to throw everything away," Charan grumbled, stuffing a warm *chapatti* into his mouth. "That anybody could take all I've built up all these years. I'm not doing that. And if you're so worried about the cattle, Father, go and attend to things yourself." At such a threat, Sadhu Singh, who had never done a day's physical labor in all his sixty years, rolled over and feigned sleep. Charan strode out of the courtyard and down a muddy village lane to the family's cattlebarn. There, hidden under a pile of freshly cut green fodder, lay a bottle of country liquor; Charan filled a dusty glass to the brim and swigged it down in a single gulp. Peloo, his crippled, palsied stableman, hobbled over to the pump to refill the glass with water so his master could wash down the fiery stuff.

Now, still angry over the exchange, Charan cursed the bullocks, "Go quickly or I'll rape your mother."

Mukhtar, crouched on a pile of jute sacking in the back of the cart, guessed why Charan was ill-tempered. "Charan is a good man," the laborer told himself, "but the old man and lady are always interfering. And they are mean, mean to the lowest." Mukhtar still felt drowsy, even after a glass of hot milky tea and the hustle of yoking the bullocks. Charan had them well trained and only a command of *"Tuk, tuk, tuka,"* delivered in a high-pitched hiss, was needed; the bullocks understood and always stepped under the yoke themselves.

Mukhtar yawned. His wife had awakened him at four o'clock so that he could see the giant star with a long fiery tail which had mysteriously appeared over the southern horizon three days before. The comet was said in the village to be an omen. The old men claimed such a star had only once before appeared in the skies and that was in 1947 just on the eve of the massacre. Mukhtar himself had been too young to remember. He was born just three days before Ghungrali's Moslem population had been slaughtered by the thousands by Hindu soldiers and Sikh mobs from the city.

Mukhtar cleared his throat and spat. "Charan, *ji,* I saw that star this morning."

"I saw it too. I had a bad attack of asthma in the night and had to wake the doctor up for an injection. They call it 'the star with a tail.' "

"Some say it appeared in 1947."

"Yes. They say that when such a star appears there will be a disaster in the village. But it has been there for some days now and nothing has happened."

After that they rode in silence. Mukhtar, his muscular body bouncing up and down in the bone-shaking cart, thought of his bed

and how he had lain awake in the morning listening to the pre-dawn
sounds. First, the chirp of the black sparrow, which always sang
first in the darkness. Then the women rising to churn milk, followed
by the sound of the *jupji* or morning prayers from the *gurdwara,* or
Sikh temple.

> There is One God.
> He is the supreme truth.
> He, the Creator. . . .
> Before time itself
> There was truth.
> When time began to run its course
> He was the truth. . . .

The prayer went on and on, the signal to Mukhtar he must rise.

> Air, water and earth
> Of these are we made. . . .

When the voices of the old people and children who still went to
the *gurdwara* died away, Mukhtar heard footsteps in the lane outside
his hut. Shrouded silent figures wrapped in shawls and blankets
moved to and from the wheat fields, to answer the call of nature. He
rose, hurried to Charan's house for a cup of tea and harnessed the
bullocks, pausing only to relieve himself and splash a little cold
water on his face.

As the cart passed the *gurdwara,* Mukhtar peered up through the
gate; on the crest of the hillock above, the priest was already raising
prayer flags although the temple's white bulbous towers were still
faint in the darkness. Unconsciously, Mukhtar observed all the familiar houses on both sides of the narrow, rutted road, the usual
huddle of brick and earthen houses, with high walls enclosing their
cattleyards, vegetable gardens and verandas. Here was Bhoondi's,
where the low-caste Mazhbi barn cleaner and his four strapping sons
lived; beyond the untouchables' quarter was the pale green house of
Sarvan Singh, Charan's uncle, an opium eater; in its courtyard
Dhakel, Sarvan's handsome son, and Sindar, a foolish braggart who
was the blacksheep of the family, were sleepily putting their bullocks
under yoke; the cart soon rumbled past them. Next, the square yellow schoolhouse, also built on a hillock and half-hidden by a high
brick wall. The cart came out into the open, a dusty, barren stretch

of earth around the stagnant village pond; the ground was brushed
with a faint pink tinge of heather. Above the pond rose Ghungrali's
giant banyan tree; some said it was a century old. Mukhtar wondered what tales the banyan tree could tell if it could speak; what
elopements, swordfights and drunken quarrels, to say nothing of the
massacre. The tree's heavy branches reached out thirty or forty feet;
roots dangled from them like heavy cobwebs. Under the tree it was
completely dark; the black shadows cast by its branches were just
beginning to creep across the pond's black-green surface.

The village came to an end at the banyan tree. Here the dirt road
split, one way going east toward the Grand Trunk Road and the
other south toward Charan's fields.

"*Chota*," said Charan, who had called Mukhtar "Little One" ever
since the fieldhand had been a child, "we will water the south wheat
field today from the canal. Take a hoe from the well shed. If someone else is using, you will have to open ten or twelve bunds, if not,
only one or two."

"*Han, ji.*"

As they spoke, the cart moved out on the broad limitless plain;
it was broken only here and there by clumps of trees around the wells
and pumphouses. One after another, almost uniform in appearance,
these small landholdings unfolded before the eyes of the two men in
the cart. The farms stretched to the horizon on both sides of the dirt
road, flowing into a faint dusty-white atmosphere. You can go on
and on in the Punjab and never see where this horizon begins and
where it ends. The scattered trees at the wells created the illusion of
a distant jungle hung with mist, but there was no jungle; the land
was too fertile and valuable. Almost all of it was planted in wheat,
mostly still green, but with a field here and there, sown early, already
ripening into a dull gold. But what wheat. It was all short, stunted
and dwarfed. A thick tangle of plump heads on short, stiff stems,
growing a green carpet in all directions. To Mukhtar, this wheat still
seemed a miracle with its lush, almost artificial appearance and its
many strange names like Khalyan Sona, PV 18, 227, RR21, Triple
Dwarf. As the cart moved ahead, Charan commented on each crop.
"This PV 18 is sick. It has a disease." "Not enough fertilizer; Nirmal
is a poor farmer." Or "Now here's a good crop; yes, that's right."

The sun made its appearance; a long way ahead of them a broad
yellow streak of light crept across the fields; in a few moments it

had come a little nearer the cart, crept to the right and acquired possession of the banyan tree's upper branches. Something warm touched the faces of Charan and Mukhtar, the streak of light rose steadily up front, slipped past the cart and suddenly all the wide plain cast aside the grayness of dawn. The dew sparkled and almost instantly the chill of the night was gone. The fields of wheat, the grass alongside the road, the ripening oats, all a rusty brown-gray and half-dead from the April heat and dust the evening before, seemed to revive. A flock of black crows, cawing and scolding, flew toward the village from their night roosts in the treetops of the fields, flapping their wings with eager cries as they did each morning. Sparrows twittered to each other in the grass; far away to the left somewhere a peacock wailed, a strange, sorrowful sound; the turtle doves began to coo and a covey of partridges, startled by the cart, rose up, and with their soft "trrrr" flew away to the wheat fields. Even the grass seemed to rustle with mice, rats and dusty green lizards.

But hardly had the cart gone two furlongs more than the dew started to evaporate, the air lost its freshness and the Punjab Plain began to reassume its languished April appearance. The grass drooped and the sounds of life died away. The perfect blue sky appeared at that moment to threaten a day limitless and listless with heat.

"It will be hot today," said Charan. The bullock cart creaked as it turned around a bend in the road. It was not far to Charan's fields now. Mukhtar saw all the while the same thing: sky, wheat fields, the hazy dust of the distance in the early, flat sun. The sounds in the grass were gone, the peacock had flown away, there were no partridges to be seen. Tired of chirping, the sparrows hopped toward shady places in the grass; they all resembled one another with their little brown heads, and rendered the plain all the more uniform.

In the distance, water splashed from a tube well; the steel pipe was set high in the air so that the farmer could see it from all his fields; it resembled a small, cool waterfall and looked maddeningly inviting. The cart passed a rich growth of wheat; a black pot was propped onto a stick in the midst of it to scare away crows and ward off the evil eye of jealous neighbors. A chipmunk ran across the road; then once more Mukhtar settled down to reverie, watching the long expanses of wheat, the unvarying trees and pumphouses. But now, thank God, a cart laden with dried cotton sticks came toward them.

A man was lying on the top of the load; he must have been watering his fields all the night. Sleepy and dozing in the sun, he just raised his head to look who was coming. Charan laughed, a surprisingly joyous, deep-throated laugh, and called a greeting, the bullocks put out their heads toward the cotton sticks, the cart gave a piercing creak in salute.

"*Sat Sri Akal, ji!*" Charan called in a loud, exuberant voice recognizing one of his drinking cronies, "*Ki hal chal hai?* Are you hale and hearty?"

"*Tik hai, maharaj. Mauj hai,*" came the grinned reply. "*Kush hun*. I'm enjoying. I'm happy."

"*Pani lugya?* You finished watering?"

"Yes. All night." The man, whiskered and hard-eyed with a large curled and waxed moustache, was known in the village as the Bandit; he had spent twenty years in prison and still always carried a flick knife in his pocket. "Why is this sun so bright so early in the morning?" the Bandit asked.

"There is so much darkness within you." Charan's eyes sparkled and his teeth flashed as he laughed again and prodded the bullocks forward.

Further on, a small weasely man with sparse brown whiskers and a dirty gray turban came by on a bicycle, headed for the village. His name was Mohinder Singh, but in Ghungrali he was known simply as One-Eye; sometimes he wore a glass eye but mostly he just went about with the empty socket gruesomely exposed. He had appeared in Ghungrali a few years before, and as a Jat, was able to buy a few acres of land with money he claimed he saved as a taxi driver in Delhi and Calcutta. Soon he had insinuated himself into the circle of the Sarpanch or village chief, who, some said fearing blackmail, had appointed him secretary of the cooperative society. He was so clever and skilled at creating enmity among the farmers and playing one faction off against the other, the Harijans said amongst themselves it was lucky he had only one eye lest he destroy the village with his gossip.

When Charan waved at him cheerfully, Mukhtar said, testing his master, "He looks a very nice person."

"No." Charan was emphatic. "There are only two or three farmers in the village who are bad and he's number one. His only business is to stir up trouble." One-Eye was soon out of sight and forgotten.

And now, behind the fields of wheat a single poplar tree was standing. Who put it there and why, no one knew. Mukhtar could hardly take his eyes off its pale green color and cool shadow. Behind it was a bright yellow carpet of mustard and a field where oats had been cut and gathered into sheaves. Elsewhere Mukhtar saw nothing but green wheat. It would begin to ripen and turn gold and then a dull, whitish brown in a week or two. The cart passed two boys squatting side by side and rocking from foot to foot, swinging sickles and cutting fodder. Together they slashed their sickles at the green *barsim,* grasping a handful at a time, advancing slowly, steadily on and on; it swished before them, as if tossed by a breeze.

One man, pausing in repairing an irrigation ditch, stood and held his back with both hands, mopping his brow as the cart passed and following with his eyes its progress. He stood a long time watching the cart without moving before he picked up his hoe again.

"Hat! Hat!" Charan coaxed the bullocks. Mukhtar looked at the landscape now with indifference. The prospect of the heat to come exhausted him. It seemed they had been creaking and rattling a good long while though they had come less than a mile.

The look of geniality on Charan's face, too, gradually wore off, leaving only a sweat-beaded forehead and a fierce frown between the grimy yellow turban and bushy black beard.

An old man, with a clean, faded blue cloth loosely wrapped around his head and holding in his hand a long wooden staff—an Old Testament figure—rose from feeding sugar cane stalks into an iron crusher and, with a word to his laborers to keep the bullocks moving around the crusher, came forward to the cart, his palms folded inward in the traditional Punjabi greeting. It was Charan's neighbor, Pritam Singh, a distant relative; a saintly, giant of a man who at seventy-two was still one of the strongest in the village, Pritam was known for his simplicity and godliness. Above the door of his house in the village hung the legend: "O Nanak, I am drunk with the wine of God's name day and night." If One-Eye was the most evil man in the village, Mukhtar thought, Pritam was the saintliest.

"Sat Sri Akal!"

"Sat Sri Akal, Charanji."

"Are you hale and hearty, young man?" Charan called in his exuberant way. The cart went on; Charan's fields were just through a grove of trees; Mukhtar involuntarily looked into the white distance as the cart went to the right, lurched into a rut and then creaked around the final bend in the dirt road. Charan's white toolshed was just ahead, his wheat lay on both sides of the road. The cart turned off, went a little distance over a bumpy canal ditch and then came to a standstill in the shade of a dozen small oak trees. Mukhtar jumped off the cart and unhitched the bullocks, tying them in the shade of the trees. The two animals at once began to munch leisurely on the grass. Three crows flew up to the oak branches above them and by their cawing expressed their annoyance at being driven from their grassy shade. In a moment they hopped back down again to perch on the bullocks' backs, picking off fleas.

Two more daily wage laborers, old gray-bearded Chanan and his son Kapur, their dark brown faces identifying them as of the lowest, barn-cleaning Mazhbi caste, were already waiting at the well. Old Chanan had lit a fire in an underground pit below a big iron pan and was feeding cane husks into it. He said he was waiting for Charan to start the diesel engine which supplied power to the iron crushing machine, and complained that old Pritam's way of using bullocks as in the old days was better. Charan unlocked the white brick tool shed which gave his farmyard its distinction—none of his neighbors had built one yet—and uttered a loud oath. Someone had emptied out a drum of residue from the crushed sugar he had hidden there; Charan wanted to use it to distill some liquor.

"It was your father, Sadhu Singh," Kapur, the boy, volunteered with a sly grin. "He came last evening after you had driven the cart in and made us pour it out. He said, 'It does not behoove us to make drink. It is beneath our dignity!' "

Charan cursed his father. "I'll rape his mother! It would have made at least thirty bottles."

Mukhtar took a hoe from the shed and started across the fields. After a short distance he stopped and straddled an irrigation ditch, his bare feet sinking into the mud; he bent over and carefully opened a small earthen bund to let the water through. Then he dredged the canal bottom, deftly repairing its banks as he moved along, singing a snatch of song under his breath: "Oi, a scorpion bit me when I was picking berries from a thorny bush. . . ." After a time he rested, looking at the landscape and seeing exactly what he had seen from the bullock cart: the ripening, but still green, wheat, the trees, the pumphouses, a few men working here and there, the sky, the white dusty distance. He turned toward the village but could see only three or four houses in the mist. There was no life to be seen near the walls or roofs from this distance, nor water, nor shade, just as if Ghungrali had been overcome by the burning rays and had dried away. Mukhtar returned to watering the wheat.

In the neighboring fields east of Charan's, old Pritam Singh, having greeted Charan, went back to pour his laborers' tea. The men paused in their work and gathered in a semi-circle, squatting on the earth and holding up their dusty glasses as the old man passed among them with a brass container. Pritam, who still worked in the fields alongside his men every day, would never see the Sistine Chapel nor even hear of Michelangelo; he was unaware of his own physical beauty and would have been amazed and humbled to learn that the greatest artist of the Western world had fashioned his image of God with a face and physique much akin to Pritam's own.

"*Putchkar, putchkar,* O may you die!" one of Pritam's workers, a young boy, called to the bullocks, swatting their flanks aimlessly with a stick as he followed them round and round the cane crusher. "*Ham bol de.* You remember God." Then, as the men sipped their tea, no sound of voices; one heard the bullocks, one white and one tawny, snuffling and munching; somewhere quite far away came the plaintive cry of a peacock, the muted call of the cuckoo, accompanied by the persistent irritable cawing of crows and the high twitter of sparrows. But all these sounds and the boy's occasional cry to the bullocks and the mutter of conversation over their tea from the men did not break the silence, they did not stir the stagnant air, rather they lulled it to sleep.

The boy started singing in his aimless way, tapping the bullocks' flanks to the beat, "*Come and dance, Nasid Kaur, come and dance. . . .*"

Pritam called him to come and take tea. "We had a bet yesterday for two bottles of liquor," the boy told him. "Charan Singh, master, and that Mukhtar who works for him. They told us they had seven bales of oats to cut on their machine. They gave us a ten paisa coin to fetch some hot cakes from village Ghazipur and said, 'If we have these bales cut and loaded in the cart before you return, you will have to give us two bottles. But if you return first, we'll be giving you.' When we got back they hadn't even cut half the oats on the machine yet. What to talk about loading them on the cart!"

"Maybe you had bicycles hidden in the fields," Pritam teased him.

"No, no, master," the boy protested, sipping his tea with loud noises. "We went jumping through the fields. People were calling on the way, 'Why are you running?' I shouted back, 'Brothers, we have a bet with Charan Singh.' To some we called, 'There is a hare running before us and we are going to kill him.' We had a lot of fun."

Pritam smiled; Charan had a great zest for living and was often taking bets for liquor with the workers. The old man washed the tea tin, went to the crusher and sat on the ground to feed the cane in between the two rotating iron cylinders. The bullocks were attached to them with a log and each time they made a full circle Pritam had to duck his head because of his great size. He had done it so many years it came automatically.

"You work seriously now, Boy, like a man," one of the laborers called.

"If you don't think me a man, what are you, a pair of trousers?" The boy turned to Pritam. "He called me a chicken earlier so there's no harm if I call him a pair of trousers. O, bullocks, move forward. May you live long. The crusher makes noises, master."

"Yes, a little."

"Don't worry, we'll fix it tonight if we can." The boy saw the old man was almost out of cane to feed into the crusher. "Have you finished?" he asked.

"Why should we be finished?" Pritam smiled. "The finished are those who don't come back to this earth. We are the living."

"Some will go on working until they die," called the man stoking the fire. "Those who can afford it stop at sixty; those who can't, go on working until they drop dead in the fields."

"Work can keep your health," Pritam said. "An idle man gets lead in his bones."

Another old man, very much an Old Testament figure like Pritam himself, approached across the fields. Pritam recognized Charan's uncle, Mamaji, an old friend who lived in a distant village and did not often visit Ghungrali. *"Sat Sri Akal!"* Pritam called warmly.

"Sat Sri Akal, Pritamji," the other replied and the two old friends

shook hands; Mamaji at once settled down on a canal bank with a heave of breath and Pritam returned to his place at the crusher. In the comfortable silence of old country men, neither spoke for some time.

"There in Hissar District where I live now we sometimes sow the old kind of wheat," Mamaji said at last, raising his hoarse voice over the groan and creak of the crusher. "Because we rely on rain. We have twelve acres without irrigation."

For a time the two talked about crops and the weather and then Pritam raised his hand to the sky. "Did I feel a raindrop?"

"It's only that one small cloud overhead. It will pass over."

"We are not salt that will melt away," said Pritam. "I see Charan is also making sugar today."

"He has that diesel engine. Charan follows all those modern ways. But the camel is best for crushing sugar cane. O, Boy, you have broken the rope."

"You should have tied it nicely," Pritam scolded. "These young men just do half things. There . . . now it is all right." Silence returned for a time with only the sound of the crusher and the chirping of sparrows as the two old men reflected on how rapidly farming methods were changing in the Punjab. "These days camels are cheaper," Pritam finally said. "Here there are no Persian wells any more."

"Yes," Mamaji agreed. "It is hard to sell a camel any more here in Ludhiana District. In the old days we had beautiful saddles for our camels. These days if a man comes riding by on a camel, people don't like it. They expect everybody to be on a tractor or a motorcycle. . . . We had a saddle one time that cost us eight scores of rupees. We made the floor and rug in our own house."

"We bought a saddle in Maghiana one time. Even if you put it under a bullock cart it wouldn't jerk. It was so nice. If you are once on a camel with a proper saddle it looks like you are riding a horse."

"Heh-heh-heh-heh-eh. . . ." Mamaji chuckled, remembering the good times past, then fell into a coughing fit. He revived, some good gossip having come to mind. He told Pritam that Charan's sister Surjit, who was married to an opium addict and was struggling to farm on newly-cleared jungle land, had not yet begun to crush her sugar cane. "Charan had to take them to the crusher from here. They have none of their own, only an old broken one. The husband eats

opium the day long and Surjit must depend on Charan for everything."

Mamaji speculated Charan and his father, old Sadhu Singh, had
spent three or four thousand rupees on their new barn, mortgaging
three acres of land to pay for it. Pritam recalled Sadhu had mortgaged three acres in the old days in Pakistan also.

"Yes," Mamaji chuckled. "Do you remember how Sadhu would
go here and there, even as a young man, gossiping and doing
nothing? Ah, if a man without enough land wears white clothes he
will do badly. We also want to wear white clothes but we can't
afford it. It's a wonder Sadhu Singh never came to ruin."

To Pritam, the prosperity of Charan and his father always seemed
something of a mystery. He himself had worked hard in his fields all
his life but now Sadhu Singh, who had never taken his hands out of
his pockets, was doing well. "Sadhu is a clever man," he reminded
Mamaji. "Look how he brings all those machines from the university
in Ludhiana to do his work."

"Yes, times have changed," Mamaji mused in a disappointed tone.
"Now cleverness is as important as hard work. But it is Charan who
saves that family. Charan would be a very good man if he didn't
drink so much." Mamaji recalled how as young men he and Pritam
and others had wanted to go to America; one man from their village had even sold his lands to pay for the fare. "He sold that one
piece for seven thousand and told his father-in-law, 'You take care of
the fields; I'm going to America.' But who was to go and who was
to take him? The poor fellow remained there, losing his land. You
see what fate makes of a man, Pritamji? What he was and what
he has become. . . ." For some time neither spoke and the silence
around the two old friends was like a tomb, as though the air were
dead too.

"These are the little jokes of God," Pritam finally said solemnly.
"What he gives with one hand he takes away with another. Nobody
has any power over it. It is enough if only we fill our bellies day and
night." The older he became the more Pritam distrusted any easy
path to prosperity. He stopped to rearrange the pile of cane by his
side. "It is close and hot today. There will be rain."

"Now God is after our mustard and gram in Hissar."

"Do you think He's not after our wheat? With these thunder-
showers it goes down and becomes shaky at the root."

"You still work as hard as ever, Pritamji. These youngsters can't beat you."

"When we first came to Ghungrali, the people from Bhambadi village over there would tease us because we wore white clothes; they said we were not good farmers. Now we have shown them.... When we came from Pakistan, how long ago it seems.... One person, Wiryam, he died only eight days after we reached here. He brought my children here for me when I was left behind with the bullock carts. He brought the children this far and then died. Another of God's jokes."

"He makes them sometimes."

Pritam rose to his feet and stretched to his full height, looking like one of the vanishing giants of the earth. "Older people like us have joint pains," he told Mamaji, settling down beside him on the earthen bund.

"It is the greed of work," admonished his friend, who suffered from it not at all himself.

"No, Mamaji," Pritam said, "our life is easier now. If people go on minding their own business, the villagers here in Ghungrali can become rich. There's no doubt about it. With these new wheat seeds, we're getting richer day by day...."

"Are the hard times really over?" Mamaji asked doubtfully.

His old friend thought for a moment, then asked, "How can we tell?"

"It rained and rained that year, more rain than there has been before or since."

The red light of the open fire cast strange flickering shadows on Gurdial's handsome face, giving it a cadaverous, demonic appearance. It was late evening and some of the Harijans were gathered in his courtyard. Gurdial, with a poultry farm of two thousand birds, was the richest untouchable or Harijan in the village. Although he borrowed and lent money with the Jats and was as prosperous as many of them, as a Chamar or member of the leather-working caste, he still lived in the poorer Harijan quarter of Ghungrali. The firelight cast a flickering halo over the group of men and boys, who huddled together, sitting or squatting on the ground in a semi-circle at Gurdial's feet. He and two Harijan elders sat cross-legged on a *charpoy* and, like their audience, lit a single cigarette from time to time and passed it one man to another, as Harijans always do. Although the moon was shining, the things outside the red halo from the fire looked impenetrable and dark. The men on the ground were partly dazzled by this light, and they could see only a portion of the lane outside, and the cattle in the yard were hardly noticeable in the gloom except for the sound of their munching and snuffling. Over the fire, Gurdial's wife had fixed a cauldron for boiling water, and she bent over it, standing in the smoke of the fire, waiting for the first signs of bubbles. Bhoondi, the barn cleaner, and his sons, Sher and Bawa, sat side by side in silence, deep in thought and looking into the fire. Gurmel, a sharecropper with Charan's uncle, Sarvan Singh, was a thin, hungry-looking man with smouldering eyes who sat and absently twisted his big moustaches; his shadow danced over Mukhtar, and at times it hid and at times revealed Mukhtar's young, strong face. Everyone was resting from the day's hard labor, thinking, remembering, and listening to Gurdial recount the old, familiar story of the massacre.

Some thirty steps from the fire, just outside the gate by the edge of the road, stood a large Moslem gravestone leaning to one side. As Gurdial spoke, Mukhtar thought there was something very melancholy about that lonely grave. He could almost hear its silence, and feel the presence of the soul of the unknown being who lived beneath that tombstone, one of the fifteen to twenty thousand persons who had been slain within a few hours that afternoon so long ago.

"In July of that year there was a rumor there would be a separate state of Pakistan for the Moslems," Gurdial said. "Except for us Harijan Sikhs, all the people in Ghungrali were Moslem. They used to tell us, 'You get your hair and beards shaved and we'll get Pakistan all the way down to Delhi.' Then after some days we came to know that the Pakistan boundary would be to the north, above Amritsar." At once, Gurdial said, reports of Hindus massacring Moslems in the nearby villages reached Ghungrali and thousands of Moslem refugees began pouring in. At first the local Moslem families and the refugees decided to move to Malerkotla, a strongpoint the Indian army was defending, but at the last moment a decision was taken to stand and fight. "No one had any idea how many thousands would later come to attack here," Gurdial said. He reached into his shirt, pulled out a cigarette, lit it, took a puff and passed it on to the next man. The fire flared up and in the gloom along the road the tombstone flickered in the shadows.

"Aye thousands. . . ." sighed Gurmel. "Such a cutting and harvesting. . . ." Gurdial said the Harijan women and children fled to the neighboring village of Majari, already inhabited only by Sikhs, but the Moslems kept the men back to help them guard Ghungrali. "Some young men also wanted to stay here to look after their property," he said. "I used to come and keep people informed, going between here and Majari." Gurmel kept silent, thinking how Gurdial had made his fortune by looting.

"From dawn onward that day no one could slip away. There were seven hundred Moslem families living in Ghungrali then, and with so many refugees fleeing here there must have been fifteen to twenty thousand Moslems in all. The Moslems thought they were safe; they were ready to fight back as soon as they saw the Sikhs start to surround the village at daybreak. At two o'clock in the afternoon, Dogra soldiers opened fire. Those soldiers were all clean-shaven Hindus. A Hindu general sent them in. The Moslems had muzzle-loading rifles. They answered fire. From outside the barrage was heavier. Some Moslems had positions on the tops of houses. All the young men of the Harijans, Mazhbis and Chamars alike, gathered in the courtyard outside their houses before a big iron gate that used to separate us from the Moslem quarter."

Gurmel interrupted. "That gate was open, I remember. We watched the Sikhs come from the rooftops. Tens of thousands there were, like herds of sheep surrounding the village. Countless. Everywhere you looked you saw men. This village was very strong. The Sikhs knew it and were afraid. They didn't dare attack until the army came to help them. At about four o'clock in the afternoon, those Dogra soldiers brought in machine guns. That's when we locked our houses and gathered at the big gate; some said you could escape toward Ghazipur."

Annoyed at this interruption, Gurdial picked up his story. "When the Moslems saw they couldn't cope with the heavy incoming fire, they all ran back to their own houses, and the Sikhs came pouring into the Harijan quarter. They demanded we give them kerosene and matches as proof of our loyalty as Sikhs. They were rushing about like maniacs, with spears, *gandasas,* hatchets, swords. The firing stopped and thousands upon thousands of men came pouring into these streets. They were all shouting, *'Jo Bole So Nahal Sat Sri Akal!* Who speaks he is full of the name of God!' We crouched in our houses, certain we would be killed too. They were like mad beasts and we could hear the screams of the women and the shouts of our Moslem friends."

Gurmel broke in, "The richest Moslem in the village, Fauju Khan, was killed on his own threshhold. It was a huge family and we thought they would be spared since he had served the Sikhs in the fight against the British. After his death it just ran like wildfire. Men who were hungry for generations just started raping women right in the courtyards. Some of the women jumped into wells— those who wouldn't allow the touch of even another man's hand. I saw them tear a baby from one woman and spear it in the air in front of her eyes."

"I saw no rapes!" Gurdial sounded angry. "Nobody could think of rape! It was like a burning pyre, this village. It was a moment when sons forgot their mothers and mothers forgot their sons."

"Did you rape, Gurmel?" someone asked.

"As God may not bring lies on my tongue, I never killed nor raped," swore Gurmel. "At that time I was but a soft boy. But I saw many others do it."

Gurdial ignored him. "Some were killed inside their houses, others while trying to escape. Many ran into the cane fields. Some of the Ghungrali Moslems escaped but most of the refugees fell, not knowing where to run or hide. Women jumped into the wells in their courtyards or flung themselves from the rooftops. Some jumped into ponds and drowned themselves. We had the heaviest rain in memory that year and all the ponds were flooded. Some of the young girls were carried away but we heard the police later got them back and sent them to Pakistan."

Old Bhoondi, whose real name was Kishan Singh—but whom everyone called "Little Bug" because of his black, jolly face, short, thick-set body and white teeth—cleared his throat and spoke for the first time. "I ran when the attack came. Before that the Moslems would not let us go."

The men laughed. Someone said, "O, Bhoondi, what a rascal you are!"

"No, no, *maharaj,* don't say that. The wells were filled with women and there was a cutting and a harvesting of human heads. I ran to a sugar cane field and hid myself there. That's all I know."

"O, Bhoondi, tell us more."

"That's all I know. I have done nothing except spend my life cleaning people's barns. That's all. *Bas!*"

But they persuaded him to go on.

"I heard the fire open from the Majari side and saw a lot of men running through the streets. I was afraid only that I might be caught and get my head cut off. A Jat shouted at me, 'Run away! Leave the village or we'll kill you!' I just ran to a cane field and those hooligans started cutting and harvesting and picking up utensils and other things from the houses. My children were still inside my house, pray to God they'd locked the door! I ran into that field and dug a ditch and pulled canes around me without taking my breath inside my chest, without moving or leaving that place until late at night. My children came searching for me in the field lest someone had killed me. It was so dark and there was much shrieking and yelling. 'O, people, we are being killed! We are being looted! Save us!' I heard the fire of a Bren gun. *Kar! Kar! Kar!* Some hungry persons were riding the women. I saw a lot, there in the dark."

Everyone looked at the tombstone in silence. Somewhere, probably near the banyan tree, came the mournful sound of a bird: "Trrrr, trrrr, trrrrr. . . ."

"There are many terrible things in the world," remarked Mukhtar.

"Many, many!" affirmed Bhoondi, who drew nearer his neighbors just as if he had grown apprehensive.

"After the attack we all went to Majari," Gurdial went on in a low tone. "I saw some people taking away bales of loot on their heads."

"I also looted some grains and utensils," said Gurmel defiantly, watching Gurdial to see if he would admit his own guilt. But the other passed over this. "I had a round in this street," he went on. "The dead bodies were jammed into the wells, the courtyards, the houses. It was three months before people stopped coming to dig in the ashes. A few days after the attack, the police made us Harijans take wood and whatever we could find and burn the bodies, thousands of them. There were no vultures, no dogs. I don't know why they stayed away. Even six months later you could smell the stench. Almost all the women and children were killed. Some men got away.

"After the attack, we Harijans had in mind that now we'd get the land. We told ourselves, 'Now the land is ours.' But after only fifteen days, the Jat refugees came from Pakistan and the government gave the land to them. We were already cultivating it for harvest and had allotted it out to all the Harijan families. But the government gave the land to these strangers. They confirmed how much each Jat family owned in Pakistan and gave them land accordingly, even though our families had lived in Ghungrali for generations and generations and Mahatma Gandhi tried to help the Harijans. When the Jats first took over the land, they promised us two-thirds for tilling it for them, but little by little they reduced our share. Now only twenty-two acres of common land is left to the Harijans, and even if we get a third of its earnings all the money goes to pave streets or to the school."

"Yes," sighed Gurdial. "We all assumed that once the Moslems were gone we would get their land. We all took possession. I harvested two hundred maunds of grams that year and ploughed the lands. But we had to vacate."

"Now we are yoked by these Jats." A murmur of grumbling went through the men.

"Ah, but there is a difference between these Jats and the Moslems," cautioned the prosperous Gurdial. "Now we can touch the drinking glasses of these Jats. We never dared touch a Moslem's. The Moslems hated us. A Moslem would never let a Harijan cross his threshold. We were like serfs in those days." His story ended, Gurdial looked around at the listeners. No one spoke but their eyes were still fixed on him. The men thought over what had been said. Life was so fearful and wonderful in the Punjab that, however much the horror or strangeness of a story, it always evoked in the minds of listeners that which had been in their own lives. Alone among the audience, Mukhtar, who had nine years of schooling, might listen with skepticism, mentally noting the contradictions. But the firelight flickering on the tombstone in the lane, the massive blackness of the banyan tree at night, the wide endless plain that stretched beyond the horizon in every direction and was the only world they knew, these and the fates of the men gathered in the courtyard seemed in themselves so wonderful or fearful that the lurid unreality paled and mingled with the real. Each of them, even the youngest, had grown up aware of the crumbling Moslem graves and the sealed old wells still filled with the skeletons of women and children.

In a few months Charan would be forty, a giant of a man who towered over most of his fellow villagers. His eyes were deeply shadowed but underneath his bushy black eyebrows the eyes themselves sparkled with life. When he laughed—so deeply you could see down his throat—he had a look of great physical strength and vitality. Yet his asthma had grown worse over the years in such a dusty climate and, during a bad attack, as he lay helpless on his bed, a horrible rasping sound arose deep inside his throat and chest, almost like the crackle of a death rattle. Like a pond filling with rushes and reeds, Charan seemed as if he were being choked by the very life within him. But it was his laughter you remembered.

As a boy, the eldest son of a prosperous land owner, Charan had studied through the ninth class and hoped to become a doctor or an engineer. He might have had a reasonable chance of realizing such ambitions had not the partition of India and Pakistan come in 1947. When word arrived that the new frontier would fall well to the southeast of their village, near the holy Sikh city of Amritsar, Charan's family and their neighbors and relatives had fled one afternoon, without much preparation, leaving behind houses, possessions, lands, everything. Charan was sixteen then and although the caravan his family joined numbered twenty-two-thousand bullock carts, it moved in single file and was highly vulnerable to attack on the journey south. One day he found himself joining the older men from the carts around him in fighting off a marauding band of fierce tribesmen from the Baluchistan desert; a homemade, muzzle-loading cannon put together by his father, Pritam Singh and some of the other men from their village, killed twelve of the attackers. The remaining Baluchis, about fifteen men, fled into an abandoned Sikh village. When they were captured and asked why they had attacked the peaceful caravan of bullock carts, the Baluchis spat in their faces and declared, "It is our will! *Allah-O-Akbar!*" Charan watched as the older men of the village, over Pritam Singh's protests, locked the Baluchis in a house and set fire to it.

Charan had never forgotten the landscape as they moved southward: the fields scorched with fire and strewn with decapitated heads and corpses like sheep in a slaughterhouse, the wells filled with poison or dead bodies. He lost many of his school friends on the way; one of these believed a band of Moslem soldiers guarding a bridge, who told him he could pass to the other side provided he submitted to a search; they stripped him and cut him to pieces. Another joined several hundred families from the caravan, who trusted some Baluchi soldiers who promised them that in the main square of Jarawala town they would be given truck transportation across the frontier to India; instead, some ten thousand people were mowed down by machine guns positioned on the roofs. Several other school friends were swept away along with two hundred bullock carts and hundreds of refugees when a flash flood rushed into a gulley they were crossing. Charan himself had just reached the other side with his family's carts when he saw a nine foot high wall of water surging into what moments before had been a dry river bed; the waves were higher than a man's head and the victims barely had time to cry out before they were gone.

He had experienced starvation. The journey should have taken three or four days; the family carried provisions for ten. It took them twenty-seven days to reach the frontier. Cruelly, they had no sooner crossed it and reached safety, on the twenty-seventh night, when cholera broke out; it had claimed Charan's youngest sister and his only brother; his father, lacking medicine, tried to save them by pouring a mixture of country liquor and raw onions into their months, but to no avail. Finally the family reached Bija, Sadhu Singh's ancestral village, just two miles from Ghungrali. They had covered a distance of two-hundred-and-fifty miles altogether, weaving back and forth on country lanes to avoid Moslem villages and the city of Lahore. To Charan, the journey had seemed much longer. Even in Bija they found little but desolation; most of the surrounding villages had been razed, looted and abandoned. But an uncle who was the local chieftain had collected the possessions and protected the crops of some fleeing Moslem families, and these he distributed to his refugee relatives. With his assistance, Sadhu Singh and his brother Sarvan, Pritam Singh, and other neighbors in Pakistan were also allotted fifteen acres each in Ghungrali under the Delhi government's refugee resettlement program. Charan first saw Ghungrali the day the family passed through it on their way to Bija. The massacre of the Moslems had taken place only fifteen days before. The stench was terrible, not a single house was standing, only the charred rubble of a big brick mosque. Even the mudhuts of the Sikh Harijans had fallen in, and their thatched roofs were burnt away. Corpses lay everywhere, and soldiers were still sealing the wells filled with bodies. Only a little sugar cane stood in the fields. No one could live there.

Moreover, the land around Ghungrali was watered by Persian wheels powered by camels, which walked round and round drawing water up by buckets. Charan's family had never used one; their old village had been irrigated with canal water. A Chamar sharecropper who had looted bullocks and equipment from the Moslems agreed to farm their allotment on a fifty-fifty basis, and the family set out for Rajasthan in search of better land.

In Rajasthan's Ganganagar district, where the Indian government had just started to irrigate the desert, Sadhu Singh managed to obtain a new government allotment of twenty-five acres. Charan's father still refused to do physical labor despite the family's impoverished state, and flatly told his relatives, "I have never taken my hands out of my pockets and I never shall take my hands out of my pockets as long as I live."

Thus Charan, at seventeen, became the sole supporter of his parents and four surviving sisters. To make ends meet, he joined the Harijans as a hired field laborer during the day and cultivated his own fields at night, often working sixteen to twenty hours each day. As Charan never tired of retelling it in later years, "I've worked like a Harijan most of my life. I had to. There was no alternative." Then with an odd smile, he would add, "But you know, those hardest years of my life were also the happiest. Maybe work is good for a man. I used to be in the fields, sixteen, eighteen, twenty hours a day. Seems like I never stopped, just slept wherever I was. There was a system of canals there and the main outlet in our village had sand dunes and grass, perhaps as high as twelve feet on the sides. Every time you irrigated fifty acres you had to go work on the canal. And I had to do double since I was irrigating a hundred acres. But I would finish double the work before the others did their single portions. Then we'd play *kabaddi*. I used to enjoy that work very much. All young men, Jats and Harijans together, and always cutting jokes. They used to find a place for me where you had to throw sand the highest, ten or twelve feet. How we used to laugh and enjoy ourselves. I would enjoy reliving those days, hard as it was!"

A. Hindu tax collector proved to be the family's benefactor. He provided them with a house and made Charan his sharecropper for fifty acres. Charan rented another twenty-five besides the family's own allotment, so that he farmed a full one-hundred acres. Hiring two bullocks and a laborer, he was able to practice the economies of scale. One year, when the rains were favorable, his friends from the canal came with twenty-two bullock pairs to help him with sowing, and he was able to reap an abundant harvest of wheat, oil seed and gram. It sold for a small fortune and enabled his father to pay the Punjab government for the land in Ghungrali. In 1952, the year a consolidation of land holdings in Ghungrali was completed, the Rajasthan government passed a law that no one could hold two allotments in different states. When the Indian government started advancing low-interest farm loans the following year, Sadhu Singh and his brother Sarvan took a combined loan of 2,500 rupees for a tube well and the family moved back to Ghungrali and the Punjab for good.

Once Charan had rescued the family from poverty, Sadhu Singh set about rapidly marrying off his now-eligible daughters. Husbands were found for two of the girls in Malaya, a Sikh policeman and a Sikh moneylender. A third daughter was wed to a draftsman in the nearby town of Ludhiana. Charan himself was married in 1954, to the daughter of a wealthy landlord whose farm was ten miles west of Ghungrali; the dowry paid him included a bicycle, a large chest of clothes, blankets, cooking utensils and some silver. The neighbors marveled at Sadhu Singh's shrewdness in arranging such good matches for his children, considering he spent only a niggardly five hundred rupees on each of his daughters' dowries and broke tradition by cutting down the marriage celebrations from three days to one, an innovation soon copied by other practical men in the village.

Ironically, Surjit, the oldest daughter, who had been married when the family was still prosperous and living in Pakistan, became old Sadhu's biggest problem. Her husband, Saroop, having lost his fortune in the partition days, had become an opium addict and sank so low as to mortgage his land allotment to buy opium. When old Sadhu came back from Rajasthan, he found Surjit and her three small children living in destitution; he packed the family off to Ghungrali, gave Saroop all the opium he needed to be content and cannily got his son-in-law to sign a *mukhiarmanam* or legal transfer of financial responsibility. Then he brought a successful law suit against those who held Saroop's mortgage, on the grounds his son-in-law was incapable of handling such transactions, sold the land for sixteen thousand rupees and bought a new farm in jungle lands not far from Ghungrali, which he put in Surjit's name. Gradually Charan cleared and built up this land so that by the late 1960s, Surjit's two adolescent sons could begin to work it themselves.

In recent years, Charan had done less and less physical labor, relying mostly on hired Harijans, sometimes sharecroppers but more often daily laborers such as Mukhtar. Freed from his old bondage to the land, Charan drank and caroused more, but nevertheless, despite his great size and fierce appearance, he seldom got into trouble. As Charan would tell his cronies, "There are three kinds of drunks in the Punjab. The first worries about his bullocks and runs to water and feed them. The second is like my cousin, Sindar, who fires a shot in the air and tells everybody how brave he is. The third gets a gun or a sword and goes off after those for whom he feels enmity. I will never drink with a man if I have a grudge against him. Such men are fools."

Indeed, since returning to the Punjab, Charan had been in only two serious quarrels. There was a popular saying in Ghungrali that most fights and village factions revolved around wealth, women and land. In Charan's case it was both times what he felt to be a question of his honor.

The first quarrel had taken place six years before, during the hottest, driest week in May. A neighbor, with some canal water to spare, agreed to let Charan divert its flow for two hours to irrigate some sugar cane. Late one night when he went to open the canal, followed by old Chanan, the Mazhbi, who was then his laborer, Charan was stopped by his uncle Sarvan, his cousin, Dhakel, and another cousin, Sindar, an easy-going vagabond who was the black sheep of the family. All three were drunk. Old Sarvan, red-faced, cantankerous and reeling about, claimed the neighbor had not promised Charan the water but rather had given it to himself. The matter might have been settled amiably had not Dhakel, then a skinny seventeen-year-old stripling who had long resented his giant, popular cousin, suddenly staggered over to Charan, swung at him and shouted in his face, "I'll rape your mother, you big bastard! That's our water!" Sindar said nothing but stood to one side holding a *kirpan* or Punjabi sword, foolishly running his finger up and down the sharp edge. As a precaution, Charan sent old Chanan back to his wellhouse for a spear. When he himself attempted to pass by, the three of them blocked his way. Charan cursed his drunken relatives, tossed the spear Chanan brought him at their feet and started to walk away in a gesture of contempt. Old Sarvan and his son Dhakel rushed him from behind and grabbed his arms. Charan easily shook them off and they fell to the ground. They rushed him a second time and again he knocked them down.

Meanwhile, old Chanan, alarmed by such foolishness, crept up behind Sindar, grabbed his sword and ran with it toward the village as fast as his legs could carry him. A short man, with a thick-set body, white beard and round, brown face, he presented a spectacle that was long remembered in Ghungrali as he ran into the village, shouting at the top of his lungs for Sadhu Singh.

Left alone, Charan grabbed his uncle and cousin, cracked their heads together and proceeded to give them a good shaking. Who knows what might have happened had not Sindar crept up behind him and seized his testicles, squeezing as hard as he could. Howling, Charan released his hold and the three of them were able to bring him to the ground and overpower him. While Dhakel and Sindar sat on Charan, pinning down his shoulders and yanking at his hair and beard, old Sarvan ran to his well for a brick, came running back and proceeded to beat his nephew with it as hard as he could. Drunk, hysterical and exhausted, he finally fell back and Dhakel and Sindar helped him to his well to wash. Charan, his body streaked with blood and his clothes torn and shredded, was left lying there. For some minutes he appeared to be dead, then his eyes opened, he struggled to his feet and staggered out into a field. His face looked terrifying in the shadows, and waving his bloody arms like a maniac, his long hair flying all directions, he thundered at them, "Now I'll fuck your mother! I'll rape your sister!" In the darkness beneath the trees of their well, old Sarvan, Dhakel and Sindar rushed about, arming themselves with bricks and staves and preparing for the worst, when Sadhu Singh and old Pritam came running from the village. Sarvan, his voice quavering, called to his brother, "Now do whatever you want! We have taught your brave son a lesson, older brother. We have taught your son how to water his fields!"

Panting for breath and in a foul temper after such unseemly physical exertion, old Sadhu was aghast and furious. "I'll see who touches his water, by God!" he roared in a voice some claimed could be heard all the way back to the village. "Now you have enjoyed beating my son to the full!" As the two brothers stood abusing each other at a distance, Charan staggered over to the canal and let the water flow into his cane field. "Look! Look! I'm watering again!" he shouted like a madman. "You can't stop me from watering my fields. Now do whatever you want. I'll see who touches this water. You have beaten me all you can and I'm still standing here and you are three! Come one by one and let's see how brave you are!"

Sadhu Singh, seeing Charan had got the upper hand, and his wrath now fully aroused, heaped scorn on his younger brother. "Yes, you have beaten him to the full but he's still standing there. Do me another favor, my younger brother, go and throw him to the ground and kill him. Are you afraid? He shouldn't be standing. Harumph! You are supposed to be a wise and elderly person, Sarvan, yet you have behaved like a child. If Dhakel and Charan were fighting you should have intervened instead of joining in. Now you have left him standing. Why didn't you leave him slain in the field?"

For eighteen months after that night the two brothers did not speak to each other. Only a few villagers knew their reconciliation followed a secret visit by Sarvan to Sadhu on the night of Dhakel's marriage celebration, when Sarvan wept and begged Sadhu's forgiveness, imploring him, "Look, you are my elder brother. I live next door to you. If you refuse to come to Dhakel's wedding, what will my in-laws say? I shall be disgraced."

For the two older men the incident was forgotten. Sometimes, when he got too drunk, Dhakel might boast, "We taught that drunkard a lesson he won't forget and he doesn't bother us now." Sindar pretended it had never happened although a few years later when he was working for Charan and they drank together one evening he sighed, "O, this liquor is a dangerous thing. We brothers were fighting like dogs that night. I'm sorry for that." Charan himself never really forgave them. "O, now we speak, we talk," he would tell his drinking companions. "But we can never be good friends. Can we?"

The second quarrel had begun four years before. A farmer, Dhan
Singh, who lived in Bhambadi, the next village to the south of
Ghungrali, asked Charan to sell him some seeds Sadhu Singh had
managed to obtain through his carefully cultivated contacts at the
university in Ludhiana; he wanted twenty-five kilos of a new high-
yielding wheat and twenty kilos of an improved hybrid maize.
Charan named a price; the two together came to two hundred and
eighty-five rupees. Dhan Singh gave Charan three one-hundred
notes and asked for his change. Charan did not have fifteen rupees
at the time; he promised to pay Dhan Singh the next time he saw
him although he thought to himself that he had probably priced
the seeds too low in any case. To Charan's surprise, Dhan Singh
came to Ghungrali three times to ask for his fifteen rupees, an
amount Charan himself thought nothing of spending of an evening
for two bottles of liquor. Each time, as luck would have it, either
Charan was away or had no money in the house. In time Charan
forgot about the debt; two years went by. One day as he was returning on his tractor from Surjit's farm, Charan passed Dhan Singh's
bullock cart on the Grand Trunk Road. When he stopped his tractor
to greet him, Dhan Singh, who had spent the day drinking, jumped
off his cart and ran toward Charan waving the stick he used to prod
his bullocks. "Aha," he shouted drunkenly, "now I will settle it one
way or another. You are a cheat, Gurcharan Singh! You never gave
me my fifteen rupees back. It has been two years now."

Charan had forgotten all about it and said so.

"O, no! You know better."

Angry to be pestered over so small a matter, Charan told him,
"If I know better, I know only that you owe me something, Dhan
Singh. I sold you seed for three rupees when all the others were
asking five. It is you who should owe me money."

Dhan Singh slapped his stick on the ground. "All right," he
bellowed. "If you are the real seed of your father, you will give me
the money!"

"Are you calling me a bastard? You say I am not the real seed of
my father. To pay you anything now would be to accept this insult!"
Several men passing by, hearing the angry exchange, hurried to
intervene, saying, "Charan, Dhan Singh is drunk and foolish today."
"Let him go his way and you go your way." For such quarrels often
led to bloodshed in the Punjab.

After that Charan and Dhan Singh did not speak although their fields were not far apart. Then one day Charan spent the afternoon drinking with some cronies in Bhambadi, and as they drove home on his tractor, the Bandit sitting on one fender, and a neighbor called Nirmal Singh on the other, they found their way blocked by a herd of buffaloes. Charan beeped on his horn impatiently and a barefoot farmer came running to shoo his herd forward. It was Dhan Singh. Recognizing Charan, he seemed to go berserk; he leapt in front of the tractor, holding out his arms and shouting to his sons behind him in the fields, "Come! Come! Bring sticks and clubs! Today we won't let him get away! We'll settle everything!"

Charan kept moving the tractor slowly forward, pushing Dhan Singh who refused to get out of the way. "Get aside! Get out of my way!" Charan shouted. "All right. If you want to kill yourself and fall under the tractor tires, just keep on." Charan's words seemed to make Dhan Singh all the madder; his eyes turned red and he dug his heels in and spread his arms out so that the tractor pushed him back against his will and his feet skidded along in the dust. As soon as Charan reached a wide place in the road near some houses he stopped the engine, leapt to the ground and seized a heavy stick. "All right!" he shouted. "Let's settle it today!"

Men came running from all directions, everyone crying at once, "No, no, no!" "Leave, leave!" "Stop this fighting!" Two of Dhan Singh's grown sons appeared, clubs in their hands and as hysterical as their father. Charan's friends jumped off the tractor; Nirmal grabbed a stick and the Bandit pulled out his switchblade knife. Women and children appeared at the doors and windows of the houses and they, too, began to wail and cry.

"Either you kill me today or pay me my fifteen rupees!" Dhan Singh shrieked like a maniac.

"I warned him," thundered Charan. "Now I'll fix him." Tall, his black beard flying, snarling like an animal, his eyes bloodshot with drink and anger, Charan looked truly terrifying.

"Either pay me or one of us will die!" Dhan Singh swung at Charan with his stick but missed and whacked the tractor tire instead. "Now I won't leave!" roared Charan. "He has damaged my tractor! He'll pay for this!"

Sticks were raised to strike blows, outstretched hands tried to prevent blows from being struck, screams arose on all sides, "No,

no!" "Someone will be killed!" "Help! Help!" when an old white-
beard, Dhan Singh's father, appeared, quivering with anger. He
collared his son and dragged him into a nearby hut. In a moment,
Dhan Singh, red-faced, outraged, humiliated and bellowing at the
top of his lungs, was shoved into a room and the door bolted after
him. The old man hastened to Charan to apologize, and Charan
agreed to go. "All right! But if he bothers me one more time, I'll
get him."

To everyone's relief, Charan, Nirmal and the Bandit jumped on
the tractor and Charan started its engine with a tremendous roar.
With a jerk it took off and thundered down the road. But Charan
stopped a few hundred yards down the road in the Bhambadi
village square to drink a glass of liquor to show he was not afraid
of Dhan Singh. One bottle led to another and that to three; by the
time Charan and his friends were on their way back to Ghungrali it
was dark and they were all giggling and carrying on as if their
brains were numbed.

"We'll fix him, Charan," the Bandit muttered ominously. "Have
no worries on that score. Now he's afraid of us. He's having loose
motions back there in Bhambadi."

"No, no," Charan said. "He's afraid we may beat him when he
comes to the fields. But we won't. But I'll never pay that son-of-a-
bitch his fifteen rupees. I'll pay him only if he comes and apologizes
and admits his highhandedness."

Several days passed. Then one evening as Charan was driving on
his tractor with only Mukhtar on the fender he saw Dhan Singh
and his two sons working in their fields. One of the sons stood up
when he saw Charan and came running toward the tractor. Charan
greeted him warily but the boy told him, "Charan, what has happened is bad."

"It doesn't matter," Charan said. "We have been acting like fools.
Tell your father to forget all about it. Here. . . ." Charan reached
into his pocket for the fifteen rupees then remembered he had left
all his money at home.

Still, as he drove toward Ghungrali, he chuckled to himself and
felt lighthearted. The sun was setting and over the wheat fields,
around the bushes and from the open spaces between the clumps of
trees at the wells, rose a thick, dusty mist, white as milk. Then as
darkness came apace, one by one the lights from the tube wells

blinked on and it seemed as if the mist was hovering over some mysterious and unknown land.

There was a slight chill in the air and the smell of newly-mown hay, and Charan breathed deeply watching the night fall. He had worked for twenty-five years to build up his farm, suffered asthma, survived repeated petty quarrels with his father, and been guilty of so many follies and injustices it was painful to remember them. He knew he neglected his gentle and kindly wife, that he was remiss in helping a sister saddled in marriage to an opium addict, and that he was partly to blame that his half-educated sons looked down on him and were disappointing. Charan clearly realized he was a mediocrity, a bit of a drunkard, short-tempered, a companion of some of the worst wastrels in the village. And yet he felt resigned to it and looked forward to an evening's laughter over a bottle with some friends, for he knew that every man must be satisfied with what he is.

So instead of going home he drove the tractor to a friend's house and there he and Mukhtar had something to eat and drink; from this friend's they went to see a mechanic in Pyal village; from the mechanic's to a farmer's; from the farmer's to the house of another crony in Majari and so on. In short, by the time he and Mukhtar reached Ghungrali, they were so drunk they had to hold each other up on the tractor. It was already late and when they reached Charan's cattleyard, Mukhtar staggered off down the road to his hut, waving his arms and breathing heavily, "Charan is a prince. A prince among men!"

The crippled stablehand, Peloo, waked from his dreams by the tractor's roar, stumbled to open the gate, and with cries and sobs from his twisted mouth, helped Charan to maneuver the tractor safely into its shed. Charan stumbled out through the gate and with drowsy, drunken eyes looked now at the village pond, now at the banyan tree. Jubru, his Dalmatian, came running to sniff at his master's legs; the dog growled at the darkness, affirming in Charan's mind that the black shadows on the pond's surface were not shadows but a dream: that the banyan tree, the sky, the stretch of plain had something blessed to say to him. The past was trivial and tedious, the future insignificant and all he had was this magic moment, this one moment of life. And Charan listened, first to Jubru's growl, then to the midnight silence and saw the pond shivering in a silvery light, a silver he had not seen before. Then he shook his head drunkenly, as if the dark shadows, the moonlight and the banyan tree really meant to betray him, to delude him into thinking his life was more than the fragile insignificant thing it was. "Ghosts," he whispered. "Ghosts, Jubru." He broke into a great peal of laughter as he staggered up to his house. "Ghosts! I'll eat them!"

Everyone said Basant Singh, the richest farmer in Ghungrali, was hard as flint. While the other villagers might fritter away their days in gossip, drink, chasing women, petty quarrels and the like, Basant Singh's thoughts never strayed from economy of operations and returns. In matters relating to religion, politics, morality and money, he was harsh and relentless and kept a strict watch, not only over himself and his family but over his servants, fieldhands and acquaintances, and, indeed, the entire village. God forbid that anyone should ever enter his office without being announced.

This office off the veranda of his big blue house was like Basant Singh himself and, needless to say, was the only one in Ghungrali: straight-backed chairs stood at attention along each wall below framed photographs of Basant Singh with a national Cabinet minister, with the vice-chancellor of the agricultural university, with visiting foreign technicians and economists and other such luminaries; at one end of the office, directly confronting the apprehensive visitor, was Basant Singh's desk, with its neat stacks of files, documents and government periodicals reporting the latest technological advances; against the back wall, steel cabinets held a formidable collection of bound records, for Basant Singh kept detailed accounts not only of all his own farm's operations, but of those of the rest of the village as well.

Every conceivable item relating to the cost of production on his own fifty-four acres was there, including amortization of every thing that was amortizable, and not excluding food for the seventeen members of his family, four permanent hired men and twenty daily wage fieldhands. The last item in his ledger, "Return to Management," summed up the profits of the last season: it showed a net income of 1,600 rupees per acre. The figure was made up of sales of wheat seed which commanded a price of 180 rupees per 100 kilos as against the market price of ordinary grain which most of the year ran at 76 rupees per 100 kilos, but fell to 66 just before the harvest. Had he devoted all his land to grain only, Basant Singh was wont to explain, his net income per double-cropped acre would have amounted only to 600 rupees.

Basant Singh did not need to tell his fellow villagers his business; they all knew it by heart. His success story was legendary in the surrounding villages. He had started out as a poor man with only two acres when he first came to Ghungrali twenty years before. He and his older brother had married village girls who together inherited fifty acres of land from their fathers. When the government sought to build a canal through their land, Basant Singh saw to it that each of the wives was awarded 10,000 rupees for right-of-way titles. With this money, he managed to get the sole franchise for selling liquor in Ghungrali, and his fortune rapidly grew. When the new dwarf varieties of wheat were first imported from Mexico, Basant Singh was ready with capital.

In the Punjab, they were first sold by Dilbagh Singh Atwal, a wheat breeder who marketed his seed crop at two to five rupees a kilo for a return of 70,000 rupees in 1964. The following year, Basant Singh, profiting God knows how from his connections at the university and agricultural ministry, planted the first of the new wheat seeds in Ghungrali. At the harvest he sold 30,000 kilos of seed for three rupees a kilo, making 90,000 rupees. The next year he planted a still newer variety, PV 18, and sold the seeds for a profit of 70,000 rupees. When Khalyan Sona, the most popular variety in Ghungrali, came the next year and the Punjab government purchased his entire seed crop, he made another 90,000 rupees. Now each year he was sowing more and more acres in still newer varieties, making triple the profits of the farmers around him.

Basant Singh's neighbors grew envious but they learned to listen to what he said and take his advice. "The profit we get from our farm production has diminished," he would tell them in his metallic calculator-machine voice. "We have to cut back in investment. These new seeds can double production. But somebody hears about it in New Delhi and they reduce the price of grain. Whenever I get a chance, I'll sell my land. There's no money in farming. Business, industry, that's the place to be. Wheat prices may be over 16,000 rupees an acre but the yield doesn't give you the interest that a 16,000 investment in industry does." To the chosen, Basant Singh would bring out his statistics and charts. "In fact, when we calculate that for the old-fashioned varieties of wheat we needed only five waterings and only half as much fertilizer, and for these new dwarf varieties eight to ten waterings and double the fertilizer, we see we have to spend double but don't get anywhere in terms of profit. Ah, the nation increases its food supply all right. But I'm not talking about the nation. I'm talking about the ordinary farmer." By that he meant Basant Singh.

As time went by, so obsessed was he with the economy of operations and returns, Basant Singh began to talk about Ghungrali's landless Harijan laborers not as people but as "the labor problem." He looked forward to seeing a modern agricultural version of the trinity—the tractor, the combine and electric power—displacing hired labor to the vanishing point. What happened to the Harijan laborers involved did not concern him.

A few of the more traditional landowning Jats worried about this. Old Pritam Singh was heard to remark, "Basant Singh has really done good for this village but he's too hot tempered with the Harijans; he has been unfair in his dealings with them."

Once Basant Singh had made his fortune, he also stopped selling liquor, handing the franchise over to another man for a steep price; instead, he began to advocate legal prohibition, telling his friends, "That's the touchstone of all Ghungrali's problems—drink! All this drinking in the village is enough to make a decent person move into town." Gradually two factions sprang up among the village Jats; the richest, most technologically advanced and best-educated farmers rallying behind Basant Singh, and a second group of younger, poorer Jats tending to gravitate around Charan and spending much of their time drinking, carousing and skirmishing with one another.

Finally Basant Singh announced no one could enter his area of the village after drinking. "Now we have challenged them," he told his followers. "I carry a rifle these days. Why? Because we'll teach anybody a lesson who dares to show up around our houses drunk and disorderly. They have no other business except drinking, those young men around Charan. O, Charan himself is not bad but they are an evil influence over him. Charan can't hide anywhere. They'll find him, they and their bottles, and he can't escape."

Basant Singh predicted that Charan and his father, Sadhu Singh, would be in deep trouble in a few years. "That son is very fond of alcohol. If anybody drinks and stays sober, I don't mind, but Charan and his friends create trouble, shouting and laughing and carrying on. There is no law and order in Ghungrali. Absolutely none."

If grim, righteous, progressive Basant Singh was the richest landlord in Ghungrali, Charan, with fifteen acres and renting three more, fell just about in the economic middle of Ghungrali's sixty-five Jat landowning families. With nine family members—he and his wife, old Sadhu Singh and the old lady, two teenage sons and three small children, plus Peloo and Mukhtar, he had to feed eleven persons each day to say nothing of the constant ebb and flow of guests his father was always inviting.

During the winter *rabi* season, Charan usually raised fourteen acres of dwarf wheat which he harvested at about 1,800 kilos per acre for 76 rupees per 100 kilos. He also raised grass and oats to feed his cattle: six buffaloes, two bullocks, one cow, two female calves, and six small male calves. During the hot summer *kharif* season, Charan harvested about 1,200 kilos of cotton, which he sold for 136 rupees per 100 kilos; 5,600 kilos of corn for 52 rupees per 100 kilos, 1,400 kilos of sugar for home consumption and 700 kilos of mustard oil seeds. Once the Green Revolution began, his land spiralled in value to 15,000 rupees an acre. (While the legal rate of exchange was 7.50 rupees to the dollar, it was perhaps more realistic to think of the real value of a rupee as about equivalent to a dollar.) Four acres had been mortgaged for a 15,000 rupee loan to build his cattleyard and a concrete cowshed; it would have to be repaid to a government bank at 9 percent interest over ten years. Each year Charan and his father also borrowed about 1,200 rupees from the village cooperative society to buy seeds; this they always repaid after the wheat harvest.

Old Sadhu sometimes suggested Charan borrow more, but Charan had seen some of his friends slide deeper and deeper in debt and he told his father, "The real problem is when you borrow money like taking a loan for fertilizer and then use it for a marriage instead. Since the man hasn't used the fertilizer, his crops are poor and then he is really in trouble. It's a question of management, Father. In Ghungrali, you can do well with ten acres and have a thresher, a tube well, three bullocks, a tractor and a laborer or two if you manage well. Some do."

Many did not, and in their search to find cash for the seeds, fertilizer and tractor fuel, some of the other Jats in Ghungrali began to echo Basant Singh's arguments about the "labor problems." Harijan labor accounted for half the expenses on just about every landholding in the village. In time an alliance formed between such poor, marginal farmers as One-Eye, the village gossip and troublemaker, and the rich ones like Basant Singh, seeking to mechanize all farm operations as soon as possible. Gradually they formed a common interest in trying to weaken, if not abolish, the traditional Punjabi *jajmani* system of exchanging labor for a fixed share of the harvest.

Basant Singh, while remaining in the background himself, encouraged the formation of a thirteen-member committee of Jats to negotiate field wages with the Harijans. The committee, a front for the rich farmers, composed of the village's opium addicts, drunkards and gossipmongers like One-Eye, decreed that daily wages should be reduced from five rupees plus all meals to four rupees, without supper, breakfast or morning tea, food which had been provided by a Punjabi landlord to his workers as long as anyone could remember. Basant Singh, who with the most workers benefited the most, threw up his hands and told his own men he could do nothing: it was a general village settlement and he had to abide by it. While the wage cut generated ill will, few of the Jats and Harijans suspected Basant Singh secretly intended it as only the first step in doing away with the traditional *jajmani* system altogether.

The *jajmani* system was more than simply an economic arrangement between landlord and laborer in the Punjab; it was rooted in caste, the most important of the delicate balances which had always held together village society in India.

Sikh religious teachings condemned the Hindu caste system which divided Indian society into racial compartments and excluded Harijans, or untouchables as they used to be called, from its benefits. Yet caste was still practiced in Ghungrali as elsewhere in the Punjab. There were, in actuality, three castes: the Jats or farmer-landlords like Charan, old Pritam and Basant Singh; the Chamars or traditional leatherworkers such as Mukhtar, and the Mazhbis or barn-cleaners and sweepers like Bhoondi and old Chanan. All were Sikhs and in Ghungrali all had access to the *gurdwara* where they sat together, prayed together, and on religious festivals, ate together. There, with some irony, they heard such teachings as:

> The Hindus say there are four castes
> But they are all of one seed.
> 'Tis like the clay of which pots are made
> In diverse shapes and forms—yet the clay is the same.
> So are the bodies of men made of the same five elements.
> How can one amongst them be high and another low?

Yet in practice the Chamars and Mazhbis suffered constant discrimination; they could not intermarry with Jats nor eat at their homes on an equal basis—they sat on the earthen floor, while the Jats sat on chairs or string cots—nor could the two Harijan castes themselves intermarry or eat in each other's homes. Why the caste system endured so tenaciously in the Punjab, where few other Hindu beliefs were accepted seemed partly to be explained by race and partly by economics.

The Punjabi Jats were relatively late-comers to India; an ancient ethnic group of Scythian origin, they did not migrate into northern India from the plains of central Asia and Russia until the time of Julius Caesar. It was not until the collapse of the Mughal Empire in the late nineteenth century that the Jats spread to the most fertile areas and occupied the whole of the Punjab plain's best farming country. The Scythians were a nomadic people, displacing less warlike rivals on the great Eurasian steppes, winning richer pastures for their flocks and establishing themselves as overlords of settled agricultural populations. Even today the Punjabi Jats retain some of the old warrior spirit, glorying unabashedly in strength of arms, in destruction of foes and the number of their cattle; they never came under the domination of the priests and holy men of the Gangetic plain who succeeded elsewhere in India in setting the whole spiritual, life-negating tone of intellectual life. In Ghungrali, Hindu philosophical beliefs such as transmigration, the existence of an all-embracing holy spirit or *atman,* and supernatural rewards and punishments for degrees of ethical behavior were strong only among the lower castes.

Ghungrali's Mazhbis, with their dark brown skin and short, sturdy stature, were descended from India's aboriginal Dravidian race, perhaps enslaved and brought by conquerers from the south. The Chamars were a mixture of the two races, with some blood perhaps from the ancient peoples of the Indus Valley, themselves probably migrants from Mesopotamia.

Quite different blood flowed in the veins of most of the village Jats, Chamars and Mazhbis; physically and in their mentality the Jats had more in common with the Cossacks of the Ukraine than their fellow Indians. A second reason caste was perpetuated in the face of its disavowal by the Sikh religion was economic: the Harijans provided a source of cheap labor and to some degree allowed the Jats to continue the ancient Scythian tradition of maintaining themselves as overlords of peasantries who did most of the actual cultivation. It was Mukhtar, not Charan, who did most of the hard physical labor.

Until its Moslem population was massacred in 1947, Ghungrali had been a large village of some 900 houses, 5000 Moslems and just under 1000 Sikh Harijans, both Chamars and Mazhbis. Now it was much smaller. Within weeks of the massacre the land was reallocated to 65 Jat refugee families uprooted from Pakistan. Twelve more Jat families were given land in Ghungrali but chose to live elsewhere. There were also 26 more Jat families who had no land and followed non-agricultural occupations, such as the Jat barber or a retired military doctor who ran the village dispensary.

The Jat families were greatly outnumbered by the Harijans who served them: 15 families of weavers, 15 families of shoemakers, 3 families of blacksmith-carpenters and 101 families of agricultural laborers. All but 15 Mazhbi barn-cleaning families were of the Chamar caste.

Politically, these 160 families of Harijans had potentially much greater power in modern India than the 91 Jat families. Together all the Jats, Chamars and Mazhbis in Ghungrali, men, women and children, totaled 1415. They farmed slightly more than 1600 acres of land of which only 1500 were actually cultivated, irrigated and sown.

Wheat, grown from November through April, was the main crop and planted on 1100 acres, along with about 100 acres of sugar cane and 300 acres in oats and grass for fodder. In late May, the summer crop was sown: 100 acres of oil seed, 350 acres of hybrid corn, 300 acres of cotton and 200 acres of groundnut.

The true modernization of agriculture in Ghungrali began in the early 1950s with the installation of the first tube well; water was everything in the Punjab; with it you could turn a desert into a garden. From one in 1953 the number rose to 46 by 1957 and 95 by 1972. All but 11, fed by canal water, of the village wells were run by electricity, and the village also had 51 electric motors and 35 diesel engines.

The year after Basant Singh first introduced the new dwarf wheat into Ghungrali, in the winter of 1965–66, all 65 farming families had planted it in seed plots. The next year, 1967–68, every single acre of wheat land in Ghungrali had been planted in the new seeds, and so it had remained ever since. Most of the Jats, like Charan, planted seed plots of ever newer varieties each year, to be planted on all their wheatland the following season. Since the dwarf wheat tended to lose its high-yielding characteristics over a three-year period, Charan and his neighbors hoped new seeds would continue to be produced at the universities and government research stations; often old Sadhu Singh's days were spent keeping up contacts in such places and carrying on reconnaissance to see how some newer variety might be obtained. As Sadhu told Charan, "It's just a question of a bottle here and a bottle there, son."

Always in the forefront, Basant Singh bought Ghungrali's first tractor in 1962; ten years later there were 36. The consumption of fertilizer rose from almost nothing to 450 tons of nitrogen and 150 tons of phosphate. Moderate amounts of insecticide were introduced but no pesticides were used because the farmers could not get together on a village-wide effort.

Credit was first provided by the Indian government in 1967 with 77,000 rupees advanced for 30 pumping sets; by 1968 a state land-mortgage bank was issuing loans and a village cooperative credit society was started with government help. By 1972, it had lent 170,000 rupees of which some 50,000 had not been recovered. One-Eye, who had maneuvered himself into position as the cooperative society's general secretary, warned that if the remaining debts were not paid, the society would confiscate their property and land. While no land was seized, since seizure would have led to bloodshed, it was clear the rich were getting richer and the poor poorer; Basant Singh and some of the more prosperous farmers began giving loans at 5 percent on 100 rupees a month; a few villagers mortgaged eight or ten of their twenty-four acre allotments and feared they could not get out of debt and would have to mortgage more. Only a state law limiting individual land ownership to thirty acres prevented the rich like Basant Singh from acquiring much larger holdings.

Basant Singh predicted the government would eventually have to subsidize small farmers. He told his friends, "Inputs have risen in cost much faster than wheat prices and the actual profit we are getting is diminishing; we have to cut back on investment and expenses. Without government subsidies, those with fifteen or twenty acres of land or less will sink. Looking to the future, the prosperity we see now in Ghungrali is illusory. The reality for a Jat family with fifteen or twenty acres is that they will have to get more and more loans just to farm. The picture will become clearer as more of the mortgages become due. But I foresee either government subsidies for the small farmer or direct government control. With this land ceiling of 30 acres, a man can't practice the economies of scale. The government is not thinking now in these terms, but it will have to later on. With all this talk of a Green Revolution the politicians in Delhi think that wherever they find flesh on the farmer's bones, they have to pick it clean."

The Harijans had benefited unevenly from the new village prosperity. When the breakthrough to agricultural modernization came, much of the *jajmani* system, going back to the Jat's original conquest of Punjab, still survived in Ghungrali. The *mistry,* whose caste occupation was to repair farm tools, still received 50 kilos of wheat, 50 kilos of corn and 5 kilos of sugar from every Jat family in the village each year. The *nai* or barber, who not only shaved the Jats and cut their hair but acted as a host at weddings and social occasions and washed up the dishes and pans afterward, received 20 kilos of grain from each Jat family every six months. The Mazhbis, who gathered cattle droppings in the barns, made cow dung cakes for cooking fuel, removed dead mules or donkeys and sang and danced at weddings, still received grain according to a Jat family's number of cattle: 10 kilos of wheat for each buffalo, 5 kilos for each bullock, 3 for large calves, 5 for one-year-old calves and nothing for calves before they were weaned.

For these castes the ancient system operated, since it was profitable for the Jats to keep it going. Not so with the Chamars, whose traditional caste occupation of leather-working was no longer relevant. With few horses or camels left to care for, most of the Chamars worked as landless laborers. But a growing number, perhaps 40 percent in Ghungrali, earned their livelihoods by raising buffalo and goats, and sold their milk at a new government dairy a few miles away.

A few raised poultry; like the sale of milk this had become profitable as the cities and towns grew larger. The most successful of these enterprises was a poultry farm started in 1962 by Gurdial Singh, the Chamar who got his financial start by looting Moslem houses after the 1947 massacre. By the 1970s, Gurdial had a thousand birds, most of them White Leghorns and Rhode Island Reds obtained from the United Nations. It was a modern operation: he made his own feed and netted about 5,000 rupees a year on a total investment worth 22,000 rupees. In 1970, he took out a 10,000 rupee loan to build a second story on his poultry building to expand his operation. Since none of the Jats would sell a Harijan village land, he had to expand upward!

Gurdial's success, plus some sophistication and knowledge of English gained while serving in the casteless Indian Army, made him the natural leader of the Harijans in Ghungrali. Some said he had ambitions to become the *sarpanch* or popularly-elected village chief; like Basant Singh and One-Eye, Gurdial had an interest in stirring up discontent since he stood to benefit by any caste polarization.

This put Gurdial potentially at odds with the majority of his fellow Chamars, those like Mukhtar who worked as field laborers and were the true farmers of Ghungrali. It was in their interest to remain on good terms with the Jats since they worked side by side with them every day. Some were sharecroppers, usually receiving one-eighth of the crop for their labor; others worked for cash, from 1,500 to 1,700 rupees in yearly negotiated contracts. But a growing number of Chamars, like Mukhtar, preferred not to be tied to any single Jat family and instead worked for daily wages. Mukhtar, only twenty-three, had worked in the fields of fifty-two of the sixty-five Jat families in Ghungrali. This freedom demanded by some of the younger Harijans to pick and choose their masters was a further erosion of the old *jajmani* system.

At the very heart of this system were the terms of harvest. Under centuries-old custom, the landless, Harijan laborer received a fixed part of the wheat crop—one out of every twenty bales cut—which was enough to feed his family for a year. He also received the right to cut grass for his cattle on the Jats' land undisturbed. This worked out so that every family had enough wheat and milk, the staples of the Punjabi diet.

Most of Ghungrali's Jats and Harijans were still deeply imbued with these traditions. Old Pritam considered it unthinkable to assert his claim of ownership to the land if some Harijans came to cut grass along the edge of his fields. Most Harijans considered it unthinkable to refuse help to a Jat whose grain was ripe and shattering in the fields. To these men, Ghungrali was not only a place; it was their whole universe. It could be seen, its 87 land allotments marked out in boundaries, pinned down on a map. Here was the banyan tree, there the white-towered *gurdwara,* the mill, the school, the many houses of brick and mud. The wheatfields were round about, located in terms of canals, wells, roads and trees. All these things could be perceived; they had a feel, smell and sound to them. The village was also much more; its huddle of houses was a community. It was not divided into mere economic units like Basant Singh's statistics, but into men, women and children, who thought in terms of relationships, factions, ties, family, kinship, rights and obligations. This feeling extended outward also to the other Sikh villages of the Punjab, as Ghungrali's daughters married and moved away and were replaced by girls from some four hundred surrounding villages. Between these other villages, as within Ghungrali itself, there were duties, privileges, connections, links, each with its own special flavor and unique value, a meaning in terms of the life of the whole.

Ghungrali had really made the shift from subsistence agriculture to modern commercial farming in five short years; it had gone from nothing to ninety-five tube wells, thirty-six tractors and consumption of six hundred tons of fertilizer a year. For the first time, a majority of Ghungrali's people found their lives no longer circumscribed by traditional agricultural tasks and values. Forced to compete with the Punjab's biggest landlords whose holdings operated with the new technology—dwarf wheat, machinery, irrigation, the application of chemical fertilizer—and faced with the ups and downs of a market economy, a few like Basant Singh grew rich, some like Charan prospered and others like One-Eye sank into deep poverty. Fearing debt and faced with the unfamiliar pressure of needing money to buy fertilizer, diesel oil, the ever newer varieties of seeds and other expenses, the Jats were torn between trying to cut down on the cost of labor or preserving the delicate social balances which had always held the village together.

Some, like old Pritam, feared and resisted the change, some like Basant Singh harnessed it, Mukhtar challenged it, One-Eye exploited it and Charan made the best of it.

The wheat was ripening now, the sky grew paler each day and the clouds that had hung in high puffs for so long in February and March were dissipated. The sun flared down on the ripening wheat day after day. As the sky became pale, the earth became yellow, a burnt gold in the once-green wheat fields, and almost white in the fallow land where the sugar cane had been cut. Then it neared mid–April; on the thirteenth, known in the Punjab as *Baisaki,* the harvest would traditionally begin. As the sun shone more fiercely each day, the golden lines on the wheat leaves widened and moved in on the central ribs, and the heads of grain paled into yellow. The air seemed thin and the sky more pale, and every day the once-green landscape faded into a deeper gold. In the roads where the bullock carts moved, where the iron wheels milled the ground, and the hooves of the bullocks beat it, the dirt crust broke and the dust formed. Every moving thing lifted the dust into the air. By the first week of April, the dust was so fine that it could not be seen in the air but it settled like pollen on the tractors and bullock carts, on the trucks and cars on the Grand Trunk Road. The people brushed it from their shoulders and Charan began to have bad asthma attacks in the night.

Five days before the harvest was to start, the Jats gathered at the *gurdwara* and called a meeting to fix the terms of labor during the cutting, baling and threshing of the wheat. Basant Singh's men declared they had suffered a financial loss the previous few harvests; they maintained the *jajmani* system of giving the laborer one of every twenty bales harvested was no longer economical. They proposed the laborer's share of the harvest be reduced to one out of every thirty bales cut and tied.

It was left to the thirteen-member committee, which had reduced daily field wages from five to four rupees a few months earlier, to announce this decision. One-Eye, with his two weedy acres of wheat, demanded that this be made a general rate for all sixty-five farms in the village, whether the crop was good or poor. Basant Singh's faction agreed and it was broadcast over the *gurdwara* loudspeaker for three days as part of the Jat committee's decision.

In Ghungrali's Harijan quarter, there was anger and dismay. The Harijans felt the thirtieth bale was too little payment for all but the richest stands of wheat in the village. They too formed a thirteen-member committee, and after three days sent their response to the Jats, a declaration that: "We Harijans do not agree to reap your crops on the thirtieth part. We will only accept the twentieth bale or fifty to eighty kilos of grain per acre."

One-Eye answered for the Jats. "Grains, we won't give. We can talk about some arrangement in terms of bales, but we want you to accept one out of thirty."

The Harijans were furious. "We won't go!" "We'll see how they'll cut their wheat!" One-Eye returned and told the Jats, "The Harijans have insulted us. They are not willing to talk to us." And he went back and forth exaggerating the differences, sowing division and planting rumors. And so, as the wheat ripened in the fields, there was talk of trouble in the village. But the field work went on. The sun lay on the fields and warmed them, water flowed from the tube wells, and Mukhtar moved about making sure it reached all of Charan's wheat; each day he went around with his hoe, opening and shutting the gateways of earth, and when the water moved deeper on part of a field and around the stems of ripening wheat, he would skim off the surface dirt between the stalks and throw it into the water until the earth was watered evenly. And the days got hotter and hotter.

One evening when the sun was about to descend toward the west, the Sarpanch passed Charan's fields carrying a shotgun. He was followed by One-Eye, who scurried behind, bent over, his voice never stopping, carrying two dead partridges by their necks.

"Go straight to that white pumphouse over there," Charan called. "There are peacocks in abundance."

"Yes," echoed Dhakel from his well. "There was one here in the morning. It was here, right here."

"It was here," joined in Pritam, calling from his oat field. "I saw it yesterday."

As they followed the bund paths through the ripe, dry wheat,

One-Eye talked incessantly. "Basant Singh agrees that the Harijans are in the wrong. They are exaggerating things. I heard the Harijans are going to the police. How can they go to the police when there is no fighting?" His voice was high and obsequious, sometimes rising to a whine and sometimes almost fading away entirely in a confidential, shocked whisper. "They wrote to the prime minister in Delhi. They can write to anybody they like. Basant Singh says how can the prime minister or the police tell anybody how to run their farms. Those Harijans who have two or three cows or buffaloes and are getting farther and farther away from farm labor, they meekly go and cut some wheat or oats and hide it under their grass; they are getting rich off our bones. . . ."

"Go straight toward Bhambadi," Charan called from the distance. "The birds are near that well."

"The people there will mind it," One-Eye warned.

"Nonsense," the Sarpanch told him. "I have killed hundreds of birds there. They don't say anything. Come with me."

"The Harijans have progressed faster economically than the Jats," One-Eye went on; he took no real interest in hunting but welcomed the chance to talk to the Sarpanch alone. "That's why the Harijans complain when they get less. Now they've had a taste of prosperity. They're forgetting their place."

"O, last night I was full of liquor up to here," the Sarpanch said, not caring to listen to the other. "You find so many partridges in open places these days. This is the right season for partridge. Ducks don't come here any more; there is no water and it is not lonely enough. The best time is early in the morning or evening such as now when the evening sun is coming through the grain. But tonight there is too much wind. Most of the partridges will be killed when the wheat is harvested. The children and dogs will get them. The dogs chase the partridges until they are tired and then the children kill them with sticks and stones. . . . If it goes on like this it may storm tomorrow. It's very windy."

". . . Before last year the Harijans exploited us because we Jats were not united," called One-Eye, falling behind as he stumbled into a furrow. "There were political Jats, pulling our legs to win friends among the Harijans. But we have shunted them out, those vote-seekers, and replaced them with people who don't worry all the time about getting the votes of the Harijans."

The Sarpanch frowned, knowing One-Eye was alluding to himself. "No, Mohinder," he snapped, addressing One-Eye by his proper name. "Now the poor people, those Harijans who have no livelihood but what they earn as daily wages, they will suffer. And it is always evil to make the poor people suffer. It is those Harijans with dairy or poultry operations, like that Gurdial, who are stirring up this fuss."

"Ah," hissed One-Eye, pleased at the opening. "It is Gurdial Singh who is seeking to replace you as *sarpanch*. Heh, heh, heh, that is his game. He is very close to the police I have heard. He gives them free chickens and eggs. Basant Singh told me . . ."

The Sarpanch cut him off. "We can't say anything. We'll call the Harijans and we'll discuss everything. It will be settled in a day or two. Now hush up about the matter. I want to hear no more about it."

One-Eye's face, had he turned around to see it, was not pleasant. Even if it had not been distorted by an ugly sneer, it would have been bad enough since the gossip-monger had not worn his glass eye, and where his left eye should have been there was only an empty socket, a dark recess one feared to look into, afraid of what one might see.

Back at his well, Charan watched One-Eye follow the Sarpanch off toward Bhambadi. "That man is an evil soul," he told Mukhtar. "He is trying to poison the mind of the Sarpanch."

The air was heavy the next morning. The rising sun looked faint and wan, the sky white and gloomy, the mist very dense and the distance hazy. All the Punjab plain seemed apprehensive and languid and even early in the morning there were some faint, distant flashes of lightning. Heavy with sleeplessness, untidy, unattractive, Charan rose from his cot and stumbled over to the pump to splash cold water on his face. His father, who had also started sleeping in the open cattleyard during the hot weather, was still lying on his *charpoy* as usual, coughing, demanding his morning tea and gazing around in a foul temper. Charan sent Peloo to fetch his tea. Mukhtar and Kapur came into the cattleyard and Charan brightened. "O," he groaned, watching for any signs of ill will on the Harijans' faces, "I drank too much last night."

Kapur laughed. "Our Charan can move lightly even after a full bottle of rum. He's not affected by two bottles even."

Charan laughed. "So, come young men," he said cheerily, "we must haul manure today and the weather looks bad. I've backed up the wagon outside so you can start loading, and I'll come and drive the tractor."

As the two Harijans went to work, Charan's wife entered the cattleyard with Sadhu Singh's pot of morning tea. She was a plain, gentle woman who lived mostly for her children; she suffered in silence the constant stream of complaints and abuse showered upon her by the old lady all day long. The old man groaned, gave Charan's wife an indignant look, muttered something about how ill-served he was and sat up in bed to enjoy his tea. Outside in the road there was the sound of drums and bagpipes, and Charan's wife went inside the cowshed to unhook the shutters from a barred window and peer outside. It was the Mazhbis playing for a group of men and women who were loading a wagon. "Charan, it's a wedding party," she called in her soft voice. "It's the village watermen. The *rajas*. O, there stands one of the Mazhbis in white clothes. Sometimes he comes to our house. O, how clean he looks today and how happy he appears." Charan joined her at the window. "O, look," he told her, "they are just leaving now."

"They are taking a band also," she said. "O, now the children are scrambling for coins." Then, realizing she had forgotten herself in front of her father-in-law, Charan's wife held her scarf to her face and hurried from the barn. A scolding screech outside heralded the old lady's arrival.

"There's not a drop of milk in the house!" She stormed in her loud, angry voice. "Now you two sit here like kings and order tea all day five times each!" She swept past them, her pendant stomach protruding under the loose shirt and pajamas she always wore, and with a great banging of pails and muttered oaths she started to milk a buffalo.

Old Sadhu, annoyed by this outburst just as he was starting to enjoy his morning tea, grumpily shouted back, "You could have arranged for more. Ask the milk sellers from the dairy, don't scream at me!"

The old lady gave a loud squawk. "Three times I sent tea to

Charan yesterday and five times to you here at the barn!" She addressed the buffaloes, angrily waving an arm at her husband, "What is this man doing sitting in the barn all day and inviting people to tea? Does he drag them in from the street?"

"It's none of our business," said Charan, coming to his father's defense as he saw the old man's face was getting red. "Women know what's what about food. Why don't you order two kilos every day from the dairy? You know we're always short of milk this time of year."

"Harumph!" Sadhu Singh sat up in bed and thundered grandly, "I will order tea ten times a day!" He was outraged to be the target of his wife's ill humor so early in the morning. "It's none of my headache to look in the milk bucket! What are you here for?" He harumphed again with indignation.

"Why don't you stop now, mother. You are making a scene," Charan said. "Go and milk your buffalo and arrange from tomorrow for two extra kilos a day. That's all."

But Sadhu Singh was aroused now; he huffed and puffed with annoyance. Charan called to the stableboy, who had been watching the family quarrel with some interest. "O, Peloo, go to the house and get your breakfast and come back at once and then we'll go."

"Why should this dirty pig eat first?" Sadhu Singh sputtered, seizing upon the poor Peloo as a target. "He was roaming about all day yesterday. Come, come, come, Charan, we will go and eat first." The old man with some effort lifted his fat body out of the cot. "You have a bottle hidden somewhere. I know what you want." His voice rose again. "There should be an end to that thing!"

Charan ignored him. "Go, go, run, and come back right away, Peloo."

"Come, Charan," the old man said, moving to the gate himself. "We'll send one of the children back to the barn in our absence. Why are you dragging your legs? Come!" But Charan, angry now, remained sitting. "Let Peloo eat first," he called to his father. "He's hungry. He's been up with the cattle since four, while you were lying in your bed, and he's a poor, crippled man."

"Have the calves milked him?" Sadhu Singh roared back. "What's he hungry for? He was roaming about this street and that street all day yesterday, and you say he's a cripple. Ha! The dirty Chamar, he's a dog!"

Charan was too angry to speak. His father stomped down the lane muttering angrily, "I know what Charan wants. He has a bottle hidden somewhere, the dirty dog! I rape his mother! He's like a dog, wagging his tail after anyone who has a few drops of liquor. The dirty dog. I know what he wants. He'll go into the streets and beg one day, if he doesn't mend his ways." Then feeling wide awake now and having worked up quite a healthy appetite, he hurried to the house, feeling a zest for breakfast. Bhoondi, the Mazhbi, his wife and two daughters, attracted by the loud voices and hoping for an entertaining spectacle, came to clean the barn. As the women began to work, Bhoondi joined Charan, sitting on the ground near his cot and lighting up a cheap cigarette. Seeing him the old lady at once squawked, "Look! Here is old Bhoondi sitting with his legs crossed. He's enjoying life."

"O, I have worked enough in my life," Bhoondi said in an impertinent tone. "I have four grown sons and don't have to work any more now. How can a man go on working till he dies?"

The old lady concentrated on milking the buffalo for a moment then moved into the offensive. "Bhoondi, your grandchild came here and destroyed our chili plant!"

"No, no, dear lady," Bhoondi chuckled in his deep, rich voice. "There are so many children around. It could be any. Not my grandchild. We've never brought him here. How could you have such an idea? Besides, if some child has pulled up your chili plant, dear lady, it won't bring your house to earth."

"O, I know that," she called from her milking stool. "But you know children can be very naughty. We have some vegetables and pumpkin planted here. They may spoil them tomorrow."

"Give me a basket of that green fodder you have," Bhoondi teased slyly, knowing the old lady would not give so much as a pin away to save her life.

The expected shriek of indignation came. "You want that somebody should bring a dish of prepared food and put it in your mouth so you can eat! You don't want to do anything for yourself! Why don't you go to the fields and cut some fodder?"

Bhoondi chuckled. "What? You can't tolerate such a small thing, dear lady? By evening this fodder will get dry. If a poor man's buffalo needs this fodder, it won't ruin your health."

She rose and carrying her full milk pail advanced toward Bhoondi

[155

threateningly. "You are just sitting here and gossiping and moving all day around the barns." Her voice rose to a piercing squawk. "Move your limbs and get some from the field, you gossipmonger!"

Bhoondi's wife anxiously called from the gate. "Now you come with me. Let's go clean the other barn."

Bhoondi kept sitting and thundered to his wife, "Don't make such a noise standing over there! Get along with your work! I'll reach there myself! I have legs! This gentleman is talking to me and you are just screaming over there." When his wife and the old lady had gone away, Bhoondi chuckled to Charan, "These women. They scream too much around here. They need to be sent to an asylum. They'd teach them some good things there, heh, heh, heh."

Outside by the manure pile, Mukhtar and Kapur were joined by Gurmel, the Chamar sharecropper of Charan's Uncle Sarvan, and Bhoondi's oldest son, Sher. "I heard the police are furious with the Jats," Gurmel reported to them. "They say the thirtieth bale is unreasonable and that the Jats are just trying to use force. Today some of the Harijans are going to the police station at Khanna town. Gurdial has sent one telegram to the deputy commissioner in Ludhiana and another to the prime minister in Delhi. All the Harijans are united behind him." As a sharecropper Gurmel said he was not yet affected by the boycott. "I don't know what to do. That Sindar's a fool, barking vulgarity all the time, but I'm happy working with Dhakel and old Sarvan Singh. They don't ask me to do too much work and they're soft spoken." Gurmel, who was slightly hard of hearing particularly resented Sindar for habitually calling him "Deaf Man."

"But they're Jats. And Jats are all alike."

"Even Charan abuses us too much," Gurmel agreed. "Like he says 'you're not my wife's brother' or 'I'll rape your sister.' "

Sher, who reported that so far the Mazhbis were staying out of the dispute, said he had heard the Sarpanch wanted the Jats to compromise and not try to force a fixed share of the harvest on the Harijans.

"Yes," Mukhtar said, "he's a good man. If someone's ill, he'll take him to the hospital; he and Charan are fast friends."

"It looks like trouble in the village now," Gurmel fretted, but not without a touch of relish at the prospect of excitement.

Mukhtar said he felt the thirtieth bale was fair for only a few of the best wheat crops. He estimated wheat prices had risen ten-fold in the previous five years, while the new seeds needed only four times as much water and fertilizer. "The Jats are getting richer and don't want to share it," he told his fellow Harijans. "All the Jats are united and we must stay united. If there's not a settlement we might have to stop working for Charan."

"He's coming now," Sher said. "Will you tell him?"

"Keep quiet, don't speak."

Charan was laughing jovially—"Let's go to the fields, young men!"

Before lunch they were able to haul two loads of manure to a cane field Charan had burnt off the day before. The horizon grew slowly blacker, and by eleven o'clock a pale light was already blink-ing on the northern horizon, and the blackness, just as if it had weight, was beginning to bend to the right. It looked as if a thunder-storm was coming, and as each one glanced at the darkening north-ern sky from his work, he thought: May God grant us time to gather in the wheat harvest. Then they remembered the harvesting terms still were unsettled, and between the sky and the uncertainty, though they were cheerful, they were a little uneasy.

At lunch, the Harijan youths squatted on the ground in Charan's courtyard and held out their hands to receive wheat cakes and a pea and potato curry, as was the custom, while Charan and old Sadhu sat on chairs and ate from a table. The women waited to eat until after all the men and children were finished.

"Shall I put for all of you?" the old lady screeched as she ladled out her tasty curry onto their *chapattis* as if it were her own life's blood; her stinginess was legendary in Ghungrali.

"Give me more *lassi*," said Mukhtar, holding up his glass for more watered-down buttermilk.

"More *lassi!*" The old lady gave a loud squawk but went to fetch some. As soon as she was out of sight Charan's wife put a plate of pickles on the ground between the Harijans; the old lady spied it as quick as she returned, and rushed to retrieve it, but not before Mukhtar and Sher grabbed fistfuls. "O, that much!" the old lady screeched as she hurried to put her precious pickles back under lock and key and the Harijans winked at each other.

When they returned to the fields with another load of manure, there was almost a steady drone to the north of distant hollow thunder. Then, as they neared Charan's well, between the distance and the right of the horizon the lightning flashed so brightly it illuminated all the plain with a strange white light. A tremendous cloud, with large black shapes hanging from its edge, slowly moved into one compact mass.

A little boy, one of Pritam's grandsons, who seemed oblivious to the approaching storm, shouted at them from Pritam's well, holding out a slingshot, "Look, look, I've killed a parrot."

On the road near Charan's land, two young boys with bales of green fodder on their heads, were running toward the village, trying to reach it before the storm broke.

Charan roared with laughter when he saw them. He called, "You are Waryamo's and Sarjito's!" To the men he said, "Their mothers are very useful women." He laughed again and called after the children, "Hurry, hurry, I rape your mothers!" Then he told Mukhtar, "Hurry, let's get this unloaded, my brothers. It can start in ten minutes." Similar clouds were gathering on the left and right of the horizon, reaching toward the black central mass. Sharply, and no longer dully, sounded the thunder. "Come, come, men! Get your bodies wet with sweat not rain," shouted Mukhtar as he and the others shoveled out the manure on the ground as fast as they could, waving from time to time to Charan to move the tractor forward.

"Pray God there's no hail, and the rain and wind don't come together," Charan shouted above the roar of the tractor. At their nearby well, Dhakel, Sindar and Gurmel were frantically trying to get their diesel engine started. Beside them was a large pile of oats which had to be run through the fodder cutter before the rain came.

"They're having trouble again with their engine," laughed Sher, as he shoveled. "Let's go, men! Show your strength. *Bas! Tik hai. Sardarji,* move ahead."

"One starts working and another rushes in and Sindar stands there all the time telling them what to do," laughed Sher. "That's why they can't fix it. The spirit of a Moslem lives on that well; his tombstone is there. That's why the engine won't go. They must please him."

"They've already whitewashed the grave," Mukhtar said.

"You men are as black as Africans!" roared Charan over the engine, although in truth Mukhtar was fairer than he was, and he added pointedly, "If the village has a fair Harijan, we know it is a bastard." He laughed at his joke, which the others ignored. Suddenly a wind got up, and with such violence it nearly carried away Mukhtar's head cloth, which flapped violently across his face. The wind whistled and tore over the plain, whirled about frantically and raised such a noise in the wheatfields that it deadened the sound of the thunder. It blew from the black cloud, bearing with it swirls of dust; one saw the fog of the dust and its shadow rolling hurriedly along the side of the road. But through the dust, which started flying in their eyes, little was now to be seen but the flashes of lightning. "Run for the wellhouse!" Charan shouted, and he revved up the engine and turned the tractor toward the well, wagon and all, because he feared to be caught in the open field in the storm.

The thunder rolled over the sky from right to left, then back, ending somewhere near Dhakel's well. The sky opened its mouth and breathed white fire, immediately the thunder roared; hardly had it ceased when there flamed such a brilliant flash of lightning that Charan saw for an instant all his fields to their farthest ends, the towers of a *gurdwara* two miles away and even the rooftops and trees of Bhambadi in sharp definition. He reached the wellyard and left the tractor and wagon under the oak trees, running to join the others in the house.

The rain, for some reason, was very long in coming, and for this Charan silently thanked God, for by then the wind had died. The sky was a very intense blue, deep blue. Inside the wellhouse it was dim and dark for midafternoon and he could barely see the Harijans. Now finally, one last time, the wind shuddered through the ripe wheat and fled away somewhere. Charan stood in the doorway; as he looked out a large cold drop fell on his forehead, another on his hand. He saw he had left some grass out for the bullocks and thought of gathering it in but at that moment there was a pelting and tapping on the road, the ground and the roof. The rain had come.

Inside the wellhouse, there was an uncomfortable chill and dampness; it must be snowing in the Himalayas or hailing somewhere, Charan said, for the temperature had fallen very fast. "These days," he said, "if it's rain without wind, it's like God come to earth. But rain and wind together would mean ruin for our wheat. If the wind stays down, the profit from this rain may outweigh the loss."

"Such a storm Old Grandfather has sent us," said Sher. "The bastard must be after our wheat, after all."

Just then Gurmel came running into the wellyard. He had been caught in the rain, and the sleeves and back of his shirt were wet and clove to his body. Water dripped from his thick moustache as he went on loudly and incoherently about enmity in the village, its foolish leaders with their "all heat and no wisdom."

"Why are you shouting so?" Charan asked.

"You know I don't speak generally," Gurmel babbled on. "But now I must speak my mind. Then, Sardarji, you may have mercy upon us if things get worse. If not, you may kill us."

"Speak, Gurmel."

"You do not know?" He paused for breath. "It was declared over the *gurdwara* loudspeaker this afternoon. The Jats said, 'No Harijans can enter our fields. No Harijans can take grass from our land to feed their cattle.' It is a boycott. Because we refused to cut their wheat on the thirtieth bale."

"But that is impossible," Charan said calmly. "We won't be able to survive in this village without a settlement. It is all foolishness. The reaping will start in a few days. If my wheat stands eight or ten more days it will start to shatter. We must reach a settlement. Those fools!"

Suddenly, with a fearful, deafening din, the skies crashed just above their heads; the men crouched and held their breaths, involuntarily closing their eyes and then opening them to see a blinding bright light bursting and gleaming at Mukhtar's startled eyes, on beads of sweat on Charan's forehead, along Sher's arms, and glittering from the water on Gurmel's hands. There was another clap of thunder, louder and more frightening than before.

"If the Jats 'boycott' us, then we must 'boycott' them," said Mukhtar, also using the unfamiliar English word, for none existed for it in Punjabi. "It means I cannot work for you any longer, Gurcharan Singh."

As the thunder crackled as before and lightning streaked the skies, Charan quickly turned to Sher. "And you. You are a Mazhbi. You, too?"

"We are all Harijans, *Sardarji*. Today you boycott the Chamars. Tomorrow it may be us."

*Cruelties of Landlords Against Untouchables
in Village Near Ludhiana*
Orders of Inquiry from Deputy Commissioner Believed to Have
Been Lost at the Police Station

April 16—In Village Ghungrali-Rajputan, near Khanna, the Harijans have been cruelly mistreated by the landlords. The *zamindars* have totally blocked the women of the Harijans inside their houses. Harijan women, young girls and children are sitting inside the four walls of their little houses and have dug small ditches for answering the call of nature in their own courtyards. They are not allowed to move outside in the streets and the fields. In the village there are about 125 Harijan families and 60 Jat landlords. During the last harvest Harijans were compelled to accept minimum wages for cutting and threshing their crops. On such wages they cannot possibly meet their ends.

But this year, the landlords have imposed another cut in daily wages. When the Harijans refused to accept such a meager amount, the landlords totally boycotted them. The panchayat (village council) of Ghungrali has appointed a 13-member committee which always goes on imposing such new orders so that if any Harijan tries to lift his head a little he will be totally crushed. The Harijans' deputation from this village met the Deputy Commissioner in Ludhiana who ordered the officer in charge of the police station in the nearby town of Khanna to go to Ghungrali and inquire into the matter. But today six days have already passed. And the orders of the Deputy Commissioner appear to have been lost in the police station. The Harijans of this village go on leading a life of misery. Even the Harijan member of the Legislative Assembly in Chandigahr seems unable to do anything to alleviate these cruelties.

—DAILY HIND SAMACHAR

The story, published in a newspaper known for its political slant, claiming Harijans were Hindus and not Sikhs, was a mixture of truths, half-truths, distortions and outright fabrications, and was quickly followed by a second story, planted by the police and equally misleading, that normalcy had been restored to Ghungrali. The boycott was beginning to draw outside attention.

As soon as the Jats had banned Harijans from their fields, Gurdial, the self-appointed Harijan leader, had sent the story to the newspaper in a nearby town to support his strategy; besides seeking to polarize Ghungrali on caste lines for his political benefit, he wanted to make it appear that the Jats had infringed on the civil liberties of the Harijans. With the help of a lawyer from the nearest city, Ludhiana, he drew up a petition, charging that Ghungrali's Jats had been "insulting women . . . not allowing Harijans into the fields to answer the call of nature and not allowing Harijans into the fields or country roads and lanes for the purpose of grazing." Indian law, imbued with the teachings of Mahatma Gandhi, was committed to ending untouchability and all forms of social discrimination; if Gurdial could get the police involved, the law was weighted in the Harijans' favor.

The Sarpanch realized Gurdial's ambition was to replace him as village chief. He told Charan, "Now the Harijans are in Gurdial's hand. Once they fall apart again he'll lose them. I'll compel the Jats to compromise and arrive at reasonable harvest terms." But no one listened to him. Instead, most of the Jats were won over by Basant Singh's argument: "We Jats have been suffering a heavy loss, giving these laborers the twentieth bale. They have benefited more the past few years than the small farmers. That's why they're creating this trouble. They've had a taste of prosperity and they want more. Well, they're not going to get it at the price of farmer after farmer going into debt."

Yet opinion in the surrounding villages, where other Jats were giving anywhere from the twentieth to the thirtieth bale, depending on the crop, and old traditions were stronger, ran against Basant Singh and the Ghungrali Jats. Within Ghungrali itself there were Jat dissenters. Old Sadhu Singh, for one, thought the whole dispute was so much nonsense, and said so to anyone who would listen. It was he who first started calling the Jat's thirteen-member wage committee *dahulis,* the Punjabi word for wastrels or troublemakers. He told Charan, "Among the Jats, the real *dahulis* are such fools as One-Eye who can cut his two acres of miserable wheat himself. Among the Harijans it's those like Gurdial who have some business of their own and don't depend on Jat wages. The whole business is all a fuss over nothing. You'll see. Once the wheat gets ripe and starts to shatter, how the Jats and Harijans will go running to each other!" Old Pritam had misgivings, warning, "What we have sown, we shall reap also." But Basant Singh dismissed the sentiments of these old men with an impatient wave, saying, "Either we shift to machinery or get labor from outside. It's the only solution. Some say this boycott is harmful to the village. But the poor are making more money than ever and spending it on hashish, tobacco and liquor. Their real enemies are their bad habits."

Despite the gathering tension in the village, ordinary life went on. The afternoon before *Baisaki* the Jats invited farmers from all the neighboring villages to compete in a bullock cart race. It was a splendid day, the wheat had ripened into a burnt gold and the oats, too were ripe and shone in the sunshine like mother-of-pearl. The sky was a pale blue, there was dust and it made a white mist among the trees in the far distance and as the hot afternoon breeze came up in sudden gusts, little whirlwinds twirled through the ripe wheat. But no one had watered for some days now and there was no longer fear of the wheat lodging before it was cut.

By three o'clock the dirt road beside Basant Singh's fields was lined with hundreds of men and boys; the sun looked almost white and in the dusty luminescent light, everything was in beautiful pastel color: the wheat, the sky, the trees, the men in their clean white shirts and yellow, pink, pale green, red and lavender turbans.

"Clear the way! The first cart is coming now!" rose the shouts. "O, come with pomp and show," declared an announcer over a loudspeaker at the finish line. "Come with courage, come, O Bhajan Singh of Mal Majra, come!" In a great cloud of dust and pounding hooves and cheers and shouts, the first cart rolled down the eleven-acre-long course.

Charan and his friends had goaded his cousin Sindar, the cheerful braggart, into entering the race. All morning long at the wellhouse Sindar had fussed about importantly, washing and brushing down the bullocks and swigging down homemade liquor. "O, today you shall run like the wind," he would tell the bullocks, breathing deep to fill out his flat, hairy chest. "Ah, today I shall crush someone under the hooves of my bullocks. I shall ride them across the wheat fields like the wind."

When Charan told him he should go home and rest, the nervous Sindar was indignant. "O, what should I do there? Should I grab someone's penis? We'll go straight to the race."

Charan laughed. "You'll break your leg."

"When you have to fight a battle, why worry about your arms and legs," Sindar boasted grandly. "I don't know about the others.

But in this village no one can beat me." A crow in the oak branches squawked derisively at this and Sindar cursed, "Kill that bastard. I'll rape his mother." Charan roared with laughter. "Just hit him with a big stone," he told Sindar. "Then he'll understand."

Charan and his friends were already drunk when it came Sindar's turn to race. The Sarpanch, red-faced and staggering, led them down the track, waving a bottle and crying out, "For God's sake, please clear the way, brethren. You are masters of your wills. It is your village. But clear the way."

Near the finish line the announcer's voice was deafening. "Bring that red flag up, just watch the red flag. These bullocks are running eleven acres. That is something. Run! Go! *Shabash, shabash!* O, green and red turbans, please clear the track. Here comes Mukhtar Singh of Jarg. One minute and twenty-nine seconds. Now it's number twelve, Ajit Singh of Majari. Look how the bullocks come. Like air. Look with your full eyes wide open but clear the way, my friends. . . . Slow! One minute and forty-five seconds. Now *Sardar Sahib,* take the red flag up. Our starter today is an old army officer and knows how. He can kill a battalion for just one flag. *Shabash. Shaba-a-ash!* Gurbach Singh of Ghungrali is coming. He's running like a railway train. Look at that man over there. He's making mischief. O, black-turbaned man, don't make mischief. Shabash. One minute, twenty-four seconds. Now comes on line . . . Sindar Singh of Ghungrali. The flag is up! The cart is coming at full speed! Friends, clear the way. Sindar Singh, Ghungraliwallah is coming! See how he flies. . . . Oop! What's happened? Friends, clear the way. Stop running this way and that. What? Ah-h-h-h, the bullocks are running towards Bhambadi across the wheat field! Clear the way! We can't see! Friends, Sindar's cart has left the road and is headed across the wheat field. O, O, look! Now he's turned them around. O, he's bringing them back. Ah, they're back on the road again. Clear the way, clear the way! The bullocks are coming with great dignity. Don't worry, friends, they'll reach here some day. Now they are back on the road and the cart is coming. *Shabash, Sha-a-a-aba-a-a-ash,* Sindar Singh of Ghungrali. . . ."

A great roar of laughter went up from the crowd as Sindar's cart finally rumbled across the finish line. Charan yelled to the Sarpanch, "Seeing Sindar race, I get drunk without liquor"; he laughed so hard he went into a coughing fit.

The next morning, as they braided ropes for the harvest under the banyan tree, the humiliated Sindar, who had gone off to get drunk by himself after the race, was back in his old form. He told Charan, "Our game was wrong. The people frightened us. Those Ghazipurwallahs. They kept standing in the road. The fault lies with those bastards. Those who blocked the way. Those seeds of a dog, penis of the great God, I'll rape their mothers. In the evening, I'll show you I can come in one minute and fifteen seconds and beat all of them. I can show you today. If I take five seconds extra I'm ready to buy you a bottle of wine."

"At least you're up and around," Charan told him. "You can move around in the streets. If you had really lost the game, you'd be in bed the rest of your life."

"Sindar has been having diarrhea all day because he lost," Gurmel, the Harijan who always worked with him, joked.

"Why should I have diarrhea?"

Charan laughed. "Seeing you race, I got so drunk I threw away my bottle."

"Even if my bullock cart falls in a well I won't have diarrhea." Sindar called to Gurmel, who was holding the other end of the braided rope, "O, *Shabash,* Deaf Man, move back quickly. We'll be through in half the time Charan and Mukhtar are taking. We'll show them how to make rope. Nobody dares beat us."

Just then One-Eye came down the road; when nobody spoke to him, he sat down beside them under the banyan tree. "Do you know how far things have gone?" he asked Charan in his whiny, obsequious voice. "Do you know, Charanji, that today they stopped cleaning Basant Singh's barn, these Harijans. Tomorrow they'll stop cleaning all of ours if this keeps on."

"It doesn't matter," Sindar called to him cheerily. "The Jats should install underground drainage anyway. You could have manure just pouring right into the fields, Mohinderji. Just dig a deep ditch and when your cow wants to piss, you can just lead her to it." Sindar guffawed at his own joke.

"You brag too much and you were last in the race yesterday," One-Eye sneered.

Sindar's grin faded and he was silent until One-Eye went away. Then Gurmel, who normally traded obscene insults with Sindar all day long, rose to his defense. "That One-Eye!" Gurmel said. "His father must have had his mother at some odd time and he's the seed of that. He's like a mad dog. If he sends his wife to my old father, only then will he get a child. The impotent bastard. That's why he abuses people. He doesn't care about the boycott. He has the worst crop in Ghungrali. A weed patch." Charan looked up, amused to hear a Harijan defending a Jat. Sindar himself muttered, "He's a fool. God will ruin this village if the Jats listen to him and hurt the poor people."

Since it was the traditional first day of the harvest, old Sadhu Singh went to the *gurdwara* that morning to pray for a good crop. Only a few other old men joined him inside; the rest of the Jats were holding a meeting outside on the temple grounds to force a show-down with the Harijans. Sadhu felt this was a disgrace and ordered the public address system's amplifier turned up to full volume. As the prayers began, the quivering voices of a few old men, Sadhu Singh's loudest among them, boomed out over the entire village.

When he finished braiding, Charan wandered over to the meeting where he was met by Basant Singh, waiting with a group of the wealthier Jats under the shade of a neem tree. "We have decided to try for a settlement this morning," Basant Singh told him. "If the Harijans don't come today, it's finished. More than forty-five Jat families are represented here this morning. We sent word to the Harijans, 'You discuss among yourselves first, but if you want a settlement, come to the *gurdwara* this morning. If you don't come now, we'll never talk."

"Maybe the Harijans are waiting for the police," Charan suggested. Just then a young boy came running up the hill to the *gurdwara* grounds. "They have left their meeting hall and are moving this way," he called. Then feeling he should add something more to this impressive audience, he shouted, "They frightened me with their eyes!"

Pritam wandered by looking bewildered. "I understand we have been sending them messages all morning." Then all of them turned toward the road. About twenty Harijans approached, mostly dressed in the gray, torn rags they wore for field work, but a few in white shirts and colored turbans, looking indistinguishable from the Jats.

The Harijans formed a semicircle in the road below the *gurdwara* and the crowd of Jats went down to face them. Surjit Singh, a dignified, white-bearded former village chief who was Basant Singh's chief lieutenant, went to the front of the Jats. A bare-headed, clean-shaven youth, no more than a boy, came forward to speak for the Harijans.

"Now come forward with your conditions and demands," Surjit Singh declared, but his voice was suddenly drowned out in a deafening roar from the *gurdwara* loudspeaker as the old men inside started to pray again. Old Sadhu Singh's voice thundered above the rest, demanding in an ear-splitting bellow that the Lord cleanse and purify the hearts of these men so they would stop this foolishness and get on with the harvest; Charan suppressed a laugh; he guessed his father had done it deliberately.

"Turn off that loudspeaker!" Basant Singh bellowed.

When it was quiet again, the frightened Harijan youth said in a trembling voice, "We want according to the field, that we should be paid for reaping according to the crop of each field."

"We can't form a committee to go to each and every field to decide the worth of the crop," Basant Singh snapped testily, moving forward.

"We don't know about everyone's field, but each Jat knows his wheat crop."

Surjit Singh hastened to speak in a more reasonable tone. "The Jats want that they should be giving less and less. You want more and more. We have to decide where the common area of agreement lies. Traditionally the wheat in our village has been cut for the twentieth part of the crop. But now new varieties have been introduced. If you go to Basant Singh's fields you can cut cheaply because the crop is rich, but those with poorer crops will suffer."

The young spokesman looked cowed, and Gurdial rose from the back of the Harijan group and came forward to face the Jats.

"We have thought things over the past few days," Gurdial said with authority. "We have decided we do not want a fixed rate but will settle field by field, farmer by farmer, as do all the Jats and Harijans in the surrounding villages. We can only judge when reaching the field what payment will suit us. Now you can go and decide if that is agreeable to you."

A murmur of approval seemed to go through the Jats, but Basant

Singh intervened, speaking out even more testily than before. "If anyone wants to make trouble, he has no place here. We are here to get a reasonable settlement. We want a generalized rate."

"Some people can be cheated on a field by field basis," Surjit added, in a mollifying tone.

"That depends on the man," Gurdial replied evenly. "A Jat should think about whom he is hiring. This trouble is quite serious for us. You don't allow us in your fields, although Harijans have enjoyed this right in all other Punjabi villages for hundreds of years. You must decide, once and for all. I suggest you consider the enormous consequences of your actions."

"If you don't want to reach any settlement," snapped Basant Singh, "well, that's up to you. You may do what you like and we will do what we like."

"You must fix rates according to each man's field. That is the way it has always been in the Punjab."

"We can't do that," Basant Singh said flatly. "I have been authorized by the thirteen-member committee of Jats this morning to offer you one compromise, the thirteenth bale for a good field and the twenty-eighth bale for a bad field. Beyond that we will not budge. An individual rate for each farm would be too much trouble, too much trouble."

Gurdial's voice betrayed an edge of anger. "It can't be any more trouble than this village is facing now. We can't go into your fields. We can't cut grass for our cows and buffaloes. . . ."

Basant Singh interrupted, "If you will not accept a generalized rate, there is no reason to talk further."

For some moments there was a stunned silence as if neither wanted to speak the words that could mean a final break. Charan couldn't believe what was happening and old Pritam shook his head back and forth in dismay.

Basant Singh bowed his turbaned head and raised his hands, palms folded together in a formal Sikh gesture of farewell. "It is all over," he said in a harsh voice. "Finished. Now you are free to do what you will and we are free to do what we will. *Sat Sri Akal!*"

The confrontation was over. As everyone milled around, the Sarpanch came up to Charan and said, "The Harijans are very determined. But I'll try to bring them around."

But the Sarpanch no longer had the village under his control. Basant Singh's men quickly spread the word through the village that the boycott stood and each Jat was to hire workers from outside. Not all the Jats went along with this. Charan's friend, the Bandit, got drunk and went to the Harijans, saying, "Come and cut my wheat. Harijans are allowed in my fields. I damn this village and the Jats' decision." But Gurdial forbade anybody to go. He called all the Harijans to a meeting and declared, "The Jats want to be dictators. But this country is free and we want to live like free men in a free nation. They will not share their new prosperity if they can help it!"

Storming back to his fields, his rifle slung over his shoulder, Basant Singh met an elderly Harijan who had worked in his fields many years. When he ordered the man to return to work and the Harijan refused, Basant Singh cursed him, "Don't get funny with he or I'll throw you out for good. I'll throw you out of my fields forever, you black seed of a dog! I'll rape your mother!" News of the incident swept through Ghungrali and since the Harijan was a respected, saintly man, resentment of the Jats grew among the Harijans.

Sadhu Singh, the harvest prayers at the *gurdwara* over, went back to his cattleyard for a leisurely bath in the warm mid-day sun; he wanted to think. He sat on a footstool by the pump, with only a wet towel around his enormous belly, pouring sudsy hot water over his head. His brother, Sarvan, came by and reported the Jats were sending a delegation in Ludhiana town to hire migrant laborers from neighboring Uttar Pradesh state. "Brother," he said, "you can give me your demands and deposit five rupees for bus fare for every laborer you need. We are also collecting ten rupees from each Jat in case of legal battles. Suppose a person goes down the road and the Harijans start beating him on the pretext he has abused their women. Then we'll use this money for fighting a court case against them."

Old Sadhu had never heard of such nonsense: he had no intention of parting with a single penny. "Uh-huh . . . h-m-m-m," he grunted absently. "Yes, Brother, you take an active part, don't worry. . . . Just hand me that other bucket of warm water. Just push it a little closer, please. Ah, that's it. O, yes, it is very good if you have this arrangement. It is safer for everyone . . .Ooop! I can't reach it yet. Just push it that way, ah, that's it. This water is not as hot as I wanted it. Peloo!" Sadhu poured the pitcher over his head, splashing Sarvan, who cried in exasperation, "We'll take five rupees per laborer you need. Just give me twenty-five or thirty rupees."

"Right now?" Sadhu Singh's indignant bellow could be heard all the way back to the house so that the old lady hastened to heat some more hot water. "I'm taking a bath!" And old Sadhu splashed about so gustily his brother gave up and went away.

The sun was warm on his bare back and Sadhu Singh had looked forward to spending the day lying on his charpoy, drinking tea and listening to music on his transistor radio. Now he felt compelled to stir himself; he rose with surprising swiftness, dried off and dressed with care in a clean white shirt and pajama pants, a cotton vest and the deep blue turban he wore only on special occasions. Then, dispatching Peloo with a message to his wife, he grabbed his umbrella and hurried across the fields toward the bus stop on the Grand Trunk Road. He moved with a vigor and determination that startled everyone who saw him. For the old man knew there were times in life when it was necessary to go into action, and with the wheat ripe for harvest this was one of them.

Charan, Mukhtar, Sindar and Gurmel, back again braiding ropes under the banyan tree, saw the old man streak off. "My father really has big steps when he's going someplace," Charan said, and Sindar agreed, "After taking a bath, he gets light and walks fast."

That afternoon Charan's drinking friend, Nirmal, and One-Eye also headed for the city, sent by the Jats to hire laborers in Ludhiana. They stopped by the banyan tree on their way, and One-Eye, in clean clothes and looking almost presentable with his glass eye in place, told Charan they planned to bring back a hundred men.

"We're not hopeful of a settlement," he hissed in Charan's ear, so the two laborers would not hear him. "Even if the Harijans are ready, we won't agree. O, many of the Chamars will be ready to desert Gurdial and join the Jats when the harvest is riper. We'll break their will." He giggled, leaning closer. "We don't want that the Harijans and Jats should get loose from our fingers. The Harijans can't stand this for more than six months. It's impossible. They'll starve."

"Maybe they will move away, get jobs in the city," said Sindar, who was braiding rope near Charan and had overheard.

"They won't leave the village altogether," One-Eye snarled at him. "And we won't bother if they do go. We'll bring more here and give them places to live."

One-Eye said he had heard on the radio that seventy thousand migrant harvest workers from neighboring Uttar Pradesh state were pouring into their district alone. "If we don't get outside labor, our local labor will eat us up," he added, repeating Basant Singh almost word for word. Charan asked why they didn't go directly to Uttar Pradesh themselves and get men, as some of the richer Jats in the village were doing on their own. Nirmal, who was already growing bored with the whole business, said he was confident they could find all the men they needed at the Ludhiana railway station. He sprawled his flabby body on the ground and scratched his nose; although he was still young, it was already red and pitted from drink. "Ah, I rape their mothers," Nirmal groaned. "We should settle for the fifteenth bale and watch old Basant Singh yell. Let the rich Jats suffer. Maybe if we create real trouble we can go to jail and other people will cut our crop in sympathy. What do you say, One-Eye? Tonight we'll enjoy a good girl in Ludhiana. . . ."

When One-Eye and Nirmal had gone their way, Gurmel said, "If we accepted anything from drunkards like Nirmal and that one-eyed gossipmonger, we'd be fools. Who respects men like that?" The Harijan sharecropper spat in their direction. "Never mind. City life is good."

"Take your children in big baskets if you go there," Sindar joked. "When they go hungry you can always throw them on the railroad tracks."

"We're afraid the Jats won't even allow our children in the village school if the boycott keeps on," Gurmel said. "I'll go to some big city after the harvest."

Sindar laughed. "If you throw cow dung in a clean sack it will still give off a bed smell. Wherever you go, they'll know you're a Chamar."

"Never mind," retorted Gurmel. "A law is going to be enforced where we'll only work eight hours a day. Then we'll apply to the government for a paved road and we'll buy bicycles and go to town every evening." He laughed. "You'll see Sindar's face after harvesting. He will look as black as a railroad guard. This time half the Jats will die of hard work. We'll make them real skinny, cutting all their own wheat. They have too much fat on them anyway."

Sindar hooted. "C'mon, Deaf Man, move back. When the harvest comes, you'll get your bottom torn by stubble. Work faster. Don't let your shadow fall on me; I'll get lazy like you. *Shabash,* O, Deaf Man, *Shaba-a-a-ash!*"

Old Pritam came by, still looking confused. "It is a dangerous day," he told Charan. "There is every possibility of a storm. My body tells me because of those thin clouds; it is perfectly close. . . ." His eyes scanned the fields and he sighed. "Who would leave this lush grass by the roadside if the Chamars were allowed to cut fodder for their cattle? . . . I do not understand what is happening, Charan. So much ill will. Why would Basant Singh abuse such a gentle old man? There must be something."

"Such things can happen without any reason, Pritamji," Charan told him.

"Ah, well . . . Whatever our leaders decide, it must be all right. I will follow them."

That evening Charan, Sindar and Dhakel got drunk at Charan's well after cutting fodder in their fields. Charan was surprised to hear both his cousins opposed the boycott.

After several rounds from a bottle he had hidden in an oat field, Sindar told them, "My thinking is, there should be some agreement. The Jats should give according to each crop like the Harijans want. It's unjust to give them the thirtieth part for bad crops and the Jats know it. It's those bad farmers like that one-eyed person who make trouble and benefit. The people who have good crops, the wise men, they should tell people like that One-Eye to shut up."

"If we could get Chamars from Ghungrali, I'd pay one bale after twenty-two or even twenty," said Dhakel, who was slight and did not look forward to having to cut his wheat crop himself. "We don't want those Hindus from Uttar Pradesh. You can't depend on them. Any person from outside our own village is not dependable."

Charan laughed. "That Basant Singh," he said, passing around the bottle. "I think he drinks in secret and is also an opium addict."

"In the morning he takes opium and in the evening he takes liquor," agreed Sindar, who had scarcely ever laid eyes on Basant Singh.

Charan produced another bottle from his haystack and for some time, as they drank one round after another, they enjoyed abusing Basant Singh.

"You can't really know about a rich man," Charan told them. "A poor man, when he needs opium, he has to run and borrow money."

"Basant Singh used to abuse Harijans, telling them, 'You bastard, you must vote for my faction or else.'"

"Basant Singh is his own air."

"Yes, the bastard is arrogant and proud."

"He is making the lives of the Harijans a living hell."

"Fuck Basant Singh. Let's go to America."

Dhakel's voice was suddenly serious. "Our America is here in Ghungrali. . . ."

It was late when Charan finally left the bullock cart at the cattle-yard and staggered home, so drunk that when the old lady opened the gate he took two steps forward and fell flat on his face. His mother and wife had to drag him inside and put him to bed. An hour later Mukhtar, now without work for a week and needing forty rupees Charan owed him, approached the house; the old lady opened the gate a crack, saw it was Mukhtar and let him in.

Charan's wife was distressed. "He's not eating," she told Mukhtar. "He's drunk." In her anxiety she had forgotten her usual shyness. "Brother, just ask him to eat something. Otherwise, he may have a bad asthma attack in the night."

The old lady joined in. "There is milk lying there for him. There is curry lying there for him. Please, my son, bring him around so he can eat some food. He shouldn't have an empty stomach with liquor only at night. My husband has gone to Ludhiana. Tomorrow the harvest may start and what are we to do if Charan can't work?"

Just then One-Eye and Nirmal pushed open the gate. Both were red-faced, breathless and drunk after returning from the city empty-handed. They could find no men at the railway station.

"Charan's not in," the old lady screeched, but Charan groaned from inside the house. "He's in. But he's sick. Go away!"

"When he entered the courtyard, he fell flat on the ground," Charan's wife explained. "We have put him to bed." Nirmal staggered toward the two women while One-Eye remained at the gate, leaning on one side for support. "Come now, Nirmal, let's go home," he called drunkenly.

Nirmal staggered up to the old lady. "O, I'm your smallest child, mother." He giggled unpleasantly. "O, don't worry if we don't settle with these Harijan bastards. Then you will go to the fields and cut.

O, you are a great mother!" The old lady snorted and shoved him aside but Nirmal lunged toward Charan's wife and tried to climb onto the cot where she was sitting. He reached out to touch her feet and she shrank back, crying, "No, no! I'm younger than you. I'm a married woman. Don't do this thing."

Mukhtar helped the old lady push Nirmal back into the road and bar the gate; he entered the house to find Charan lying face down on his cot, his pillow on the floor. Mukhtar put the pillow back under his head and told Charan, "Get up and have some *chapattis* and milk. Otherwise this liquor will wreck your stomach at night."

After some argument Mukhtar persuaded Charan to come outside and he managed to stagger to a chair in the courtyard; his wife and the old lady at once brought food. "Why don't you give milk to Mukhtar?" Charan asked roughly and pushed the young Harijan into a chair, although by custom he should have squatted on the ground. For once the old lady did not protest about giving up her precious food. "O, there is a lot," she screeched. "He can have as much as he likes."

Charan drank two glasses of fresh milk and downed some of the unleavened bread before he rose and lurched toward the gate. "O, I just want to piss," he told his mother, who started to follow him. Outside he whispered to Mukhtar, "C'mon, I've got another bottle in the barn." Mukhtar said he had already eaten, after which Punjabis usually did not drink. "No, you want some," Charan coaxed. "Just a little teeny weeny glass." After some argument, Mukhtar finally got Charan to go back to bed. By this time all the children were awake and watched their father; Suka, the oldest boy, made no attempt to conceal his disgust. As Mukhtar started to leave the old lady caught his sleeve and told him in a gentle voice, "You did a good thing for him. Now maybe he won't have an attack tonight." Mukhtar agreed to look in on Charan at the cattleyard the next morning.

He arrived just as Charan was taking the bullock cart to the field. Sadhu Singh had still not returned from his mysterious errand in Ludhiana. The former master and servant shook hands awkwardly and sat down together on a *charpoy*. Mukhtar spoke first.

"We're thinking of renting some land near Ludhiana. We have no firm arrangement yet but my brothers are talking about it. Maybe get some acres to rent on a fifty-fifty basis. Or I may try for a factory job."

For some time Charan made no reply. Then he told Mukhtar, "It is not good if you leave the village. You know that."

"A police inspector is coming this morning to meet the Jats and Harijans. But we don't want the police to decide what share of the harvest we should work for."

"No, that is not good. . . ." Charan thought for some time. Then an idea came to him. "Look, *Chota,* one man on either side could break the boycott, could end all this foolishness."

"Yes."

Charan reasoned that the Jats were getting about four times more yield with the new wheat than the old varieties. He told Mukhtar he felt it only fair that the Harijans should get four times as much also. He asked Mukhtar if he would be willing to harvest on the old traditional system, abandoned in Ghungrali for some years, of *lavi* or simply carrying home each night all a man could manage after a day's harvesting. "It was a good way," Charan said. "Fair to all."

After a long pause, Mukhtar asked him how many men he wanted. Charan said he would need at least five.

"I can bring as many as you want on this carry basis. Let's forget about how many bales."

"Can you bring five tomorrow morning?"

Mukhtar agreed and they shook hands. Peloo, who had been watching and was himself a Chamar, gurgled and clasped his hands together approvingly.

"Now shall I be dependent on you? I have your word?"

"Yes, you can depend on me."

But the boycott was not to be broken this way. As soon as Mukhtar approached Gurdial with his decision, the Harijan leader called a meeting. He announced that Charan wanted Mukhtar to break the boycott and return to work for him; he accused the Jats of trying to destroy the Harijan's solidarity. "They don't even want to let our children go to school," Gurdial shouted to the crowd. "They want us to stay backward and illiterate. Now they want to destroy our unity with this offer!" Mukhtar protested, saying there had been no persecution. "We didn't provoke them," Gurdial told him angrily. "Do you want to see some Harijans beaten in the next few days?" Mukhtar stared at him, wondering if he might stage that too. Just then some Harijan men came running up with the news Jats had come from nearby Majari and Bambadi villages to hire men for the harvest.

"We are all tigers!" someone shouted. "We'll go to other villages. To hell with the Jats of Ghungrali!"

"Come men!" someone else shouted. "The Bhambadi jats want to take a contract for eight hundred *bighas* of wheat!"

"Let Basant Singh go to Bhambadi. They are cutting on the twenty-fifth bale there!"

Gurdial's face gleamed with triumph and Mukhtar realized he had lost. Men crowded around him, telling him, "Don't go, Mukhtar. We must stay united. Don't destroy our unity. We'll show the Jats!"

Across the village, Charan was also under attack. Nirmal and One-Eye came rushing to his cattleyard, One-Eye shouting, "What's this we hear about you agreeing to hire Mukhtar?"

"Don't let these Chamar bastards into your fields," Nirmal warned him. "We'll provide as many men as you want."

"Where are they then?" Charan roared back at them furiously. "All right! Bring me eight men to start work tomorrow morning. If you don't bring, I'll take Chamars from the village!"

"We'll burn your fields!" One-Eye sputtered, then seeing Charan's eyes redden, he realized that he had gone too far and turned and fled, bumping and pushing Nirmal to get out the gate first.

A police inspector came to a gathering of Jats and Harijans under the neem tree by the *gurdwara,* but could do nothing. He begged, "Don't strangle these poor people. Don't kill them. I don't say that the Jats should be giving with their four hands, but don't make the Harijans starve either. I want that this trouble should end with a little adjustment on both sides."

Basant Singh was adamant. "We have already sent men to bring in laborers from outside. We have all contributed money, and when they come where shall we put them to work? We no longer need our village Harijans."

"Then you won't prohibit them from going into the fields to answer the call of nature or from moving on common lands and roads?" This was as far as the inspector's legal authority went.

"No. We will be responsible if any of the Harijans are insulted."

Mukhtar wandered away from the meeting feeling miserable. He saw through Basant Singh's strategy. Now he could get by with paying outside laborers as little as four rupees a day. Whereas under the *lavi* system Charan proposed, a man could carry home grain each evening worth sixteen to twenty rupees. Cheap labor was Basant Singh's game, Mukhtar realized, even if it destroyed Ghungrali's way of life.

As he turned back toward the village, Mukhtar heard a great roar near the banyan tree; children were running toward it. There, approaching along the dirt track from the Grand Trunk Road, was a giant tractor pulling a big red mechanical reaper. A driver in a visor sat in the iron tractor seat, his face protected from the dust with a cloth. The thunder of the tractor's cylinders sounded through the village and people came running and crowded around, admiring the big cutting machine. Beside the driver, sitting on a fender and looking grandly triumphant despite the coat of dust that covered his clothes, face and beard, was old Sadhu Singh. When the tractor stopped, the old man climbed gingerly down and dusted himself off.

Charan came running from his cattleyard, stared at the reaper and asked his father, "But how much will it cost?"

The old man chuckled and whispered in his son's ear, "It's a demonstration machine from the university. If we had to pay for it, where's the fun?" As Sadhu Singh climbed back on and the reaper headed for their fields, Charan ran in search of Mukhtar. He soon met a crowd of Chamars, some of them Mukhtar's relatives. An uncle took Charan aside and told him, "Don't go and ask Mukhtar to work for you, Charan Singh *Sahib*. He would be an outcast among his own people. Don't do this thing."

"There is no reason that if the thirtieth bale doesn't suit I can't give on the old *lavi* basis."

"No," the Chamar said, "it is no longer a question of payment. The truth is there are people interested in keeping this trouble going. They will do anything to stir up things even worse. It is wrong, but true. I think some of us will suffer a great loss."

Charan went to the Jats wage committee and demanded they supply him eight workers then and there. After a heated debate, they produced four migrants from Uttar Pradesh who had wandered into the village that morning. They were slight, feeble-appearing youths with the shaven heads and single lock of hair that some Hindu peasants habitually wore. Charan took them back to his cattleyard, where old Chanan, the leader of the village Mazhbis, was working.

Old Chanan at first said nothing, but busied himself cleaning the yard and collecting buffalo dung in a basket. Charan, with a desolate air, sat down on a *charpoy* and watched the old man. Finally, he confided in him. "What am I to do? Father has brought a cutting machine and I need at least six more men. If I could find Punjabis I would give them all the wheat they could carry home each evening and to hell with the thirtieth bale. What am I to do?"

The old man, squatting in the dust, scratched his gray beard and his eyes twinkled in his dark brown face. "We Mazhbis are not bound by what the Chamars do. That Gurdial Singh is up to no good. He wants to change things. . . ." He sighed and scratched the dust with an old stick. "How times have changed, Charanji. Twenty years ago, Jats wouldn't drink water from a Harijan's well. There is still one Jat in our village who does not drink water from the well of a Harijan. He says it is impure."

"He is a fool," Charan said. "He is an idiot. He is unhappy if the Jats share their food with Harijans too. He should come with me one day and I'll carry some *chapattis* and tell one of the Harijans to bring another bunch and then bring along a Brahmin priest just to carry a lunch for that Jat. If that fool can tell me the difference between those two lunches then I'll agree with him. A human being is a human being."

The old Mazhbi frowned. "No, *Sardara,*" he said, using a very old form of address, "we are not happy now with all this equality."

"Why?" Charan asked with surprise.

"Why? In olden times after working hard if you sat for some time to take rest, the Jats had to bring water and serve us. Now a Jat will keep sitting and tell some Harijan to bring water. He takes a full rest and the Harijan has to run here and there. Now the Jats even ask us to carry their food. Would you have allowed me to touch your food twenty years ago? Let alone carry it? But now you think we are equal. Damn these new laws. Nehru was our real enemy. The government thinks it is favoring us. The fools don't realize they are putting the Harijans under great pressure. And now this boycott. The Harijans of Ghungrali must bring bales of grass from other villages. This is insulting to them and insulting to you."

"There are many troublemakers in our village," Charan muttered darkly.

"Yes," the old Mazhbi agreed. "If our leaders don't act sensibly how can the people know what is going on or what should be their attitude?"

Charan smiled. "It is all the fault of that star with the tail. It wanted to show its power and that star has chosen Ghungrali as its victim."

"Yes, yes," old Chanan said quite seriously. "That star was an omen. But we are men also." He stood and gave Charan his hand. "Today, Charan Singh, you had the courage to try to end this foolishness. I shall have six men for you in the morning."

That evening, when Charan told his father he would have Mazhbis for the harvesting, he added, "I didn't go to Mukhtar."

The old man harumphed. "Well, he's not been here and if he's not coming, why should we keep running to him?"

"All right," Charan said. "It doesn't matter. I don't want him."

But in the morning, Mukhtar was waiting alone at the cattleyard, having kept his promise.

Old Chanan and five young Mazhbis had arrived at Charan's house at dawn and after the old lady served them tea they went directly to the fields. Charan had gone to the barn to fetch the bullock cart.

His four Hindu laborers were sitting there waiting for him, huddled on the cots where they had slept the night, bedraggled, eyeing poor Peloo, the barnyard and his cattle with hostility, smoking *bidi* tobacco leaves and talking in their unfamiliar tongue.

Mukhtar stood by the gate waiting. For a full three or four minutes, Charan said nothing to him, but seeming to show his indifference, was absorbed in unfettering the bullocks and putting them under the cart's yoke. He beckoned to the four Hindu laborers to climb on, and then Charan himself crouched on the tongue of the cart and prepared to move the bullocks forward. Almost as an afterthought he turned and greeted Mukhtar.

"Hello. How are you, *Chota?*"

"O, I'm all right. All right. Everything is fine."

"How are things on your front?"

"Everyone has arranged to cut outside the village except me."

Charan started to speak but said nothing. Then as he urged the bullocks forward and the cart creaked and rumbled out the gate, he called cheerfully over his shoulder, "Well, then you should go outside also."

The reaper, which resembled a fallen red windmill, had been constructed by a university engineer to his own design, and might have drawn great attention had not word gone around in Ghungrali that Basant Singh was, in a day or two, bringing in a genuine combine, imported from England—one of a shipment of twenty which had just been unloaded in Bombay and would be the first to reach private owners in the whole of the Punjab. Until now there had been just two demonstration combines at the university.

When Charan learned Basant Singh would have a combine it occurred to him the latter must have known all along he would not need labor this harvest. Charan cursed Basant Singh for taking such a leading role in the boycott, when he knew he himself would not be directly affected. But Sadhu Singh told his son, "He is a man who doesn't like to take risks. Why should we bother our heads? It is his affair." Charan had replied, "There are real hypocrites in this village."

Old Sadhu, for his part, was consumed with relief to see their wheat cut; the first in Ghungrali to be harvested. As the reaper's four red-painted rakes rotated around and around, guiding and sweeping the grainheads into its sharp blade, and leaving the cut sheaves in a regular pattern on the stubble field, the old man pranced around like a child with a new toy. When the university engineer came to test its operation, Sadhu hugged him with a happy roar of laughter. "It's working splendidly, Vermaji! See our neighbors' ears flapping. We are always ready to try anything new. Harumph! Now those gossip mongers are repenting." As long as the university man stayed in the fields, Sadhu Singh strutted back and forth, shouting at the laborers, giving Charan this and that order, seemingly very much in command. When the laborers complained the reaper left some grain standing at the corners, Sadhu bellowed as if he had been personally insulted. "Can anybody dare to say anything is wrong with it? You don't lose even a single grain!"

Aside from the fuss his father made, Charan had his hands full preventing a fight between the Mazhbis from the village and the four Hindus from Uttar Pradesh. These outsiders, whom the Punjabis scornfully called "*bhaiyas*," were of much slighter build; they did not enjoy the nourishing Punjabi diet of wheat, milk and eggs, and were not physically able to keep pace with the Mazhbis. Falling behind, it took them twice the time to complete a row of bales.

To separate the workers, Charan divided them into three teams, which moved up the field behind the reaper, gathering the fallen sheaves into bales. As soon as he was out of sight, the Hindus would slip over to the shade of a tree, crouch with their sickles and, looking desolate, would smoke *bidis* until old Sadhu, waving his arms and moving his portly figure very briskly, would storm across the fields after them. "Those *bhaiyas!*" he fretted to Charan. "They don't know how to make bales."

One Mazhbi team led by old Chanan spoke little; it included Amarjit and Surjit Singh, two brothers who officiated as priests at all the Mazhbi ceremonies. Both had lean faces and broad shoulders and were staid and important looking; in build, in their long uncut beards and in the expression of their whole persons, they resembled the warriors depicted on Sikh calenders and, indeed, were very traditional, saintly men like old Chanan himself. Charan, as always during harvests, moved about in the manner of a genial host, telling jokes and laughing uproariously at the slightest provocation. "Tell me, boys," he told the priests, "whosoever gets tired I'll relieve him and he can rest." "Just take care of your *bhaiyas,*" one of the priests mumbled when Charan was out of earshot.

The second Mazhbi team was composed of young men, who joked and engaged in continuous horseplay. Their ringleader, Bawa, a son of Bhoondi the barncleaner, whose face was as black as an African's from years of labor in the sun, told Charan, "Those *bhaiyas* were asking me where I was from. I said my district was Rajasthan and my village was called Fuck Them All." Bawa, who had a deep, infectious laugh, kept shouting abuse down the field to the Hindu workers, "Go and tie up your *dhotis,* men, and drop your shorts; I'll take you to Fuck Them All Village!" Then he would gather up the sheaves very quickly. "Hurry up, boys, we have to beat those *bhaiyas* and show them how Punjabis do it."

As the day wore on and the Hindus became angrier and angrier at such baiting, Charan cursed Bawa and told the team, "Now just let those boys work on their side of the field and you work on yours. That Bawa's a dangerous man. Don't let him pick a quarrel. He can eat a live pig's testicles. They are of that caste." To distract the

Hindus he would tell them jokes, roaring with laughter and slapping his thighs himself as they half-heartedly joined in.

"We are working for a rich landlord," one told him. "How could these people dare to say anything to us?"

"Absolutely," Charan agreed. "Nothing they can say. *Bilkool nahi.*"

"If we get angry in this foreign land, it is difficult for us to work," another threatened. But Bawa and the other young Mazhbis kept it up; when Charan fetched a pail of drinking water and asked who wanted some, Bawa shouted, "Just leave a little drop on their pigtails." When his cousin Sindar came to see the reaper, Charan left him in charge of the Hindus and stormed over to Bawa. "Listen," he warned him, "you stay four acres apart from those *bhaiyas*. Otherwise, I'll play hell with you."

Sindar, glad to have a captive audience, worked alongside the Hindus, bragging of fabulous victories in bullock cart races and regaling them with dirty stories. "This is the thirteenth month of the year, boys," he told them. "If you're afraid to work now, you're in trouble. If somebody commits a murder in the Punjab, he does it because of his bumper wheat crop; he can afford to spend half his profits for a lawyer."

"How many men have you killed?" one of the Hindus asked this tall, fierce-looking Sikh with the funny nasal voice.

"I never had a bumper crop, so how could I afford a murder?" Sindar asked, giving them a sample of his logic. "Somebody once poked somebody else's bottom but he was a Qazi, you know, a Moslem priest, and he was doing his prayers and without being disturbed he just reached back and gave a rupee to that man. And the same man poked another man's bottom but the second man was a Punjabi Jat and he cut that man in two. The poor fellow thought he could make another rupee. We tell anyone who bothers us that we are Jats and will cut them in two. We are not Qazis."

"Well, sometimes you get mad," said the tallest of the Hindus, his temper cooling down.

"That's true," agreed Sindar. "Everyone gets mad, but I never get mad just because I don't understand a language. These Mazhbis only talk among themselves in Punjabi. They are not insulting you. So work hard, men, show your strength! You are not city women. Did you ever think how women who work hard have easy births? It is those wives of the *babus* in the city, those who always keep sitting and not working at all, when they give birth to a baby they cry at the tops of their voices, 'Hey, Ma, save me this time! I won't let my husband touch me again.' But ten days after giving birth they start winking at passersby and again get pregnant." As he rambled on and on, Sindar showed the Hindus how to stack and tie the bales; soon they began to catch up with the two Mazhbi groups. "O, I rape his sister," Sindar cursed, hitting his sickle on a rock. "I would be better off if I were a woman. I could sit inside all day. But you know at midnight you get a foot-long penis inside you. Then you say, it would be better if I was a man. So what God has made, that is right." His nasal voice went on without pause. "Work with an energy! Show your strength! God has made our bones of steel!" After an hour of Sindar, the Hindus had forgotten about Bawa's taunts and a fight was avoided the rest of the day. Old Chanan agreed to bring more Mazhbis the next day and Charan sent the four Hindus back to the thirteen-member committee, after giving each an evening meal and four rupees; hiring outsiders only meant trouble.

When Charan returned home that night he found his sister, Surjit, waiting for him; she was in tears. Her hired laborer had run away, her husband, Saroop, was in an opium stupor, she could not engage any harvesters anywhere and her wheat was beginning to shatter in the fields. Surjit was desperate. Charan had sown fourteen acres of the new dwarf wheat on her land for the first time and she felt all her hopes hung in the balance. Her two teenage sons, Pala and Kaka, had started to mow but there was no one else. Charan felt very weary. He had troubles enough with his own harvest. But he promised to do what he could, telling Surjit to go home and tell Saroop and the boys to cut all the wheat they could in the meantime.

In many ways, Surjit was Charan's favorite sister. A strikingly handsome woman except for the hard set of her features in repose, she had like him raven black hair, high color of radiant health, and the same air of vitality and strength. Beside her, her husband, a once-handsome man with deep-set gray eyes and a gentle manner, looked pasty, old and lined. To Charan, Surjit always spoke of Saroop with contempt, telling him her husband's opium cost only two rupees a day. "So it is all right, brother," she would say. "If you keep one laborer it's five rupees a day in our village. Whereas my husband is quite a good worker."

Surjit never admitted to her family that she loved Saroop and was prepared to go through anything to keep him. They had wed shortly before partition back in Pakistan and Saroop had been a good catch, a rich landlord's son. Unlike Charan, he proved to be too soft to rebuild a new life in India; as a refugee his whole life had crumbled, and for years he had been a slave to opium.

Yet even today Surjit's appearance spoke of past prosperity; her yellow silk *salwar-kameez* and frayed white wool head scarf did not belong in the shabby little hut where they lived, with its log beams at a slant and its sagging thatched roof which always seemed about to collapse. Their farmstead was set in the jungle, some distance from the nearest neighbors, whom the proud Surjit detested. Everything about the place seemed makeshift and mean: a cattle shed whose corrugated tin roof was propped up by stripped tree branches, two or three hungry-looking buffaloes, string cots scattered about, piled with dusty quilts and bedding, an open hearth, black with soot and buzzing with flies. Charan went there as seldom as he could and never stayed long.

If he did go he knew what she would say. First, she would carry on about his drinking. "You and father between you must spend twenty rupees by evening. You are racing to see who can ruin the family first. Ah, well, everybody has to hang himself. O, Charan, what is happening to you? You were so hardworking when you were young. And strong. How everybody was afraid of you. Nobody could touch your arm for fear of getting a push that would send a big man to the ground."

Or her loneliness. She would complain, "The children's grandmother will never visit us. She says she's got no company here and no new faces to see. And she's getting so fat, Charan. Fat as a pig!"

If Charan remained overnight, she would go and on, as in a litany: "Now I feel a little relieved. I had to really go through hell for years together and all the time I was praying to God, *Hey, Sadhe Padshah,* O, Holy King, shall I ever be able to see good days again? Now he has heard my appeal and thanks to you and father I am better off. I was only waiting for my boys to grow up. O, Charan, within a few years I shall be quite free of all my burdens. I shall bring a bride for Pala and marry off Kaka. I'll just be sitting on a bed in the kitchen in a few more years, sitting and sleeping in the same bed. I will get up and start churning milk early in the morning so that the children can have a nice morning nap. I won't give them any trouble.

"I'll make two rooms on either side of this one room here and I'll give one to Pala and his bride so they can enjoy the loneliness of their two beings. I have faith in the Maharaj. He Himself will do everything for me. You know I have a heart as big as a lioness. One hundred people can come and stay with me. You won't see the slightest wrinkle on my forehead. Everyone brings his own food stamped by God. We are nobody in between. O, Charan, I have seen really bad days. Now they are over. . . ."

To himself Charan resolved to save her harvest somehow, even if he had to spirit the Mazhbis out of Ghungrali in the middle of the night. But he confided in no one except old Sadhu.

After she left, Charan went to the cattleyard and checked the tractor to see if it was ready to pull a wagonful of men on the long trip to Surjit's farm; he found his eldest son Suka had not oiled the engine as he had been told. When he asked the boy about it, Suka lied twice to him, first claiming he had used oil from a tin at the house and then from a bottle in the barn. "You are lying again, my son," Charan told him sadly. "You are a big liar. Is that what you've learned from all these books? O, Suka, Suka. Instead of telling me the truth, that you forgot, you treat me like a fool. You should be ashamed of your dirty face. I could see the engine had not been oiled. If you go on lying and behaving in this way, you won't go anywhere in life."

Suka, a handsome sixteen-year-old, said nothing but turned his eyes back to a book. Suka loathed the village and field work and wanted to become an army officer and get away from home as soon as possible. Everyone in Ghungrali knew Suka cursed his father and was insolent to his elders but that Charan closed his eyes to it. In truth, Charan was ashamed; he suspected, rightly, that Suka looked down on him as a drunken peasant with earth-soiled hands. For this reason, he could not bring himself to discipline his son. From time to time he heard reports that Suka kept bad company at school, and one day he found a sword Suka had hidden in the wellhouse. He sought old Sadhu's advice but the old man regarded his educated grandson as a valuable ally in his disputes with Charan and he refused to hear anything ill of the boy. Charan's second son, Kulwant, had also proved disappointing. Charan would say proudly of him,

"This boy, now, has a real hand for farming." Actually both sons, when their father's back was turned, refused to lift a finger in the fields. Half-educated in the nearest town, like the sons of most of the villages newly-prosperous farmers, they lived for the day they could leave Ghungrali for good. God knows what fate would await them. The young Mazhbis observed their disobedience but said nothing to Charan, choosing to take on the extra work themselves.

In contrast to Charan's sullen offspring, as they worked in the hot sun all day, almost overcome by the heat, the Mazhbis always stayed cheerful. Charan, anxious that they be contented and go with him to cut Surjit's wheat, was sober and genial, working all day to bring them water and pails of buttermilk, and fiercely fighting with the old lady so they would be provided with plenty of good, appetizing food. "Here it is!" he would call happily, serving out wheat cakes and a thick lentil soup in the field, "Who doesn't eat of this will repent afterwards." In the fields with the Mazhbis, without knowing why, Charan felt pleasurably alive and contented.

The reaper finished cutting in two days and with eleven Mazhbis on hand now, the baling went quickly, with only Suka the target of Bawa's sallies. "Hey, Suka, you want a sickle so you can help us work?" Bawa would call. "I've got one hidden deep in my shorts. You'll get it when it's dark."

"Don't talk rot to me, you black-faced bastard," Suka would curse, vanishing the rest of the day, so that Charan alone would have to keep fetching pails of drinking water from the well.

The Mazhbis still worked in two teams, the old men and the young, and when they neared the end of a field and one or the other was not far behind, they would race to finish with great shouting and banter back and forth.

"*Shabash,* boys, we have to show our strength to these old men." "Hurry, we must beat the others; they're catching up." "Here, bring that bale." "You hold mine and I'll hold yours. No, Bawa, I mean the rope." "O, the rope broke! I rape its mother." "Hurry, hurry, you boys! Bring more bales."

"You'll see," Bawa shouted, working to beat old Chanan's group, just a short way ahead in the next row, "we'll make them spit like stallions. Those Sikh priests like Amarjit are very tricky. They know so many ways to bring women to their beds. They'll tell them, 'O, dear little girl, unbutton these trousers.' If she's foolish, she'll unbutton theirs. If she is clever, he will say 'O, no, my dear, I meant those trousers hanging there on the wall.' "

This made the usually grave Amarjit laugh, and Bawa cried in triumph, "Look! Our Sikh is in high spirits again."

"Let's go! O, hurry, hurry up, those boys are passing us." "Pull it tighter." "Bring, bring, bring more bales." "Hurry, hurry!" "Don't let them beat us, boys."

"Wah, wah!" Charan joined in. "Go, boys, go!" Both groups of Mazhbis worked frantically now, as they always did, abreast near the end of the field. "Bring, brother!" "Hurry up!" "Now, boys, watch out!" "They should not beat us. After all, we are bearded men, Amarjit, and they are children." "Take care your long beards don't get caught in the bales, old men!" "Don't worry, we'll bring them to their knees!" "Make them piss in their shorts, boys!" "Come, hurry, Bawa, we will make their shorts wet. Will these old men remember us? Just wet their shorts. When they reach home, their wives will ask. . . ." "Don't talk so much, Bawa." "Bring, one more bale!" "Ah!" "Finished!" *"Shabash,* boys, now we have shown them our strength."

When both groups reached the end, the old men usually a bit behind, the Mazhbis would flop down on the grass, their bodies and faces drenched with sweat, breathing in the air quickly before the heat came back again. Charan would hasten to pour water into their glasses or outstretched hands and one of the youths would boast, "The young men are better than the old in every respect."

"No, the old are real bulls," another would joke. "When they start they won't stop for hours. If you could see old Banta last night. How he was begging for it and his wife kicked his bottom."

"I have been where they charge one *anna* if it's as big as a donkey's and half an *anna* for smaller sizes."

"What for half an *anna?"*

"You wouldn't know because you are no size whatsoever. Yours is like a lady finger. Maybe even smaller than that."

"O, Bantee, Bantee, what can your wife do with a lady finger? She won't even know you are there."

Inevitably, conversation turned toward the boycott. "Now it's only talk," Charan would say. "But sometimes these things can lead to murders on both sides. It's nonsense."

"Boycott, boycott," Bawa joined in, repeating the strange-sounding English word. "When you speak that boycott, your whole mouth gets full of it."

The evening of the third day when they reached the last field, Charan told the Mazhbis to make extra large bales, three apiece, for their payment. "These bales must be really big ones," he said. "Don't hesitate. Now before this was my farm and your labor, but now, take it, my wheat is in your hands. Be generous with your bales. Make some really big ones. Tomorrow don't say that Charan was a miser."

"No, no, Charan," old Chanan protested. "We are not that greedy." He made a moderate-sized bale and told the men to follow his example. "This is big enough. We know you are a large-hearted man, a real lion. But we must not exploit your generosity."

"I'm sure you deserve these big bales. That is no untruth. . . . Now shall we save my sister's wheat? What do you say, boys? It is shattering in the fields there in Bhadson village and she can get no one to help her. What do you say? You'll get the same there all right."

After some consultation, old Chanan spoke up. "We five are ready to go: Amarjit, Surjit and his son, my son and myself. Now we must finish our work. But we are ready, and ready to go, the five of us." The reaper had returned to the university but Chanan said it would be good to cut the grain with a sickle in the traditional way; he was fiercely opposed to any form of modernization and told Charan, "These machines are awful. It is very difficult to make good bales when wheat is cut by a machine."

After some discussion all the other men agreed to go as well. Charan, who was relieved to see all his wheat now lying in bales on the fields, felt very pleased. "Make your piles of bales and we'll load them on the wagon," he said. "Now it's all settled. We'll start at five."

"No," said old Chanan. "Better to go before the village stirs. We'll rise and come to your barn when the moon comes over our beds.

Two hours before dawn, the Mazhbis crept through the sleeping streets of Ghungrali and gathered at Charan's cattleyard. They piled straw in his wagon and scrambled aboard as Charan started the tractor engine and roared off before any of the other Jats knew they were going. Three hours later, as the sun was rising over the fields, they arrived at Surjit's farm near the village of Bhadson, twenty-seven miles to the south. Along the Grand Trunk Road there was little traffic; hundreds of crows, startled by the tractor's noise, rose from the high branches of the old oaks along the road, screaming and cawing. As they neared Bhadson, trees no longer obscured the view, and they could see the sky and country far ahead. The Mazhbis seldom ventured far from the village, and as the tractor bumped along they looked around them with curiosity. Through breaks in the semitransparent dust, the world exposed its fairness: the white mist lay unevenly around the bushes and haystacks and wandered in small cloudlets, clinging to the surfaces as if not to spoil the view. Surjit's farmstead, in the middle of a great expanse of dry, brown wheat, was reached along a small dirt road, and great clouds of dust rolled up from the tractor tires; the men covered their heads and noses with their shawls and blankets so as to breathe. A few hundred yards beyond the farmstead began the low, flat jungle.

It was hotter in Bhadson than in Ghungrali and, perhaps because of the nearness of the jungle or the scorching wind which blew day after day, or the absence of big shade trees on the newly-cleared land, the sun seemed to beat more fiercely. The air was thinner here, the sky whiter and dust was everywhere, settling on the wet backs and shoulders of the men as they worked. By late morning a gray haze of dust would spread over the sky, and the sun would turn a livid white. Hot winds unceasingly stirred the wheat. The Mazhbis tied rags over their mouths and noses to keep out the dust, and, with only their grimy wet foreheads and eyes exposed, resembled bandits or *dacoits*. From the edge of one field to another, fifteen men moved forward: the Mazhbis, Saroop and his two sons, Pala and Kaka, and Charan. Saroop, whom Surjit had strengthened with large doses of opium, was formally the master, but he almost apologetically worked alongside the Mazhbis in the fields. Everyone knew that in reality the farm was in the hands of Surjit: she arranged everything, nothing was done without her consent. Without a mechanical reaper, the Mazhbis, Saroop and his sons cut the wheat as Punjabis always have, slashing their sickles at the ripe stems, grasping one handful at a time, advancing slowly, rocking from side to side on their haunches and moving steadily and rhythmically, to the end of a field, crouched low in a wide, spreadout line, nearly buried in the wheat. All day long the sickles flashed in the white sun, all together making the same sound: *grrch, grrch, grrrrrch.* And from the glint on their sickles, from their wet faces and backs and the way they gathered up the swaths after cutting, you could see how suffocating and oppressive the heat had become.

As their muscles grew tireder, the more the younger men joked and cursed and told obscene stories, and the quieter the older men became. Charan himself, who had not mown wheat for many years because of his asthma, never seemed so full of energy and life; he ran back and forth from the house, carrying water, tea, brown sugar cakes, pails of buttermilk, steaming hot *chapattis,* kettles of delicious potato and pea curry, and sometimes even ice, for Surjit was as generous as the old lady was stingy, and she worked all day over the hearth preparing the best food she could for her rescuers. As they worked, the voices of the men arose from the wheat: "Move on, O, brave men. Try to be fast." "O, these thorny weeds, it is like the sting of a scorpion." "This wheat is dry; if your sickle is sharp it cuts easily."

Charan would hover about, as if his good will alone sustained the brutal labor, even joking with Saroop, whom he usually avoided. The younger Mazhbis were tirelessly good humored. "Once Bawa's uncle came and showed Bawa his penis," called Banarsi, one of these easy-going youths. "And the uncle asked, 'What is it, dear nephew, a dove or a snake?' And Bawa said, 'O, Uncle, it is a snake but only a very little one. Maybe a worm.'" "O, shameless creatures," one of the older men would call above the laughter, "look at your elders all around you and you cut such filthy jokes. Now better you stop this kind of talk." But Saroop, anxious to please the family's deliverers, encouraged it. "O, Bawa," he called. "Today you don't speak at all. I have not heard you yelling."

"Today they have not shown me anything. How can I yell?"

"Come, some to me. I shall show you something right here."

"In the presence of all these men? No, I feel ashamed. I'm not a boy without a beard, *Sardar* Saroop Singh."

"Now race with me," a voice would rise from the wheat a few rows down. "Beware, I'm coming like the wind."

"Come," challenged Bawa. "I'm running like a dust storm if you are the wind." Or one of the youths would start to sing, rocking on his heels as his sickle flashed in the light.

> I'm dancing like a peacock
> And my bells are jingling
> You come from somewhere, my love
> Like a great white pigeon you come
> I'm dancing like a peacock
> My love, my bells are jingling
> I'm cooing like a female pigeon among the dancers
> Come from somewhere, like a great white pigeon

Down the field other voices joined in singing:

> She rises from the pond
> Like the opium pipe's flame
> And presses hard against the temple pillar
> She, the soldier's widow

As they neared the end of the rows, the men would pick up speed, their sickles flashing across the width of wheat. "Come, boys, show your strength!" *"Shabash, shab-a-a-a-a-ash!"* *"Shabash,* make the parrots fly!"

When Surjit brought tea, old Chanan would silence them, and the men would leave the fields for the shade of a tree, flopping down, seemingly exhausted, on their backs. Always the landscape was the same: the bands of reaped wheat, the empty fields of stubble and the patches still standing, the crows flapping their wings and cawing to one another, the high-soaring vultures and the cloudless sky. And as the second day replaced the first, and then it was the third, the air became even more stagnant from the heat and stillness. Sometimes there was not a breath of wind, nor a cheering cool sound, so that the hot breezes, stirring the furnace heat, were a relief when they came.

Old Chanan steeled his men; "We won't leave until Sister says, 'Now I cannot afford any more food for these men.'"

Surjit protested, "I won't say that ever, Brother. You can stay here as long as you wish. I won't run out of food. After all, I am Charan's sister. I have the same blood running in my veins."

Always the talk came back to the boycott. "Some of the Jats will really be afraid by now," speculated Bawa. "Their wives will tell them, 'Now, little Pritam's father, go and arrange for some Harijans to cut your wheat. You must cut it at once before it shatters or we'll starve.'"

Chanan was optimistic. "Surely the boycott will be settled by the time we reach the village."

Charan thought it would have to end soon one way or another. "They may reach some compromise or there will be some killing. But ultimately they will have to stop this foolishness."

"Have you heard the new thing?" asked Bawa. "That some of the Chamars burned Basant Singh's effigy and women beat his likeness with sticks and cried, 'May he die! May he die!'"

"Who says that?"

"Women."

"Nonsense," Charan growled. 'You know those gossip-mongers in the village. Those Chamars. . . ."

"Never believe the Chamars," old Chanan advised; he was also opposed to any erosion of the caste system even though he himself was of the lowliest Harijans. "They are nobody's friends. Stay with your own caste. Chamars will be your friends if you go on serving them tea, but if you go to their houses and ask for tea, from that day on they'll not look you straight in the eye."

"Yes, they are a greedy lot, Uncle," echoed Bawa. "Where there is tea, the Chamars are your friends."

"Bawa took too much opium," called Kapur, old Chanan's son. "See how slow he cuts." As was common during the harvest in Punjab, Charan provided the men pellets of opium to swallow to keep their strength up and sometimes they ate too much and went into a stupor.

"He has a ghost inside him."

"You had that same ghost yesterday, Kapur."

In mid-afternoon, the Bladson *mistry* or carpenter came to sharpen everyone's sickle, an old custom during harvest for which he would receive grain. In an equally old harvest custom, since he was from another village, the Mazhbis teased him and cracked jokes at his expense. The *mistry*, a bony, slack-jawed youth, bent over his work and pretended not to hear them.

"O, what is this, *mistryji?*" Bawa asked, after his sickle had been sharpened. "It has gone dull."

"He looks dull himself. He needs sharpening."

"You should help him, Bawa. Put some energy in him."

"If he agrees, we will. He doesn't know how much extra energy these Ghungraliwallahs have. If he needs some he should come at midnight. We will all give him a drop of energy, each one of us."

Hearing enough of such banter, the *mistry* looked up and addressed Bawa, who had sprawled out on a grassy bank. "Do you have a stomachache, boy?"

"Yes."

"If you have a stomachache, come with me. I shall set your stomach right. Only you will have to spend the night with an old man in our village. He is a real good doctor. He applies some medicine at midnight. Are you ready?"

Encouraged by this daring retort and gleeful, all the Mazhbis began to taunt the poor carpenter in high falsetto voices. Just then Surjit arrived with a fresh tin of tea and offered him some. But the poor man stammered something about having to reach home "come what may" and fled the laughter of the Mazhbis. Mystified, Surjit poured the tea, telling the workers, "Brothers, all the neighbors are jealous because we are finishing our harvest so quickly. You see, this is the first year I've had as much wheat as my neighbors. Before they used to graze cattle in our empty fields. Now Charan has sown all this land."

At last, when the sun was about to descend toward the west, and the plain, the fields, and the air were no longer suffocating but took on a tolerable coolness, the Mazhbis carried their sickles to the farmerhouse for the last time. Most of them flopped down on cots strewn around the yard, too tired to talk. Old Chanan came last of all; he called to the others, "Boys, give me your sickles. Let us try to collect everything for the trip home."

"O, Brethren, do you want to take your baths with cold water or hot?" Charan asked. "I shall get hot water for you. It's my duty. We'll light a fire and heat a drum of water." He was already quite drunk. The Mazhbis, after a brief rest, began to wander about the yard, stripping off their dusty clothes.

"O, Charan, what will we say to the Jats when we get home tonight?" Amarjit asked. "They will accuse us and say, 'You are running to other villages and here we are short of men; instead of bringing men from outside, you are taking them away.' What shall we say?"

"That, Charan will have to explain, not us," said old Chanan with a smile. "We will tell them to ask Charan Singh who took us out."

Charan laughed and waved a bottle of liquor at them. "Ho, ho, don't worry. *Wahiguru Ji!* God is great!"

Several of the Mazhbis crouched around a fire. "The flames are coming out of the pit." "You used too much oil. Sprinkle some water around the edge." "Shall I take a bath here at the pump?"

The Mazhbis stripped off everything save their loincloths and poured hot water over themselves, using no soap but rubbing their glistening, muscular brown bodies clean and dry with oil. Charan hastened to pour a drink for old Chanan, who was still resting on a cot with another older Mazhbi, Banta. Banta downed a large glass of liquor in a single gulp and, looking pleased with himself, declared loudly, "Listen to me. Charan treats us as if he were our father. It is a great honor for us. We are poor men and he is our master." Several Mazhbis drank a toast to Charan, glad of the chance to quickly refill their glasses. "Charan, you are one of the finest men in the world," old Chanan joined in, himself enjoying a glass of liquor now that the work was done.

Bawa wandered over, coarse black hair dripping wet and brown face and shiny shoulders clean and oiled. Charan poured him a full glass of liquor. "O, Bawa, you are a naughty boy," Banta said at its size. Bawa downed the glassful in a quick swig, and smacking his lips, held it out to Charan to pour another. He leered at them and said, "Be sober and enjoy your life." Banarsi joined them, waving his glass in their faces. "Drink up, boys. Tomorrow you may be dead." Bawa laughed. "Then you'll work for God. Cutting His crops in heaven."

The rest of the men crowded around, sitting on cots or the ground as Charan hurried about, filling their glasses and Pala ran to replenish the supply from the house. "We are here because of Charan's good tongue," declared Amarjit rather formally, who with his long beard seemed to add a priestly aura to the occasion. "The way he treats us we can sacrifice our lives for him. He is a gem of a person. . . . Yes, where men work, there is God. Our Guru respected work and we are all laboring men." Surjit passed among them with a dish of her best pickled chillies, expressing to each her gratitude. Charan sensed the feeling of well-being among the men now that the harvest was over. "You know, my brothers," he told them, "I have seen many harvests in my life, but I have never seen one like this. We have been three days without a fight."

"All these boys are real good workers," Chanan agreed. "No one has run off to answer the call of nature all the time or made other foolish excuses."

"Ah, the neighbors are looking across the field," Surjit remarked in an undertone. "I don't want them to cast their evil eyes on all this pork we are going to eat. How jealous they will be! O, brothers, I have seen bad days here but now we have a fine wheat harvest thanks to you."

Charan poured another round and still another, with great bursts of laughter. Saroop had brewed twenty-five bottles of liquor from brown sugar, a liquor which numbed the brains of those who drank it, just as if they were suffering from concussion. It was not long before Charan and the Mazhbis sat around in a great circle, exhausted, satiated, drunk and looking as rascally as any Romans at a bacchanalia, especially the younger men who had not yet dressed nor wound on their turbans but sat with towels wrapped around them like togas, their wet, uncombed hair sticking out every which way. Charan was soon very drunk and he jumped into the center of the circle and with a bottle in hand, roared, "I'm now at your disposal, my beloved ones. Now you will have a pig! We won't serve it on plates. We'll put it on a big platter and have it here in the middle of all of us."

Surjit brought a large white cloth and spread it on the ground before them and the men settled in a circle, sitting crosslegged or with legs sprawled out in every direction, the row of precious bottles before them. It was almost dark now; as the fire from the hearth flicked red shadows on their faces, the world seemed to have shrunk to their circle, the star-filled sky and the croaking of angry frogs on the edge of the nearest fields.

"Let me serve my friends!" Charan bellowed, and suddenly, in the glistening faces of the Mazhbis, in the warmth from the liquor, in the din of shouts and laughter was discernible to him a great vitality, youth and revival of strength.

"Drink up!" he shouted at the top of his lungs. "Enjoy, for we only live once!" And he rose to his full height, and waving his glass, and so bursting with feeling that water came to his eyes, he cried, "I'm not only happy, I'm super-happy. Happiest of all the world! I'm so happy I can jump up to the sky!"

Saroop came running from the house, his arms full of bottles. "Here!" cried Charan. "Have you ever seen so many bottles? These are the young ones of the last. Who wants more?"

Surjit called Pala to come and get the pig. She whispered to him, "See the neighbors over there. How those dogs are looking with their big wide eyes! They are having heartfailure to see our great kettle of pork." Pala carried the platter to the men, straining under the weight of the huge mountain of meat and gravy. He set it in the midst of the Mazhbis, and Surjit came running with a stack of hot wheatcakes. "Do like this," Pala said, "come and take whatever you want." And the hungry Mazhbis fell to eating like birds of prey, each leering and seizing and stuffing it down as fast as he could, for few had meat but once or twice a year. After eating, many sat as if paralyzed from the food and liquor, with foolishly happy expressions on their faces.

Pala declared in a loud voice, feeling a speech was required from the host and seeing his father was too drunk, "Brothers, you have worked hard and done everything for us. I'm too glad. If I did anything wrong, please excuse me. I'm a poor man. I did to the best of my ability. I think what I served was very poor food. If I'm guilty, please pardon me." Some of the men cheered and applauded and Bawa knocked over a bottle of liquor. "So, let us start for Ghungrali," old Chanan finally called and there was great confusion as the Mazhbis staggered to their feet and lurched around in the darkness, bumping into each other and searching for their possessions. Bawa picked up the large platter and lifting it into the air, poured all the gravy and remaining scraps of meat down into his throat. Surjit screamed, discovering someone had stepped on a basket of baby chicks. "O, who has done it? O, God, forgive me! Someone has crushed the poor little things." Amarjit rushed to help her, calling, "O, God, what a mess someone has made!" Surjit recovered herself and cried, "Only two are lost. Forget it, brothers. It was an accident and what has happened has happened."

Charan mounted the driver's seat and shouted for everyone to climb into the wagon. Pala and Kaka came running with fresh hay for the Mazhbis to ride on. The tractor started with a great roar, everyone shouted at once, Saroop drunkenly ran around the wagon fervently shaking hands with all the Mazhbis, and Surjit came running to give each man a piece of brown sugar. "Here, brothers," she called above the din, "take this and sweeten your mouths. Godspeed on the journey home!" Amarjit's voice rose above the others. *"A Jaikara;* I'll yell a religious cry." And his deep voice bellowed into the night:

"Jo BOLE SO NIHAL! *Who Speaks He Is Full of the Name of God!"*

Everyone roared back, "SAT SRI AKAL!"

"JO BOLE SO NIHAL!"

"SAT SRI AKAL!"

The next morning in Ghungrali, One-Eye cornered Charan on the road. "Charan," he called in an ugly voice. "Now we'll have to talk to you. We have an objection."

Charan whirled around. He was hurrying to the land of the Sarpanch to help his friend harvest his fields, and his head was splitting from the revelry of the night before. "Aren't you cutting with us today?" he asked the one-eyed man.

"They didn't invite me. Don't ask so many questions before you hear me. . . . O, I don't say anything myself. But your own friends are objecting too much."

Charan scowled at him. "Bring those friends to me. Let them talk to me straight. Don't convey messages in that sneaky manner. You say whatever you have to say to me."

Taken aback by Charan's fierce manner, One-Eye's voice rose to a whine. "No, no. I don't say anything. I was just telling you the truth. Your own best friends are talking against you."

"You forget about them. They should come and talk to me straight. Don't try to play the messenger and give an evil twist to their words. Now you come out with whatever you have to say, Mohinder."

"No, no, Charan. I don't have any objection. I don't even know where you went with the Mazhbis. I myself was not here in the village."

Charan grabbed One-Eye by his collar, and lifted him off his feet and gave him a good shaking. "Then shut up!" he shouted into One-Eye's face. "Keep your evil mouth quiet! Don't always try to make trouble. Do you think my sister's crop is not my responsibility?"

One-Eye gasped for breath and Charan dropped him to the road. He scrambled away on his hands and knees, then rose trembling, fearing that Charan might strike him a powerful blow. "Now, *Maharaji,*" he pled, "don't shout at me so. I fold my hands before you. I didn't mean anything."

"All right. Go your way. But never again try to twist things around. You will make us quarrel. All of us are good friends. And while we respect you as a Jat, that is all."

Shaken, One-Eye hurried on to his fields, as the father of the Sarpanch came out of his gate to greet Charan. An elderly gray-whiskered man, he took Charan's hands in his own and said, "It is good, my son, you are here. We don't need anything except your presence. You go and sit under the shade of a tree on a *charpoy.* But be here."

"Don't worry, uncle," Charan smiled. "I'll be here all day. I can't mow these days because of my chest, but I'll serve as water carrier."

"No, we have others for such jobs. You just be here, that's all."

Nirmal was already in the field with some fifty men, the friends and relatives of the Sarpanch who had volunteered to cut his wheat. Nirmal greeted Charan accusingly. "So you are back, Charan. Here people are bringing men from outside and you are taking our men to other villages."

"O, listen to me," Charan said impatiently, "that is not just some other village. That is my own farm in a way. You know I plowed those fields, I sowed them and now it was my duty to reap the wheat. Now tell me, did I do wrong? Are you all mad here in Ghungrali? Whosoever asks me, 'Why did you take the Mazhbis to Bhadson?' will get the same answer. Just now your great friend Mohinder was asking the same thing. I have satisfied that bastard."

"Now, Charan," Nirmal said in a placating tone. "You fly out of your clothes in a minute. We are just talking. You know everyone is coming to us and asking for more men. After all, we have to satisfy every one of the Jats. The day before yesterday we managed to get thirty men at the station in Ludhiana. Served them tea also. In the meantime two Jats from some other village came. They offered them more money and free cigarettes and food and tea four times a day. We were furious with those Jats, and One-Eye started yelling at them. When the *bhaiyas* heard the quarrel, all of them ran away. That is the labor position over here. I wish I'd never heard of the word boycott. Now for the last three days there is a great rush. Everyone is rushing at us and asking for men, men, men. Tell me, what should we do? We have only a few men and the demand is thirty, forty times more. And some of the wheat is starting to shatter."

"Yes, yes, I know that." Charan's voice was harsh. "I don't ask you to give me men. I arranged with the Mazhbis myself. Now, look, I'll be needing men as soon as my father comes with the threshing machine. What right have you got to tell me I can't take men outside this village?"

"O, you are really terrible," groaned Nirmal. "I didn't mean anything except I heard you took some men to Sister's."

"They were eleven. All of them Mazhbis. I took them on *lavi*. I told them before leaving that they would get the same amount from my sister as they got from me. Moreover, Bhadson is my own farm—my second farm."

"No . . . all right. You did the right thing. It is your duty to help Sister. You have done good. Good. Be a happy man. Enjoy your life."

"You know that Mohinder came to me and told me that my own friends were critical. I knew what he was up to. He was trying to stir up trouble between us."

"Leave him, Charan. Who doesn't know him? He is that way. He must make everyone quarrel. That is his strategy."

"I pressed him hard. Now he won't dare to talk with me and say my own friends have turned against me. I told him to either produce such friends or keep his mouth shut."

"You did well. He deserves that kind of treatment. He has made many friends into enemies. What does he gain by such gossip?"

"He is an evil soul," Charan said. "You know the saying, 'A one-eyed man is always dangerous.' " Charan laughed and then Nirmal started to laugh too and suddenly the two of them were laughing and shaking and slapping each other on the back as if they had taken leave of their senses. Seeing them, the Sarpanch hurried over, saying, "No, Charan, I won't shake hands with you today."

"Why?"

"Because you have come to help us and are too sacred. We'll feed you good."

"O, don't insult me. It won't be the first time I have eaten good. My mother used to feed me the whole day until I was three. You can still see her udders." Charan gave a huge laugh.

"Have you noticed, Nirmal?" the Sarpanch joined in. "Even today they have no milking buffalo. They make tea out of her own milk; she is a real twenty-four-hour queen."

"It's true!" roared Charan. "She's not like your mother, who's as small as a goat. She could hardly feed milk to a baby sparrow. Here, just see my body, though it is half of what it used to be. Even then I'm as big as any two of you. It's all because one old woman had pails and pails of milk."

Across the fields, One-Eye heard the hoots of laughter and watched the three friends carrying on. His good eye narrowed to a slit and he told his sharecropper, "That Charan and his father are real crooks. They'll eat up his sister's land in drinking. Ah, what they have done to that poor girl! They have played tricks on her and misused her property. For years they've taken money from that farm of hers and used it to buy drink." His face twisted into a pious expression. "But why should we talk? It is their own private folly."

Near Bhambadi village, Mukhtar and two other Chamars from Ghungrali were buried in a sea of wheat mowing, their sickles flashing, their shirts wet with sweat and dust and their faces sunburnt and glowing from the hot wind. The wheat belonged to a Hindu *pandit* from Bhambadi; the three of them had taken a contract to cut and thresh it for 68 kilos of grain per acre, more than they had ever earned in Ghungrali.

"What will you do if the boycott goes on, Mukhtar?" his fellow worker, Uttam, asked him.

"I don't know. I'm thinking of going to a town and trying to get a job in a factory. I'm hopeful the boycott won't last too many days more. But one thing is certain. I shall try my best to give my son a good education. The government gives help to Harijans, and my parents wanted me to go on with my studies but I couldn't master the English language. I was very poor in it, and gave up my schooling after nine years. So here I am. I'm determined my boy will not follow in my footsteps. My children will not become sharecroppers or daily laborers in Ghungrali. I'm sure of one thing, no matter what happens: my son will never work for the Jats. He may be an electrician, a factory worker or a mechanic if he doesn't become an educated gentleman, but I will never let him work for Jats. Never."

"This wind is nasty. It spoils everything."

"I'll try to make my son a real gentleman, well-educated and well-fixed in life. What I couldn't be, I'll make my son that."

"You can't work with high speed in this wind."

"It doesn't matter." Mukhtar worked with a steady rhythm as he talked, grasping the stalks with his left hand and slashing at them with his sickle in his right hand. "Here we are not under any Jat or anything. We are masters of ourselves. If the wind doesn't stop we will take rest until it does."

"It won't stop so soon once it starts."

"Very well. We shall be working and try to do our best. Maybe God will hear us and be kind enough to end the wind."

After a time, Uttam told Mukhtar, "Your Charan never came into this boycott trouble. He has always played a good role. He still wants both parties to reach some settlement."

"You can't find a man like Charan for ten miles around," said Mukhtar, with so much feeling Uttam was surprised. "He is always for the poor. He says, 'What is wrong if these poor people earn some grain? They are also like us Jats—they are human beings. They also want to share in the prosperity of the village.'"

"Basant Singh is always for himself. He doesn't care at all what damage he does to the village. He only knows his personal business should flourish. Now his combine has not arrived in time and he has hired men from Uttar Pradesh for four rupees a day."

"Charan gave the Mazhbis four times that much."

"As they say, 'Money makes the mare go,'" Uttam said cheerfully. "It is true with Basant Singh. He is not concerned with anybody except his own little family."

"We could have reached a settlement if it wasn't for him and that Mohinder and Nirmal. They want to play their own little game. They are really nasty fellows. But Charan is a man of silver."

"I always heard he was a drunkard and abused his workers," Uttam said. "I would never work for him."

"He drinks and abuses both," Mukhtar agreed. "But he is also a man who is always true. He stands for the right thing and disagrees when there is injustice, and for that you cannot find a better man miles around."

Mukhtar fell silent, thinking. And he thought not of his work but of the boycott and those who were responsible for it. First, he passed sentence on Basant Singh, One-Eye and the other trouble-makers, but the more he thought the angrier he became at Charan, Dhakel, old Pritam and all the good men of the village who allowed themselves to be manipulated. For without them, were not the others nothing? For two days he had such thoughts, and gradually he began to feel contempt for them and sorrow for them also. And so, when he and Uttam met Charan on the road one afternoon his words came with unexpected harshness.

"Listen, listen, Chota," Charan called from his bullock cart. "The harvest is almost over. It is better you reach some settlement and come back to work for me on daily wages."

"We are trying to settle," Mukhtar said as they came abreast.

"Then what is wrong?" Charan asked. "This dispute was over cutting wheat on the thirtieth bale and now the cutting is almost over. If you quietly start working for me on daily wages, everything will be all right."

"Will it?" Mukhtar asked in his harsh new voice. "Will it be all right then, Charan?"

"Are you mad? If you want that someone should come to you and beg forgiveness and ask if you are ready to work for me, then I shall come to your hut this evening. If that is all, I shall come and ask you, for all to see."

"No, Charan. If that was all, there would never have been any trouble."

"That's what I mean. That now we should end all this nonsense. It has been more than enough now on both sides. What has happened has happened. I mean there shouldn't be any more trouble."

"Look around you, Charan." An anger growing inside of him, Mukhtar's voice rose. "Look around you. Do you think it doesn't hurt us to see the crops of our village shatter in the fields? Do you think it will be all over if everyone apologizes to everyone? Do you think Ghungrali can ever go back to what it was or that Basant Singh or that one-eyed person will let it, or if not they, others? Do you think the Harijans can ever again trust the Jats in Ghungrali to

always give them the right to gather fodder for their cows and buffaloes undisturbed? Do you think any Chamar will ever trust his
future again in the hands of the Jats? Do you, Charan? Can we go
back?" Mukhtar's voice had risen to such a pitch that Uttam anxiously tugged on his shoulder and said, "Let's go, Chota." And as
they moved down the road Mukhtar was angry, with such an anger
as he had never known. Time would pass, and the trouble in the village, but Mukhtar's anger perhaps would not pass, but remain in his
mind all his life long.

Charan stared after them, speechless. Of all the villagers Mukhtar
was perhaps the best farmer, although at twenty-three, he was young
enough to be Charan's son; and Charan knew he had such a skill
and knowledge of the land as his own sons would never possess, and
that without him, his own life would be immeasurably harder. And
Charan stared after him a long time, numbed by the realization that
Mukhtar was right.

In the lives of all men, there are times for pausing, reflecting and
taking stock. And this Charan did until the threshing began, spending the days at his well, cutting fodder, preparing the threshing
ground, working alone; in the afternoons when the hot winds rose
to furnace heat and the sky was gray with flying dust, he dozed on
a *charpoy* in his toolshed, and thought, and thought, his only companions two sparrows who had made their nest in a water pail hanging from a hook on the wall, who flew in and out the open window,
feeding their young. So Charan reconciled himself, and added his
missed opportunity to break the boycott to all his other follies and
failures.

And then Sadhu Singh brought a threshing machine he had con-
trived to borrow free of charge from a government office and Charan
was busy again. The Mazhbis, who had been cutting the wheat of
other Jats, returned, and old Chanan, Bawa, Kapur and Amarjit first
used hoes to cut away the stubble at the threshing ground and then
swept the bare earth clean with cotton stick brushes. Charan brought
the bullock cart to the fields and put in place the iron drummy his
father had produced with the help of some back slapping and six
bottles of liquor, and old Chanan erected a curtain of jute bags sewed
together to prevent the dust and the chaff from blowing back on the

men who would feed grain into the drummy's steel hammers. The other Mazhbis brought bales from the fields, stacking them into an enormous pile, and finally they were ready to begin.

Charan climbed onto the tractor and started the engine, and then with a shout, *"Wahi Guri Ji!* God is Great!" he put the tractor into gear, the belt began turning on its pulley, and with a deafening roar the hammers inside the drummy began to beat down; old Chanan and Bawa, working side by side with gloves to protect their fingers, began pushing handfuls of grain into it. On the other side of the machine, Sher, who had at last rejoined the other Mazhbis, stood with a wooden fork; he tossed the grain and chaff that came out of the machine into the air to further separate them; Amarjit did the final winnowing, tossing the grain into the air with a wooden scoop, where the wind blew the remaining dust and chaff away. And gradually two great heaps began to form by the machine, one larger and white as mother-of-pearl and the other smaller and a milky, light brown—Charan's wheat harvest. And because of the roaring din of the metal drummy and the tractor engine, no one spoke at work, but they thought about things to themselves, and during rests they talked and joked and gossiped more than ever.

"There is much ill will in the village," old Chanan told Charan during one of the rests. "You know what the Chamars say? They say, 'We were not used to going out of our village. But now we are used to it. Now we don't care even if the Jats don't open their boycott for ten years. We don't give a damn for the Jats.'"

"Who says that?"

"If you had boycotted me and ordered me to stay out of your fields, Charan, I would be saying the same thing. You know that one-eyed person used to say, 'Now we will set the Chamars right.' But if this trouble goes on, nobody will even be cleaning the Jats' barns."

"How can we afford to make the wives of the Jats clean them?" grinned Sher. "Now we don't even let them touch a spot where there is a little dirt. You know we Mazhbis always pray for the best for the Jats' cattle."

"Why not?" asked old Chanan. "You are joking, Sher, but it is true. We always pray for their cattle. If they had no cattle, they would not ask us to clean their barns." The old man wanted things to stay as they had always been. Now he said angrily, "Here the Jats don't allow the Harijans in their fields. How can they allow Basant Singh to bring a combine into this village?" Like Mukhtar, old Chanan had read the handwriting on the wall. When he had cooled down, he said, 'You know, Charan, we did well to go to Bhadson. Otherwise your sister could not have managed."

"Yes, it was a real success," Charan said. His eye caught his son Suka beating the bullocks with a heavy stick. "Stop that!" Charan shouted. "O, don't you see what you are doing? You are a Jat's son, not a weaver. Why can't you handle bullocks?"

"Hush, Charan," old Chanan admonished him. "He is a child."

Charan snorted angrily. "Child? When I was of his age, I used to support the whole family as a laborer in the fields. You say he is a child. . . . Well, let's go back to work, men."

As they moved back across the field to the threshing ground, Chanan told Sher, "Charan has been very generous to us."

The younger man shrugged. "Everyone has to be more generous than before, uncle. The old days are over."

Charan, in threshing his wheat, was once more the first in the village. Some of the Jats had succeeded in bringing in men from outside. Others, when the thirteen-member committee proved itself a failure, were harvesting their own wheat in desperation. In the fields nearest Charan's, Dhakel, Sindar, Gurmel, two neighbor youths and their sharecropper had been at it ten days.

Dhakel, with his frail build, had become exhausted but worked quietly and determinedly, without speaking much. Gurmel, for the first time in his life, began to feel he was growing old. But Sindar, who had not run off on the eve of the harvest as many had expected, had turned out to have surprising stamina and a zest for work. Throughout the scorching days, through duststorms and whirlwinds, rain and thunder, Sindar kept cutting away with his sickle with a vigor that surpassed all the rest; perhaps he wore them all down by never pausing in his endless running monologue. "Work with an energy! Show your strength! God has made our bones of steel!" his nasal voice would rise from the sea of wheat. After Dhakel managed to get some of his wife's relatives from another village to come and reap one day, Sindar could hardly wait until they left to declare, "Today we have stomped on their bottoms. These outsiders. They can't even look straight in our eyes. They won't forget us the rest of their lives, that bunch of dead old ladies. Do you think it is a joke to compete with men like us? Now they won't dare look towards Ghungrali. They will tell even their grandsons not to compete with Ghungraliwallahs."

Sometimes Gurmel would become irritated by the incessant flow of words and snap, "Don't worry about us. Worry about yourself."

To Sindar, this was just an opening. "What do you say? Why shouldn't I worry about you? You are like my own seed. And I have real beautiful seed. Anyone who wants to borrow it I can lend to the whole of the world. My one discharge will make all the women in Ludhiana district pregnant."

When Dhakel lagged behind, Sindar would joke, "Do you know why he is tired? He was raped by all of us last night. He was drunk and couldn't even tell what was happening to him. In the morning he asked, 'Who spilt milk on my pajamas?' The poor man doesn't know he will give birth to twins before the next harvest season."

"Aaaggh! Why do you talk all the time?" Gurmel would explode.

"O, Deaf Man, have you seen my sickle dance?"

"Dance! It creeps like a tortoise."

"You say tortoise but I doubt if you have eyes in your face. Didn't you see the day Dhakel's in-laws were here? Those dead old ladies, my son, will remember me for ages. You know a tiny skinny body came up to me and started showing his feats with a sickle. But when I began to work, he didn't stay there for another second. He went as far from me as he could."

"O, yes," said Gurmel sarcastically. "I saw you running ahead of all of them. Look what Sindar is talking, Dhakel. Any person who doesn't know him might believe his big gossip."

"O, Deaf Man, you can try your hand any time you like. You will be an acre behind me, I bet. My body is made of steel. Whatever happens, we will keep working. O, I rape their sisters! After this we must get drunk for two days. Only then will my body be in tune again."

One day a family of beggars from Rajasthan came to them while they were mowing.

"God will give you more," cried an old lady among them. "We are hungry. We are from a country which is ravaged by famine."

"I won't give," Dhakel shouted angrily. "Why should you work if you can get by with begging? Run from here!"

One of the beggars was a handsome young woman. "O," said the neighbors' sharecropper, a thickset ugly little man, who was working with them, "she can serve our purpose. Give her as much as she likes. We'll enjoy her today."

"You can take a big bale of wheat if you make our boys happy," Sindar told her. "Stay a while. Ten minutes."

"Yes," the sharecropper joined in. "Nothing can go wrong if you please our boys."

Dhakel was furious with the beggars. "Shall I tell you what is what?" he called angrily. "Run away from here!"

"I can't stay, *Sardarji,*" the young woman told Sindar. "You see my relations here with me. It is all in the hands of God."

"Then you won't get anything," grinned Sindar. But he gave her three large bundles of wheat and she hurried away.

"You idiot," called the sharecropper. "You should not have given her like that. Only then could she be useful to us."

"O, you fool," Sindar told him. "I was cutting jokes. I didn't mean anything except a little joking. Here, bring that rope. Show your strength, men! O, I remember one time in Isaru. We were threshing. A real good girl came along to beg some grain and she brought two more girls back the next day. We had three trips each. How they were jumping like springs underneath! All were happy and all were the gainers. There was another time in Mal Majra village. . . ."

And so the days passed, Sindar rambling on and on, the sickles flashing in the sea of wheat, cutting it down stalk by stalk, row by row, field by field and acre by acre; and gradually, Ghungrali changed under the hot white sun and the gray fog of dust. The rocks and sheaves lay row upon row in the stubble fields, or the new-mown wheat would lie in swaths as the men gathered to pick it up; every day there were clouds, it was dusty, the white mist gathered in the distance like a blizzard of snow, the hot wind blew in sudden gusts and never seemed to rest, the earth become hot to the touch, the air dry in the nostrils, and the heat of the Punjab plain grew worse and worse. And day by day in Charan's fields the threshing continued, the white clouds of dust, wheat and chaff tossed in the air, the dust casting a luminescence over the men, the put-put of the diesel engine droning on and on, the pile of precious grain growing and growing. And the men kept on working carefully in the hot wind and sun, winnowing the wheat so as not to lose a single grain. Now the whole countryside grew bare and flat with only stubble fields and the green-brown foliage of the baked trees, and when the dust cleared as dew fell at dusk or lay on the earth in the early morning there was nothing about but stubble fields—a man could see for miles and miles. Once the wheat was cut and gathered in, the sky seemed larger, the earth more spacious, and the men working in the fields began to ponder upon their own significance and the meaning of it all.

Late afternoon. An hour before nightfall. The men had gathered under the shade of the withered oak trees at Charan's well for the final rest of the day. Charan poured tea and when Sindar wandered over to drink at his pump, Charan laughed and asked him to tell them some gossip. But Sindar, his face and turban and beard wet and gray with dust and grime, was in no mood for banter. "I have been thinking," he told his cousin, "that it is a sin to hurt poor people. God will surely punish our village."

Charan laughed. "A sin? What is a sin?"

"In my eyes," called Gurmel, who was stretched out on the grass, "the greatest sin is to rape a virgin girl."

"The real sin is if you take labor by force and refuse to pay for it," said Charan. "Or if you squander your children's property, forcing them to beg and go wander on the roads."

"A man does so many sins in his life," said Sher, the Mazhbi, lighting up a cigarette. "If you just look at someone with a bad intention, that too is a sin."

"There is one sin worse than any," Charan continued. "To show friendship with a man when you mean to destroy him. It is like helping a man in need. If he has no friends or relations, if he is shivering with cold and you give him bedding and food and make him comfortable, that is true virtue. But there must be no personal gain in it. None at all. If you do something for gain or to look good to your friends, it means nothing."

"Ho! What is all this about sins?" called the Sarpanch, coming up the road. "I have not seen any sins lately but I have seen that strange star. With a long white tail like a comet. They call it the star with a tail."

Charan shook hands and moved over on his *charpoy* to make

room for his friend. "It all began with that star. It is said such a star brings disaster to a village."

"Look what harm it brought to our own village," said old Chanan.

The Sarpanch chuckled. "It was there before the boycott started."

Sher gazed at the sky. "These whirlwinds will be more and more these days until the rainy season comes."

"Don't worry, Sher. The whirlwinds will take your share of the grain."

"O, be careful with your cigarette, Sher. This hot wind is dangerous."

"Yes," said old Chanan. "It would be the greatest sin on earth to set fire to the wheatfields."

Charan agreed this would be the greatest sin of all; he recalled hearing of a village many years ago which caught fire and the entire wheat crop was destroyed. "Sins . . . ," he mused. "It is better to speak of virtues."

"A man who lends money without interest is good," said Sher, hoping to delay the return to the fields.

"A man who helps others is definitely wise," Charan agreed, "But a man who can get a loan without interest is even wiser."

"It's good to scatter grains for birds."

"The birds can feed themselves," Charan said. "They are not beggars."

Sher snuffed out his cigarette. "Man says when he is alive, 'This is mine, this is my property, my wheat, my sparrows, to do with as I like.' But when he dies he only gets six feet of earth. We work like animals for the Jats, we go through hell. But I believe a person who does good things in life, his next birth will be comfortable." He grinned slyly. "Let's say Charan is a bad man. He drinks. He does many bad things. Well, in the next life, he'll be in my place and I'll be in his. And how I'll be taking work out of him with a whip!" The Mazhbis all laughed.

"There's no life after death," said the Sarpanch. "People used to say there couldn't be chickens without a hen sitting on them, so there must be a God. But today there are electric incubators. Man is a seed, a foetus, a child, a man, and in the end, he dies. And nothing happens. They have cleverly cooked up these things like heaven and hell. I don't believe any of it. When you have nobody around to whom you can show your happiness or anger, you can praise or curse God and satisfy yourself."

"I agree with Sarpanch *Sahib*," Charan said. "I don't believe in heaven or hell either. It's like this: Man has this piece of steel working as an engine. If he is missing some screw that machine will stop. In the same way if something goes wrong with our body, it stops. When the engine dies, it doesn't make noise any more. The same with a man's voice. When he dies, it's like you took oil out of an engine. Take it away and, *bas,* it stops."

Old Chanan was gazing off into space. "When you are dead then everything is finished. There can't be anything after death, and yet. . . ." He turned and faced Charan. "Sardarji, there are many mysteries. One night some years ago, when my wife was alive, I was lying awake. It was a cold night but for some reason I had brought my *charpoy* outside to sleep under the stars. My wife told me, 'It's cold. Bolt the door from outside or it flies open.' I told her, 'All right. I'm here if you need me.' I slept and then I awoke. I got up again and looked at the stars. Then I felt something and I turned around and saw my wife. I didn't speak to her. But she appeared to be standing at my bedside looking down. I kept looking at her and wondering how she had come out. Then she went away and I went back to sleep. The next morning, the door was still bolted from outside. My wife told me, 'I was inside all night; I never asked you to open the door.' And after some days she died. I have no superstitions or anything. But I can't explain it. She was alive then. It was no dream. I saw her."

The conversation had grown too gloomy for Charan. "There goes a whirlwind!" he exclaimed. "Now it's going toward the village. It will convey a message to Ghungrali, 'Now you end this boycott and thresh your wheat. Otherwise, I'll destroy it.'" They all turned to watch a spiral cloud of dust twist down the road and flee over the fields, drawing after it bits of straw, insects and feathers. The loose swaths of wheat scattered every which way and as the darkening column rose it lifted several of Dhakel's bales into the air.

"Look! Look how it tosses those bales like feathers!"

"O, that piece of paper! Look how it is going higher and higher in the sky. It's in the whirlwind."

"O, the paper is going higher and higher."

"O, I see it. High as the birds. There it goes."

"It goes toward the village."

"O, look, now it goes toward Bhambadi."

"Yes, I'm also seeing. Now it goes toward Ghungrali again."

"Now leave that paper, boys," old Chanan told them. "It may go up ten miles in the sky. We must go back to work."

Charan laughed. "Someone is waiting for that piece of paper because he has to write a letter."

The old Mazhbi, disturbed by the conversation, studied Charan's face. "Don't you even believe in God?"

Charan shrugged. "Who knows where God lives?" he asked lightly. Then his eyes moved from the faces of Sindar and Gurmel, to the Sarpanch, Sher, old Chanan and all the other Mazhbis, and when they came to rest they seemed to be sparkling with new knowledge. "Maybe God is within all of you," he said.

Sunset was not far away and the dusty evening sky cast a pink glow on the men's sunburnt faces. Old Chanan gave a cry of pleasure as he found an old forked stick he had placed on the side of an irrigation ditch during last year's threshing and had forgotten. Sindar had followed the others to the threshing ground and Chanan told him he had used the stick for pushing wheat into the steel hammers of the thresher after it became dangerous to do it with one's bare hands in the fading light.

"If you're so careful with this one little stick," Sindar told him, "you can save real weapons, spears and knives, for years together." Sindar hung his sickle over his shoulder, kneeled down by the threshed wheat, picked up a handful of kernels and let them sift pleasurably between his fingers.

Old Pritam Singh came across the fields in the gathering dusk. "This machine works well," he told Charan, raising his voice above the roar of the thresher. "Ours is an old one. It can hardly finish in two or three days what you do in a few hours. But here yours is—you have finished almost one acre since midday. Can you thresh for us? We have some bales sitting over there."

"How many are there?"

"About twelve hundred."

"You shouldn't rely on me, Pritamji, because from here I'll have to go to Bhadson and thresh my sister's wheat. After that I can help you but the chances are few that I'll get back before another ten days. You should not depend on me."

"All right." Pritam was weary and confused that evening. He and his sons and laborers had worked hard to cut their wheat; he had always believed in hard physical labor but somehow these days, with all the new methods and machines, a man's willingness to work was no longer enough. "We'll make some other arrangement," he told Charan. "But if you help when you return, my son, that will be good."

The old man moved slowly back to his own fields; Charan felt sorry as he watched him go. He had never known Pritam to utter a harsh or mean word in his life.

Charan took a last look at the threshers before returning to his well where the Sarpanch was waiting with a bottle. He watched old Chanan moving patiently and steadily, pushing the grain into the grinding jaws of the thresher with his fondly rediscovered old stick. Then the tractor engine died and Chanan put down the stick and looked at the sky with an expression of gratitude, as if to say the day, thank God, was over, and he was going to rest. Watching him Charan thought, there may be a heaven and hell or there may not. Who can know? Or does? But one thing seemed to him certain: if there was a heaven, old Chanan was sure to go there.

On his way to the well, Charan told Suka to help the Mazhbis carry the rest of the bales to the threshing machine. The boy grappled with a heavy load, stumbling awkwardly and cursing his father; he almost fell on the bale heap when he went to slide it off his head. Charan felt ashamed of his oldest son, the heir to the fields around him. The Sarpanch called out; he was already rinsing the glasses at the pump and Charan answered in his deep, hoarse voice that if they hurried they might have time to kill a bottle between them before the others came. Soon the workers could hear bursts of Charan's laughter drifting across the darkening fields.

At dusk in Ghungrali-Rajputan and all the other villages on the Punjab Plain, the crows leave the rooftops and barnyards in great cawing flocks for their nighttime roosts in the trees of the fields and the ancient oaks along the Grand Trunk Road. The sun sets, a dusty mist enwraps the earth, and the plain breathes evenly and deeply. The monotonous silence lulls you into peace; you move along in the bullock cart, half-dozing and tired-of-bone, when suddenly, from somewhere, comes the alarmed cry of a bird startled from sleep and you wonder what it is. To the east, all over the horizon, the sky is flushed with reddish light, and it is difficult to tell whether someone is burning a cane field or the moon is preparing to rise. Whitish dust sifts into the gray smoke from village fires, and the whole plain seems to be hidden beneath mist. There is a smell of hay as you ride along, and of dried up grass, scorched by the sun all day. When the moon does rise, the night grows pale and dim and a few last crows caw forlornly overhead.

Old Pritam's bullock cart creaked gently along in the dimness; he sensed why the warm air was so still, as if nature itself was waiting, alert for a storm, and afraid to stir. Pritam was in no hurry and the cart moved slowly, coming abreast of a huddle of dark figures who moved softly and rapidly in their bare feet in the dust. One man walked in front of the others, carrying a small boy in his arms. Several men and women followed him with bundles of freshly-cut grass on their heads. Pritam recognized young Mukhtar, the Chamar.

"It is not good," the old man told him, "the way we are treating each other. But I think it will all be settled very soon."

Mukhtar did not answer. Since he had decided to uproot his family and leave the village, he wanted no sympathy from a Jat; he was determined at least his son would be free of their bondage.

"Now you go to other villages. We mind it very much." The old man's voice quavered. "Look, we have to feed your children. Your daughters are my daughters and your sons, my sons. We must see that they are fed."

"Yes, you are right, *Sardarji,*" Mukhtar said quietly. "But it is written that we should cut the wheat of another village."

"Yes, it is written. But it will be all right in a few more days, my son."

Husen

I V

Husen

PILANGSARI VILLAGE AND

DJAKARTA

JAVA

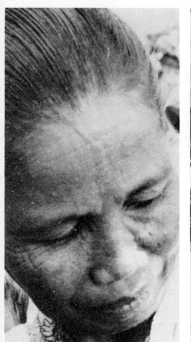

Mother

Father

Abu

I V

T HE GREATEST RISK of deepening disorder today lies in the vast migration of peasants from the countryside to the cities, a stream of the poor
and landless from their familiar, secure villages into squalid urban slums
on a scale unprecedented in history.

The great cities of Asia, Africa and Latin America are coming too
soon. Industry is not drawing the peasants in; agriculture is pushing them
out. Most of these cities have come into being far ahead of economic
development, as ports of colonialist exchange of local natural resources for
Western capital and consumer goods. They are barely part of a modern
urban-industrial system; they do not command enough local savings,
skills and resources to give jobs to all the newly arriving multitudes.
Coming more than a hundred years after the industrialization of the West,
after a further century of technological advance, modern industry provides
less untrained manual work, and, with the necessity for ever higher skills,
has to make an investment in most places of around $2,000 per man, as
opposed to $200, a century ago. In many such cities, an actual majority of
the population are new, young immigrants straight from the villages.
Lacking any skill but that of cultivation of the land, they turn to the kind
of employment which keeps a man from absolute starvation but con-
tributes all but nothing either to the country's development or their own
acquisition of skills and confidence: street vending, petty hawking, shoe
shining, errand running or pedaling a cycle-rickshaw.

They live in great new slum areas surrounding established urban cores,
crumbling ant heaps of anxious people who survive from day to day by
providing each other with the most pitiful goods and services. Often they
confront a scale of misery far worse than anything they left behind in
their villages. In most of these cities, some growing at 8 percent a year,
20 to 40 percent of the labor force is already out of work and the number
of unemployable men is expected to rise 50 to 70 percent in the 1970s and

1980s. For such men and their families, the true population crisis is not in some remote future, but right now.

Our fourth story is about one such man, a peasant who migrated from his Javanese village to the city of Djakarta. After an opening episode which takes place a year earlier, the six-month time frame is from the June rains on through the harvest season and a drought, ending with Lebaran, the Javanese New Year in December. The setting is equally divided between the village and Djakarta.

On the eve of World War II, Djakarta was just a sleepy port city of 400,000 people. It was built on the site of an ancient Javanese fortress of the same name which was chosen as a capital and port by the Dutch in 1619. Their soldiers seized the fortress, burned it and began building the city of Batavia (the name again became Djakarta in 1949), which in time grew to be the main urban center of the Dutch East Indies Empire, and remained, until the Japanese invasion, a Dutch city on the edge of the tropical jungle. Its canals and short bridges and little houses with brown-tiled roofs and diamond-paned windows were built to remind its inhabitants of those they left behind in Holland. Lying at the head of a deep bay sprinkled with almost a thousand tiny islands, Djakarta was an odd choice for a capital, being central neither to Java nor to the 7,900 islands of the Indonesian archipelago. Moreover, it was built on swamp land, and the network of canals which covered the whole city area was really a system of drainage ditches, which in the festering, equatorial heat became breeding grounds for mosquitoes and disease. As the city grew, these ditches, since many people lacked any other source of water, came to answer the need of a place to relieve themselves, wash their bodies and launder their clothes. By the end of the war, Djakarta's population was approaching 600,000; by 1951, fed by a Moslem rebellion against a secular national government, when refugees poured into the city, it reached 1.7 million.

In 1955, when Husen, the central figure in our story, arrived in the city as a sixteen-year-old, Djakarta had just over two million people. Within six years, by 1961, it had reached three million. In late 1970, when Husen turned thirty-one, it passed the five million mark. Aside from a natural growth from births minus deaths of 2.8 percent each year, the city's expanding population was also fed by the arrival of almost 300,000 migrant peasants every twelve months. In fifty years, the mortality rate in Java alone has fallen from thirty deaths per 1,000 to below fifteen. In 1959, there were 57 million Javanese; today there are almost 85 million. They are leaving the land at an accelerating pace of at least 5 percent a year, mostly for Djakarta and a few other cities. Inundated by this flood, Djakarta seems less an ordinary city than a vast conglomeration of *atap*-roofed, bamboo kampongs, held together by a network of crumbling, often dirt, roads. There are, to be sure, aside from the old Dutch city, many towering new glass and concrete hotels and office buildings, broad new boulevards and sprawling residential areas with big solid houses resting in walled gardens. These belong to the 15 percent of the population which pays property taxes, drinks purified water, gets electricity and public schooling. The rest of the population—4.5 million men, women and children—pretty much do without.

The most common occupation of newly arrived peasant immigrants has been driving a cycle-rickshaw or pedicab, which the Indonesians call a *betjak*. In the past two decades, the number has grown from about 30,000 to 150,000, and since most are driven in shifts, as many as 300,000 to 400,000 men may depend on *betjak* driving for their income. If one includes their families, the *betjak* may provide the livelihoods for a million people or one-fifth of Djakarta's population. Like other poor immigrants, the *betjak* drivers have not only a hard physical struggle to make their living, but they exist in shantytowns without sewage disposal, reliable water supplies or electricity. Add to such conditions concepts of congestion, pollution, crime, race and cultural polarization, feelings of alienation and claustrophobia, and the emergence of an entirely new kind of urban society is to be apprehended—one lacking social and spiritual balance.

When they arrive in Djakarta, as in other great urban centers in the poor two-thirds of the world, most peasant migrants are gentle men and women, plain, straight and conservative with traditional cultural and material drives. They want to stay home in their villages, cultivating a few acres of land near the burial grounds of their ancestors, building homes and raising their children in peace. They believe in a society concerned with mutual cooperation where each has his part to play in the organic whole. Village life is governed in harmony with the seasons; disaster, such as illness, death, flood or earthquake, is accepted as the lot of all creation. And as each person grows up, he creates an inner picture in his mind of his own place, his relationship with others in the village and the world outside, all securely balanced so that he feels an overriding sense of being bound into a community whose common task goes on forever.

In the city, old ties and traditions snap. The immigrant is faced with the enormous compulsion of working out new relationships, new meanings to his life. He may come to have a nagging wonder over what he is really living for, or become totally alienated and slip into crime or violence. Or he may come to see the distinction between life on the land and in the city as close to the primordial distinction between good and evil, between the unnaturalness and inhumanness of urbanity on the one hand and the simplicity and truth of village life on the other. Then he will see a return to the land as his only salvation.

IT WAS TWILIGHT. A misty rain, the last of the afternoon's monsoon storm, gently drifted down in the halos of the street-stall lamps along Djalan Thamrin. Water glistened on the pavement, on the soaked canvas hoods of the line of *betjaks* and on the lean, hard-muscled shoulders of their drivers. Welcome Circle seemed to be washed clean by the storm. Water streamed down the rusted girders of a half-built skyscraper, surged through the open drainage canals and splashed under the tires of the gathering evening traffic. Everything seemed wet: hedges, palms, buildings and people dripped with rain. The rain had washed away the oppressive heat and fumes of the day, and the air smelled of freshness, frangipani and jasmine, and the sweet, peculiarly East Indian odor of clove-spiced cigarettes. A shiny black car with a diplomatic flag splashed past the row of *betjaks* to the hotel entrance, the pale colored lights on the hotel's open terraces grew brighter, and the drumbeat of a dance band could be heard.

As the rain let up, the *betjak* drivers moved about, brown faces beaming and white teeth flashing as they joked with one another. One, Husen, did not join in but sat under the dripping hood of his *betjak's* upholstered seat, mounted on its bicycle base. Bareheaded, barelegged and without shoes, his shorts and shirt torn and soaking wet, he stayed motionless. Even if the sky opened up again with a torrent, it seemed as if he would not stir. He had not moved his *betjak* from its place in line for a long while; he had pedaled here before evening prayers and, up to now, had not had a fare.

"*Betjak! Betjak!*"

Several drivers, seeing guests come from the hotel, pushed their *betjaks* toward them, smiling eagerly.

"Hello, mister! Where are you going?"

Husen pulled out a crumpled packet of *kretek* cigarettes and hunched over to light one. He inhaled deeply, keeping the clove-scented smoke in the hollow of his chest and then blowing it through his nostrils, slowly, as if to draw warmth into his body. A vendor came up to the *betjak* stand knocking a hollow bamboo stick on a piece of wood. He balanced two heavy tin cans suspended from a bamboo pole and moved with short, quick dance steps, swinging one arm lustily and using the other to keep his shoulder pole in balance. He set his burden on the sidewalk, opened the cans and spread out a food counter of shredded cabbage, tomatoes, pieces of chicken, boiled rice, jars of spices, noodles and white china bowls. *Betjak* drivers crowded around him, squatting on their haunches to eat; it seemed to Husen he could taste the spicy soup. His stomach rumbled with hunger and he puffed furiously on this *kretek*. All around him the evening activity was beginning: a steady flow of guests, orchestra players, guards, servants flowed past, in and out of the hotel drive. Two Dutch women came out and Husen called "Always tired, madam. If take *betjak* not." But they wanted to walk and it was some time before a soldier came up and climbed into his vehicle.

"Where are you going, *Bapak?*"

"Only over there. To Blora." Husen lifted the *betjak,* wheeled it around on its back tires and mounted his leather perch behind his passenger. He pedaled briskly, his knees pointing outward and his hands clasping the handles on the back of the seat; the entire chassis, passenger and all, had to be rotated to steer, and it took strength. Just a few hundred yards and Husen had to dismount and push the *betjak* up an incline.

"Where the devil are you going, stupid fool?" the soldier exclaimed. "Go under the bridge." Husen turned the *betjak* around, just missing a man on a motor scooter, who skidded on the wet pavement and cursed him. A pedestrian, hurrying across the road, bumped his leg against the *betjak's* wet tires and looked at Husen angrily as he brushed off his pants.

"You do not know how to drive!" the soldier complained. "If there's an accident, what then?" They entered the darkness below a bridge; voices called to them from the shadows: "Hello, hello, uncle, you like to go *pooki-pooki,* you like come sleep my house?" "Hey,

Husen, have no money!" The soldier laughed. Seeing his passenger in better humor, Husen moved his lips but only a choked sigh came out.

"What?" the soldier asked harshly.

Husen twisted his mouth and grinned nervously from ear to ear. With an effort over his labored breathing, he said hoarsely, "I am sorry, *Pak,* because my boy—my baby son—he is not here. Excuse me. I beg your pardon, *Pak.* It was God who took my boy away and I cannot complain. I mean, what could I do anyway? Excuse me, *Pak,* excuse me. My son died this week."

"What did he die of?"

Husen leaned forward in his seat. "Maybe fever and influenza. He was sick a week and then died. . . . I took him to the doctor for an injection and then home to my village and he died. . . . *Inallillahi Wainna llilla hi Roziun.* God's will be done."

The *betjak* hit a pothole in the road, jolting the soldier. "Watch out! Fool! Have you not eyes?" Husen apologized and dismounted to lift the *betjak* wheels out of the hole. "Go on, go on," the soldier fretted, "hurry a bit." He feared the *betjak* driver was preparing to ask for extra money and he turned squarely to the front until they reached his destination. When they did, the soldier handed Husen a ten rupiah note.

"Wah. Not enough!" Husen protested.

"Why not enough?" the soldier bellowed threateningly, and Husen begged his pardon. "You don't be angry with me, *Pak.* All right, you haven't money, okay? I am sorry."

Husen pedaled quickly to a tea stall, sat himself in his *betjak* and stared up at the trees. Why? Why? he asked himself. My little boy was not bad. He had done no wrong. So clean and white and big and healthy with a long nose like a Dutchman's. Why should he die so young? He was but a year old. In the village Karniti had cried all week, she did not sleep or eat or anything. If I can earn money for the prayer ceremonies, ten, twelve thousand rupiah, I go back to the village. He sat numb and in silence. An hour passed, and another. . . .

Along the road, with laughter and curses came three foreign sailors. All three climbed in the *betjak,* jostling each other, abusing, joking and trying to sit at once. Husen heard the abuse, listened to their jokes and little by little the feeling of loneliness left him. He had to strain to pedal but he did not mind, to him it was all the same now, as long as he had passengers and was kept busy taking them around.

After midnight, Husen pedaled back to a *betjak* shed in Pedjompogan where he had slept since he took Karniti and the baby to his village. He took off his shirt and the five pairs of short, tight pants he wore to prevent a hernia, and wrapped on a loose sarong. He could not sleep, and smoked a clove-spiced *kretek*. Out of the two hundred rupiah he had earned that day, twenty went for a single plate of rice with vegetable soup poured over it, ten for coffee and a fried yam, and forty for a fresh packet of "Djinggo" *kreteks*. Eighty more went as rent to the *betjak* owner. This left him possessed of just a hundred rupiah—a long way from the ten thousand he needed for his son's death rites.

The bamboo shed had a red-tile *atap* roof, earthen floor and bamboo walls; it was only ten by fifteen feet, and the entire space was filled with sleeping *betjak* drivers, sarong-wrapped and bare-chested like Husen, with their arms and legs entangled and their bodies so closely packed the air was thick and suffocatingly hot. Husen listened to the sleepers, heard some of them groan and cough or gnash their teeth as Javanese do in their sleep; he scratched himself where a flea had bitten, and regretted having returned so early.

He went out into the fresh night air and sat smoking, thinking it would be a week since his son died, and although he tried to be *iklas,* the desired Javanese state of willed affectlessness, he had not been able to speak to anyone about it properly since he had come back to the city. One would have to tell it slowly and carefully; the baby was his third child and the second to die when a year old. His only son now lived with a divorced wife and the baby would have been the first in his marriage with Karniti, who had already had a miscarriage. But the baby fell ill, he suffered fever and he died. One needed to describe the visit to the city doctor for injections, the journey home to the village when these failed, the trip to the *dukun* or witch doctor and the details of the funeral. Karniti stayed in the village while he came back to the city to find money. One would have to tell about her too.

When the baby died, he took it from Karniti's arms and held it on his own lap to wash it and wrap it in fresh linen and carry it to the graveyard. He laid his little boy on his side, loosened the strings of the shroud and turned the face so that the pale cheek touched the earth. The priest stepped into the grave, kneeled down and whispered the confession of faith three times in the dead child's ear: "O, you who are already living in the world of the grave. . . .O, my child, you now know that the angels do exist, that life beyond the grave does exist, that the balancing of good and evil deeds does exist, that heaven and hell do exist and that the Lord Allah will wake each one in the grave on Judgment Day."

Some months later Husen returned to the village with the ten thousand rupiah. It was enough to pay for all the needed *slametan* ceremonies, including the last, which the Javanese believe marks the time when the body has decayed entirely to dust.

A year afterward. Around nine o'clock one evening, Husen, with some other young men, was riding in the baggage rack of a decrepit red and yellow passenger bus on the Djakarta-Tjirebon highway. The wind was cold and the roof piled high with tin suitcases and fraying wicker baskets, but Husen did not mind. He would soon reach the market town of Djatibarang after a 208-kilometer ride, and from there it was only three more to Pilangsari, his village. He enjoyed the sensation of being free, of rushing through space, and the rough jokes of the young men who preferred to brave the cold wind and the jolts through the sudden potholes rather than sit for hours inside the cramped hot bus. The reeling trip took five hours, but once outside the city nature was beautiful. Everything was green, every shade of green, and there were reds and yellows too. All along the narrow highway were houses, some of stone but most of whitewashed bamboo; their picket fences seemed to stretch in an almost unbroken line all the way back to Djakarta. The houses all had red-tile *atap* roofs, else they would be flooded in the daily downpours. They were surrounded by trees: fat, stumpy banana trees with wide, fibrous foliage; palm trees, some low, some soaring up fifty feet, clean and straight as telephone poles with towering crowns of outstretched branches; clumps of feathery bamboo, their green trunks leaning against one another; mimosa bushes hung with golden balls. Sometimes there was a big *waringin* tree, what the Hindus call the banyan, its trunk of great height and width, from which the branches reached downward to implant themselves in the earth, take root and shoot up again.

The highway was choked with traffic: cars, buses, trucks, scooters, bicycles, *betjaks*. Once darkness fell, the bamboo shacks along the road were lit with kerosene lamps, orange glows that gave the countryside a mysterious, enchanted look. In some villages, crowds had gathered for a shadow play or musical performance and for a few yards the road would be lined with stalls selling tea, coffee, cakes and *kretek* cigarettes.

The driver stopped the bus in the dimly-lit bazar of Djatibarang and Husen scrambled down the ladder; he carried no baggage—he had left his *betjak* clothes back in the shed at Pedjompogan. Husen hated encumbrances of any kind; only a toothbrush was in his pocket. Now he walked home; it was dark at first on the country road, most of the lamps were already extinguished. But soon everything was visible in the moonlight, although it was difficult to make out the colors and features of objects. All around were only trees, fields and a star-filled sky, but things looked different from what they were.

From somewhere came the sound of birds, interfering with each other's sleep. Husen trudged along, moving faster, and suddenly he could see standing before him on the side of the road a silhouette resembling that of a man; it stood motionless, waiting and holding something in its hand. The figure approached, got taller and was now in line with him, and Husen discovered it was not a human being at all but a lonely bush. Similar motionless shapes dotted the rice paddies, peeped out from behind the leaves of banana trees, hid behind the huts and mango groves; they all had a resemblance to people or ghosts and filled him with suspicions and fears since other *betjak* men had been set upon when returning with money from the city. Husen left the road, crossing a small footbridge over a canal, and followed a path along the edge of a mango grove. Ahead, almost hidden in its clearing among the mangos and banana trees, appeared a bamboo cottage with shuttered windows. Somewhat to one side a woeful little pond was discernible; beside it drooped some somnolent little papaya trees, barren of fruit. Otherwise nothing else was to be seen or heard near the house except the cicadas out on the pale open expanse of rice paddy behind him, resembling, in the night, a great body of water like an open sea.

Hardly had Husen called out, *"Ma! Ma!"* then there was a sound of glad voices from the house—one was a woman's, the other a man's; a bolt was pulled back, a swing door gave a squeak and in another moment a tall, spare figure stood by Husen, holding his hands and uttering a prayer. His father was completely bald and wore only a pair of loose pajama trousers; he seemed very joyful to see his son again. Husen took his father's right hand in both of his own and bowed deeply.

"Please, inside," his father said, as Husen's mother and a younger brother, Tarja, rushed out. After greeting them, Husen asked, "Where is my wife?"

His father told him Karniti had gone across the river to Karang-getas village to spend the night with her parents. He dismissed the subject at once, asking Husen if he had been well in Djakarta, how was his health? Husen suspected the old man or his mother had again found fault with Karniti, as they often did. As his mother went to fetch hot coffee, he asked if the river boatman had gone to sleep. His father said he had and they went outside to sit under the stars on the worn bamboo bench that was always there.

For some time they sat in silence. Husen wondered if he should wake the boatman; there had been ill will between his parents and Karniti since the baby's death; they feared his marriage might now be without issue. A lizard shrieked from its perch in a banana tree. "Gecko! Gecko! Gecko!" There was another cry from the blackness of the garden: "Knick knack, knick, knack."

"Oh, maybe a ghost," said Husen's mother, bringing them glasses of steaming, sugary coffee. "No, that is only a turtle or frog," said the father.

"In Djatibarang a small baby has died every day this week," the mother said emphatically. "I have heard many ghosts of children calling in the night. Over there where the trees are thick, many, many people are hearing ghosts these days."

"There were some in the banana grove behind our house," his father told Husen. "Tarja went there at night to relieve himself and saw the earth rising like a geyser."

Out of the darkness several figures appeared, startling the family. But they were only village youths who went about at night playing their guitars, singing the bittersweet songs of Tjirebon, or telling *dongeng,* or folktales, sleeping only when it suited their fancy. Some-times the young men of the village would stay up all night and then swim in the Tjimanouk River at dawn to revive themselves before going to work in the fields. Like all young Javanese, they slept remarkably little. Djuned, Husen's best friend in the village, was with them, and after greeting the family he suggested Husen tell a ghost story. Husen chuckled in self-deprecation, but the others joined in, "*Trus, trus,* let's go, let's go, tell us, Husen."

The lamplight cast a flickering halo over the group, which huddled together, sitting on the earth around the bamboo bench. Outside the orange circle of light the world looked dark and impenetrable, and a restless wind rustled the banana leaves with an eerie whispering sound. Husen forgot about fetching his wife as the youths edged in closer.

He described an episode that had taken place late at night in Djakarta many years before. He was pedaling along Djalan Palam street in the Menteng district about midnight and saw a girl standing under some trees. He thought, "What is this nice girl doing here?" He called, "Where are you going, Miss?" but she said nothing, just gestured down the street. He could smell her perfume.

"Why, Miss, are you out so late?" he asked. "No taxi now. It is after midnight." She said nothing but took a seat in his *betjak,* and when he asked, "Where are you going, left or right?" she only pointed to the right, to Djalan Djawa. "Where are you going?" he kept asking but she would only point, directing him down Gredja Theresia Street, into August Salim and then to Djalan Thamrin and beyond to Djalan Wahid Asim, a dark slum area.

Husen gradually became fearful and asked loudly, "Miss, where are you going?" but she said not a word. So he pedaled through Tanah Abang and after Tanah Abang up the steep hill past the marketplace.

"There is a big bridge there and usually I must get off and push. But now I feel very strong. I am very happy driving. It is very easy. I am not tired. And after Djembatan Tinggi, I think, oooh, this is very nice girl. Maybe she like with me. So I reach out and touch her shoulder and . . . aaggghhh! . . . my hand goes right through her!"

Husen's audience drew nearer, apprehensively edging away from the rustle in the banana leaves.

"Oh, I can see, I can see. But I cannot feel her. So the hairs on the back of my neck become stiff and I see we are passing Kober Djatipetamburan, the biggest cemetery in Djakarta. Now I hear the gong of another *betjak* behind me. Brr-r-r-ring! Br-r-r-r-ring! Like that. And I turn my head around to look but there is no *betjak* there. Nothing. Nobody in the street. And when I turn back again the girl is gone. I not stop. She cannot jump down. She is just vanish. Wah! I think, this is *kuntil anak!*" He used the Javanese word for the ghost of a harlot. Husen told them he then jumped down, lifted the *betjak* in the air to turn it around, and pedaled back to the stand at the Hotel Indonesia as fast as he could.

But he said nothing of the episode to anyone, since it brought bad luck to tell anyone of seeing a *kuntil anak*. Instead, for a week he was very lucky and had many customers. Then one evening he could not resist, and told some friends. They said many *betjak* drivers in Djakarta had seen such ghosts.

One said, "Husen, if you can pull one hair from the head of a *kuntil anak* it is very lucky; you will get rich." So the next time he picked up a girl late at night he reached out and grabbed her hair.

"But this girl screamed," he told the youths. "She is very angry with me, and says, 'Why you grab me like that? I'll call the police!' So I tell her the story and she is all right again and not cry for the police or anything. So after that if I take a nice girl at night, I don't grab them but just try to pull out one hair. You know, if we go fast and the girl's hair flies out, I move my hands a little on the back of the *betjak* and try to catch one hair. Always I keep trying. I think, yah, if ghost, one hair will I get; I will be lucky and get rich. So when a girl passenger's hair flies, I pull out one. If she screams I think, 'Wah! This is girl, not ghost' and I say, 'Oh, very, very sorry, Miss. Your hair is flying in the wind and it catch where my hand holds the side of the *betjak*.' But there is that lucky chance also. So I keep trying until now. If I carry nice girl late at night."

"Go on, go on, Husen," the youths cried, when he finished.

"Yah, tell us more about your life as *betjak* man in Djakarta."

"Oh, yah, it is only a routine," said Husen, pleased. He jumped to his feet, tore off a banana leaf and brought it back to sit on, dusting off the seat of his pants. "You want to hear about men going to the moon? Okay, I tell you the history. The first time there were three men in a rocket. Their name is Astronaut."

"Oh, Husen, what is the meaning, Astronaut?"

"Oh, three men inside the rocket and they are heroes. And they are all clever men. Maybe professors and so on. You see, the United States country is modern country. And American people, they want to try everything. Maybe these Americans they want to try going to the moon and the Mars and the other things in the sky. Maybe they want the same like with God. All the time try."

"That is, Astronaut not eat, not drink in rocket?"

"Maybe bring food in rocket and maybe bring air to the moon."

"Oh, very far, very far."

"No, Husen, in the moon is only one woman, Njitawok and her cat. Because if I look from here, I see Njitawok give food to the cat."

"No. No Njitawok. No trees. No water. After come to the moon, Astronaut jumps, but must slowly. Many dust over there and many big holes."

"Is that not hot place, the moon?"

"Yah, Husen, because from here it gives much light."

"Oh, because from sunlight. Look at a mirror. If you put it in front of a lamp you can see light."

" 'Sen, if the moon turns over, why the Astronaut he don't fall off?"

"Look here." Husen rose and went to dip a pail into the pond, filling it with water. He came back and swung it over the heads of his friends in a sweeping circle. "If you spin, it goes to the bottom, not fall down. People are like this, stay like this. Because there is a magnet in the center of the earth. Because go very quickly."

"Okay, go on, 'Sen. *Trus, trus.* Give us another history. Another history about Djakarta."

"Okay, yah, I have one more. I hear there is restaurant under the ocean. Maybe from Japanese. He want to make restaurant like that."

The youths laughed. One protested, "Oh, not! Restaurant under the ocean. The water go inside and the people eat over there die."

"No, no, very large. Maybe one hundred meters. Maybe the restaurant is made from steel. So the big fish don't hit the side. Maybe the people who eat in that restaurant seeing fish. Very happy. Looking left and right. You can go. Very happy. In Japan."

The youths kept wanting to hear more about life in Djakarta and Husen warned them new arrivals must be careful; they should look for a *betjak* driver from Tjirebon. He told them not to accept cigarettes from strangers since they might contain some drug like opium or morphine.

"Much money over there, 'Sen?" someone asked.

Husen laughed. "Okay, yah, if you not like me, okay, maybe much money also."

His father sighed. "I forget everything about Djakarta. It was a long time ago. I left Djatibarang by truck and came to some place. Cars and people going every direction. . . . It was confusing."

Husen warned them that if they arrived at the central railway station not to take a bus or truck but find a Tjirebon *betjak* driver first. "Find a Tjirebon man and have him take you to Thamrin or Harmonie or Banteng Bus Station. Then you can find bus. Sometimes maybe if you take bus from the railway station you can get robbed. Not for sure. Maybe. You must stay with friends at first in Djakarta. You must stay with me if first time coming."

Husen's father quietly slipped off to bed; seeing him go the youths begged Husen to tell them a *dongeng* or folk story. Djuned joked, "Oh, 'Sen, if you tell many history you are quickly old."

Husen laughed. "Maybe you like to hear about the Monkey and the Turtle?" And be began:

Once there was a Turtle; he have plenty of banana trees. And from the ground the ripe bananas are too high to reach. The Turtle is confused because he cannot climb the trees. He wants to pick the bananas but he cannot reach them. Too high.

Along comes Monkey, walking by the Turtle. And the Monkey looked at the Turtle staying under the trees and the Monkey says, "Why you stay over there, Turtle?"

The Turtle says, "Monkey, can you help me pick these bananas?"

The Monkey says, "All right. I want to pick the bananas." And the Monkey climbs the tree and picks the bananas but he doesn't bring them down. He only sits there and eats them.

And the Turtle says, "What is, Monkey?"

The Monkey says, "Here. Watch out! *Awas!*" But instead of dropping the bananas the Monkey answers the call of nature.

The Turtle calls again. "Where is, Monkey?"

"Over there! Over there! Black ones!"

"Oh," says the Turtle, "you cheated me. This is not bananas." And the Turtle runs to the river.

The Monkey too goes to swim in the river and he gets very cold and wet. And he comes up on the sand and wants to find the Turtle but he doesn't see. Instead he finds a *djengkok,* or footstool with a handle on it, and sits down. And he calls to the Turtle, "Turtle! Turtles!" And the Turtle answers in his high, squeaky voice, *"Tinul, tinul"*—for that is the sound the Turtle makes—"yes, Monkey?"

And the Monkey, hearing the voice come from under him, says, "Aw, goddam, bloody this is, my pipe has answered!" The Monkey thinks his pipe has answered because he doesn't know he is sitting on the Turtle's shell. And the Monkey runs and takes a stone and bangs it down on his pipe. "Aagggghh! Eeeoweeyeow!" goes Monkey, and he falls down, losing his senses.

And the Turtle comes running and says, "What happened to you, Monkey?" "Aw," says Monkey, "I faint because I just hit my pipe. Because I banged it with a stone for it was talking."

And the Turtle says, "Oh, Monkey, it was not your pipe that answered you. I am under you. You sit on my shell and think it is a *djengkok.* You call me and I answer, *'Tinul, tinul.'*"

"Yes," Turtle went on wisely, "you are an animal. I am an animal. So don't you lie to your fellow animals. Are you not forget before? I tell you to give me bananas but you play trick. Now you get your turn."

"Oh, yes," said Monkey in a small voice.

"So that is story of Monkey," Husen chuckled to his audience, which still sat with rapt attention. "Finish."

But they begged him to go on. So through the night, acting out all the parts with animation and sometimes breaking into laughter in his enjoyment, Husen kept his friends entertained. He told them about Koler, a luckless carpenter whose pipe became a hundred meters long while making love to a mosquito goddess, and how, while he was swimming in a river, it got hard and crossed to the other side where the king's daughter was bathing. When she had a baby and Koler, only a poor man, presented himself as the father, he was put to sea in a drum by an evil demon who himself tried to marry the princess, until Koler, now transformed into a handsome noble named Vijayakushuma and his pipe returned to normal size, appeared to rescue her in a happily-ever-after ending.

When the youths pressed him for more, Husen related how

Tangkuban Prau Mountain was formed by an upturned boat kicked over by a furious prince who fell in love with his mother but could not marry her; about a foolish Egyptian king who was always out-witted by his lazy son-in-law; and when he could remember no more folk tales, about once riding in the elevator in Djakarta's Hotel Indonesia.

As the sky began to lighten in the east, Husen saw most of his audience had nodding heads and drooping eyelids. The air seemed warmer and there was a scent of green grass wet with dew.

"Better a swim in the river," Husen suggested and in a moment all the young men were running through the garden, leaping over ditches, jostling and kicking clods of earth at each other and pulling off all their clothes as they scrambled down the steep, high river bank. Some small children were already bathing on the opposite bank; they squealed with delight when Husen dove toward them, splashing and calling "Whoever can catch me can ride on my shoulders!" With some boys chasing him, Husen swam to the middle of the river, waded onto a sandbar and waved his arms like a giant. A tiny boy across the water shrieked with alarm and ran to hide behind his mother who was beating some clothes near the water's edge.

"Hey, where you come from?" called the child, reappearing but clutching his mother's sarong tightly.

Husen shouted back in a gruff giant's voice, "I haven't village. Can I sleep in your house?"

"No, no! You're a *tjulik!*" cried the little boy, accusing Husen of being a demon the Javanese believe kidnaps and decapitates little boys. "If I cannot sleep in your house I will bring you to the center of the river where it's deep."

"Please!" the tiny boy dared him. "Come on!" But when Husen dove toward him and disappeared under water, the child shrieked again and tugged at his mother's sarong. Husen surfaced close to him and thundered in a monster's voice, *"Awas!* Watch out! I'll carry you away to my village."

"I'm not afraid," said the child, adding as if in proof of his courage, "I go with my mother to the market in Djatibarang." Husen dove again and this time emerged from the water very near with a great splash, this time frightening the boy, who turned and ran up the bank. *"Hai! Hai!"* Husen laughed and went back to join

234]

his friends, who were already drying off again. The light of the
sun now made its appearance on the treetops of Karanggetas across
the river, and in the blue distance Husen could just see the sacred
volcano, Mount Tjiremai, fifty miles away. As he watched, a broad
streak of yellow light slipped through the banana trees, glittered on
the river water, rose up to touch the bank on his side, and suddenly
the sun itself appeared in the highest mango branches, sending
shafts of light everywhere. His friends went home for morning tea,
and Husen had started up the bank toward his house when he saw
Karniti. She was waiting for him. "When did you come?" she asked
when he reached her.

"Last night. You were gone."

"Yes. I'm sorry. I took my mother some tea and sugar."

"You don't stay there, Kar."

"I wanted to see my parents, Husen."

In her flowered sarong, her shoulders bare and her long black
hair hanging loosely, Karniti still looked as she had on their wedding
day four years before. She was only fifteen then, almost a child.
Husen was twelve years older.

"I watched you with that little boy, Husen. Our son would have
been that age."

"Kar, you don't speak like that!"

"One of your mother's kittens died yesterday. I was cooking. It
was sick and sleeping on some straw by the fire. I looked to see if it
was breathing and it was. I looked again a few minutes later and it
was dead. Its life was just snuffed out."

"When?"

"Last evening."

"I was making food and all the kittens came and there were only
three. That's how I found the sick one."

"If it was already dead its mother would have come to protect
its body."

"Yes. She came afterward. . . . You came last night? Why did you
not come across the river? You maybe have another girl?"

Husen started to walk toward the house. She followed him. "No,
Kar, I got here late yesterday. The boatman was asleep. I'd had to
wait a long time for a bus; and we sat up all night telling stories.
Ask Djuned. So I am only sitting in front of the house all night,

speaking with my friends. I haven't another girl. Why, every day in Djakarta I am only going to drive the *betjak* and finish and go home. Why you think always I am having another girl?"

When she didn't answer Husen stopped and turned around and saw she had tears in her eyes. She put her hand on his arm. "Oh, Husen, I want something to do in the village. I want something to do."

"Why you not wanting to go back to Djakarta with me? I must go thère to make money. Now we have a better room there."

She did not answer.

"Okay, what do you want to do?"

She spoke as if she had memorized the words. "I would like a small *warung* by the road, a little shop to sell ice and tea and cigarettes and food."

"Better you going to Djakarta."

She said nothing.

"Okay, Kar, waiting. Maybe I'll have money next time."

Karniti took a few steps away from him and leaned against the green trunk of a small palm tree. "In Djakarta, I have nothing to do. I'm getting older, Husen. Perhaps I could make my life better. I want to take a new step. To build a new life."

Husen fumbled for words. "I know, Kar, I know. Actually, I, too, am in trouble and I'm confused. My son by Taminah is seven now and I've got to find money for his circumcision ceremony. And he's growing up with all those gamblers and whores in Bongkaren and he doesn't even go to school."

"Bring Rustani here with me."

"He won't leave his mother. You know how he cried all the time when we had him here before, even when we had plenty rice and mangoes. And I have my own life to worry about. We haven't money, Kar. Wait for some time."

Her voice was toneless. "Better you go now, work in the fields for your father." She turned and walked quickly away from the river. Husen watched her disappear into the green shadows of his father's orchard. He felt resentful over her increasingly frequent accusations that he had other women. He wondered if she was getting too deeply involved in the life of the village. The suspicion crossed his mind that she had found someone else. It did not occur to him that ever since her miscarriage and then the death of their baby boy, Karniti was haunted by the fear that he would leave her if she could not give him sons.

> *The* betjak *"boys" are Indonesians in their twenties or*
> *thirties who will probably die young.*
> —*Louis Fischer in "The Story of Indonesia"*
>
> *A* betjak *driver is like a buffalo. A buffalo is kicked*
> *by a man but a* betjak *driver is kicked by money.*
> —*Husen's father*

As a young landless peasant, Husen's father had once been ambitious to educate his children; after a hard day's labor in the fields, he had carried bananas into Djatibarang to sell in the marketplace each evening. Over the years, saving every penny and raising and selling mangoes, sugar cane, *srikaya* and *kadongdong* fruit, he was able eventually to buy almost one hectare of rice land. But only Husen, of his nine surviving children, reached high school. And Husen was his father's gravest disappointment.

In 1955, when Husen was sixteen and in a year would complete a government scholarship in teacher's training in the district capital of Indramaju, his father received a letter from the school superintendent: "Your son has been absent without permission for four days. If he withdraws you will be held accountable for the seven thousand rupiahs paid him under his scholarship the past three years."

Such a sum meant financial ruin; he would have had to sell his land to raise it, so the father hastened to Indramaju. "In one year my son has spent only one month in my house," he declared to the school superintendent. "It is the duty of the teachers to take care of the pupils. So it is not my fault if Husen has done something wrong."

"Well, what do you think?" the father was asked. "Should we carry on another year with Husen?"

"It is up to you."

"He cannot live in the dormitory any longer. Your son is a wild boy; he is a bad influence."

"I have no money to put him up with a family."

"Then he is automatically released."

"Let me see him first," the father asked. He searched Indramaju for the boy, finding him at the house of a distant relative, lying on a mat, defiantly smoking a *kretek* cigarette and steadfastly refusing to return to school. "I am ashamed, father," Husen said. "I failed my examinations in algebra and geometry. When I saw the results posted I ran away. I won't go back. I don't want to see my friends. . . . I never go again. . . . Better I go home to my village. . . . If it is like this, to be a teacher, better I am a farmer."

His father did not know what to say; the family's hopes had rested on Husen. And now this. "All right, if you like. Please. It is up to you. If you want you can become a stupid boy. But if you want to be a gentleman, and be high peoples, you must return to school. Then you will not be like other people in the village. You will have a good job, good work. Only labor with fountain pen. You will not always be tired like a cultivator. You will sit and write and wear white clothes.

At home his mother wept. "If you ran away from school, why you not tell your father? Do you like to spend your life in hard labor? To toil in the fields and always be tired the rest of your life?"

Anguished, Husen lashed back, "All right! If my parents are all the time angry with me, all the time shouting at me, I will go away. I want going to everywhere, to see many places, to make many friends in my life. I not want to be teacher, always books and papers, quickly become old. I want to see everything, to try everything in my life, Mother. I want going away."

"Oh, Husen," his mother cried. "You won't listen to your parents. Don't you even believe in God?"

"Where is God?" he shouted back at her. "I don't know. Maybe in myself." Husen ran to the fields. He told his father, "I want going to Djakarta."

His father had feared this was coming. "Do you know Djakarta? No, my son. What work would you do there? You do not even have relatives there. Better you stay home with your family." The father was silent for a long time, thinking. Then he took Husen's right hand in both of his own and told him, "If you want to go to the city, go ahead with my blessing, my son. But you must make three promises to me, promises you will never break in the many years ahead."

"Yes, father."

"First, you must be a good man. You don't be a thief; you don't rob; and you don't become a pickpocket, even if you have to starve. Second, you don't forget your parents. If you have money, you must help your parents. And third, you must look for many, many friends in Djakarta. The city is dangerous but if you have many friends it will help you. I hope all goes well with you, my son."

The train fare was eighteen rupiah; his father gave him thirty. He joined a friend, Supardi, who was two years older and sometimes went to Djakarta to sell rice; they found a place to stay near the Hotel Duta in the old Dutch city with a poor shopkeeper from Tegal in central Java, a bamboo shack divided into three cubicles with a dirt floor. In one the shopkeeper and his family slept, keeping their few clothes and possessions in a small tin trunk; a tiny kitchen barely had room for a pot on a primus stove and a bag of rice; in the third cell-like cubicle Husen and Supardi slept on a bamboo floor mat, hanging their clothes on nails. There was no electricity nor water; coconut oil lamps were used at night, and Husen had to bathe, relieve himself and wash his laundry in a brown, sludgy canal along the nearest road. There was no place else to go. Accustomed to the privacy of a banana-leaf privy at home, Husen never got over the shame of having to defecate in view of others at the canal; even fifteen years later he would pedal long distances in his *betjak* to find an overgrown pasture or grove of trees on the city's outskirts where he could go unobserved.

He soon discovered that most of the peasants who came to seek jobs in Djakarta lived in much worse conditions than they had in their villages. At first he was shocked by the pall of smoke from cooking pots, the mile after mile of narrow alleys snaking through densely-packed bamboo shacks, the slippery stairways carved from mud on the canal banks, the potholes, the rubbish everywhere, the skinny chickens picking in the dirt, the multitudes of nearly naked children, hair matted, legs spindly, skins festering with yaws or scabies, the pathetic lines of torn and ragged garments hanging up to dry. He soon learned these were not the worst places in Djakarta; deep in the city were twisting, secret lanes where young girls, lice-ridden, their faces caked with cheap yellowish powder, could be had for a pittance; where men smoked *ganja* and opium and used morphine from dawn on through the day, and where, in sudden moments of frightfulness, pain and loss, life ended with a knife in the ribs. Gradually Husen, like the other rural migrants, got used to the danger, the infested shacks, the rats in the yards, the bugs falling from broken roofs, the floods of muddy water after rains, and the sour smell of poverty that seemed to cling to the poor of the great city.

Husen could not find a job but stayed alive by helping his landlord in his small shop in exchange for rice two times a day. Within a month, his friend Supardi disappeared. He had borrowed fifty thousand rupiah from the rice merchants in Djatibarang. All Husen knew was that Supardi started out for the village one morning and was never seen again. His parents came to Djakarta looking for him and even went to the police. Some believed the Darul Islam Moslem rebels, rank-Communist terrorists from the forest near Djatibarang, had seized him, forced him to become a guerrilla, and that he was killed in a fight with government soldiers. People said, "Supardi is dead," but no one ever knew for certain. Other villagers had vanished in Djakarta without a trace.

Three months after he left home, Husen wrote his father he had a job as "a clerk in a Bombay firm." Had his father gone to Djakarta to see for himself, he would have found a squalid, ill-lit office near Pasar Senen, the city's central market place, with an imposing sign in English hung over the door: "Tarachand Company and Krishna Ltd." At two shabby desks sat Tarachand himself, a skinny bespectacled little Gujarati, who imported saris from Calcutta, and his even more worn assistant, Sital. As their servant and errand boy, it was Husen's main task to bicycle to the office twice each day with "Bombay food" from the kitchen of Tarachand's small house in Pasar Baru; he also ran messages, went to and from the postoffice and, when time allowed, helped Mrs. Tarachand with her housework. This worthy, as fat, fierce and ill-tempered as her husband was thin and gentle, was always angry with Husen. "Why do you come so late?" she would shriek, with distaste for all the unaccountably cheerful Indonesians and this grinning boy in particular. "Trouble with the cars, Madam. Very many trouble in the streets. Many motor cars and so on and so on." It was an altercation with Mrs. Tarachand that abruptly ended Husen's employment. One day she ordered him, "You make clean the rooms, boy, while I prepare food for my husband." When she squatted down in her sari to flap chapattis on and off the fire, Husen started vigorously dusting, humming and singing. When she returned he was absently rubbing the face of her cherished portrait of Mahatma Gandhi.

"Aaaaggggh!" Mrs. Tarachand screamed, moving across the

room with surprising speed to snatch the rag from Husen. "That is the Mahatma! Don't you do like that! E-ee-ee-eee! There is a dirty smear across his nose!"

Husen told the shopkeeper that night, "*Wah!* I think, who is this old man? Maybe is a god."

For some days Husen found work as a gardener and then, borrowing a *betjak* from one of the shopkeeper's neighbors, tried the labor that was to be his for most of the next fifteen years.

At first passengers were reluctant to take Husen's *betjak;* he still looked like a schoolboy. One Javanese, who said he was a school teacher, offered to finance Husen's further studies; but when the man invited Husen inside his house, asked him to spend the night and attempted to caress him, Husen fled, shrugging off his disappointment by telling himself, "My brain can't handle more learning anyway."

He drove a *betjak* for a year and then drifted from one job to another, first as a construction laborer, then as a *knek* or truck driver's helper in the waterfront district of Tandjung Priok, finally settling down as a garbage-removing coolie for the public works department. This meant filling baskets with rotten, stinking refuse, sodden with mud, filth and germs, and loading them onto a truck; soon even his food tasted of the stench. But the driver shared with Husen the illegal profits he made selling the garbage to farmers on the Bogor Road instead of taking it to the city dump, and the money was good.

When he turned eighteen, an older sister of his, Karlina, came to Djakarta to join her husband, who had started what turned out to be a very profitable general store in Bongkaren, a dusty, filth-strewn shantytown in an abandoned freightyard notorious for gambling, prostitution and narcotics. Husen moved in with Karlina, and one night while he was helping at the store, one of the coolies he worked with came in with his daughter.

Her name was Taminah. She was slim, tall and fair-skinned but her father's low occupation made it difficult for her to make a good marriage. Husen thought her very beautiful; when he told Karlina, she suggested, "If you want to marry, Husen, take that girl."

The ceremony was at her father's nearby shack. Karlina arranged everything. Husen wrote his father and mother, asking them to come to Djakarta for the wedding. He received back only a one-line telegram, "If you need money for your marriage, ask your sister or brother-in-law." After the marriage, Taminah made Husen return to *betjak* driving; at first they lived with her parents until they rented a small, two-cubicle bamboo hut of their own. After two years, a son, whom they named Rustani, was born; after six years a baby girl, Misri. For seven years, Husen was content. The future looked promising. Taminah's father rose to the position of driver in the public works department. He found a job for Husen in its car pool. It meant he could leave the *betjak* and learn to drive a truck.

Then the sores came.

At first Husen hardly noticed the inflammations on his thigh. Then they grew and grew until there were four boils, each the size of a fist, red and swollen, spreading up his right thigh and around to the small of his back. The whole area became festered; everyone shuddered to look at it. Taminah, especially, could not bear to look at him. She spent more and more time at the house of her parents. The day came when he could no longer go to work. He was badly ill. His clothes hung on his body; his eyes grew inflamed and watery and they sank into the hollows of his cheeks. Husen was ashamed to ask anybody for help. He had not seen his sister, Karlina, for many weeks.

One morning, after a night of feverish fitful dreaming he awoke and found Taminah and the children were gone. The wooden bed where she and the baby girl slept was bare, stripped of its covers. Husen staggered to his feet. The trunk where she kept their clothes was also gone; his own few garments had been left on the floor. The tiny kitchen was bare. Husen lurched to the door, opened it and stared into the bright sunlight like a madman, dazed and confused.

"Where is my wife?" he asked a neighbor sitting on the stoop next door.

"She went to her parents last night."

"Where is my wife?" he repeated hysterically.

"She's a very bad wife," another neighbor called from her door. "When you are well she is kind with you. If you are sick, she is going."

Husen tried to say something, but his voice, quavering with emotion, was lost on his feverish lips. Ashamed, he backed into the hut and slammed the door. He realized Taminah had abandoned him; as if he had come to the end of his strength, his whole body shuddered, his teeth chattered and tears streamed from his eyes. Then he fell to the floor.

For seven days and nights he lay there. His whole body was consumed by fever. The boils on his thighs and back caused him incessant pain; every so often he would gasp *"La illa hailallah—la illa hailallah*—There is no god but Allah," and then moan with pain. He did not eat, he did not defecate. His neighbor woman, who thought he was dying, left a tin of tea for him and this he drank, crawling into a corner of the room afterward to make water. When the high fever attacked him, he had nightmares and imagined the little room was filled with *setans* or ghosts. He would scream aloud, *"Aduh,* Taminah! Help, help! Taminah! *Aduh,* oh, mother, father, where are you?"

On the seventh morning, his fever subsided. He woke up quite clear headed and listened to the crowing of a cock. He watched the sun's rays try to creep through the cracks of the decrepit, darkened bamboo wall. His vision cleared and he looked at the room about him. The plaited bamboo walls he had pasted over with old newspapers and whitewashed, now torn in several places. An old, shredded mat on the dirt floor, two bamboo sleeping benches. A table, two worn rattan chairs crawling with fleas. A cupboard with the doors hanging open. His eyes blurred as he raised himself up by one arm. Vaguely somewhere floated visions of a life continuing; somewhere far away there was the cry of a small baby, a son, a small house, a small plot of ground, he and Taminah. But all this was finished now.

It's my fate, Husen thought. I am going to die in this room. He longed desperately for the village. Just to smell the freshly hoed earth again and be sprayed by the falling rain, to walk at dawn through the morning glories, the dew wetting his bare feet, to feel the morning sun warming his body, to swim once more in the river, to eat a cucumber plucked from its stalk, to sleep on the grass under a mango tree. Tears stood in his eyes and, delirious, filthy, he dragged himself up to his knees at the table. His wife had left two full bottles of aspirin. Shuddering all over, his hands shaking, Husen shoveled the contents of both bottles into his trembling mouth. He tried to kill himself. Instead his body rejected the pills and, torn by pain, he vomited and vomited, finally sinking to the ground unconscious. . . .

Then it was night again and he could hear his sister's voice calling him, "Husen, Husen! It's me! Karlina!" She was crying and he was being carried through the streets and someone was washing him with hot water and a doctor told him his condition was "very dangerous" and he was injected with penicillin, swallowed something and fell into a deep restful sleep. He slept and ate, slept and ate again and was still feverish when Karlina took him in a freight car back to the village.

He did not make the expected recovery. For four months he lay in a dark room in his father's cottage, growing thinner and weaker. His right leg and foot began to shrivel up; his parents called *dukun* after *dukun,* but the medicine men's herbs, massage and magic potions were no more help than the city doctor's penicillin. When news of Husen's continued decline reached Bongkaren back in the city, a rumor started that he was the victim of black magic. It was recalled that a certain Tjarti had wanted Husen to marry his daughter instead of Taminah and that his daughter had found no other husband. The theory was surreptitiously advanced that Tjarti's father had paid a sorcerer to bewitch Husen. In time it reached the village. Late one night a neighbor named Suleiman, a simple peasant who always went to the mosque and whom no one suspected of practicing the occult, crept to Husen's bedside. "I want to try and help you if I can," the good man whispered. "Maybe I can help you." He took a glass of water from the Tjimanouk river, spat into it and recited an Arabic verse from the Koran under his breath. He gave Husen the water and told him, "If you recover remember to tell no one about this; it is not I but Allah who will make you well. I am only His instrument. I am not a *dukun,* only an ignorant peasant. Please, this water drink. If you are a good man, if you are good at heart, you will get well. You will rise and walk as before. And if another has put a magic curse upon you, may the curse go back to him, he who made you suffer."

Husen swallowed the water. Four days later the boils burst and white, yellow and red matter oozed out. After a week Husen could stand and walk. He found he had a bad limp, and moved like a cripple. When he tried to go quickly he looked grotesque, jerkily bobbing from one side to another, one shoulder and arm sagging down. He thought to himself, "I will never go back to Djakarta again, not like this." One day an old lady rode up on a bicycle; she lived in a broken down hut in the village and had once been a *dukun* and masseuse, but was now seldom seen about. She was of extreme age and almost bent double but her long spidery fingers were still strong and when she was brought to Husen she cackled, "Oh, this is very nice boy. Sorry sick like this and not good again like before. Very sorry. If I can make him walk like a strong, young man again, I'll make this boy my son. You can call me mother and come to me when you are in trouble, Husen."

The old lady, her sparse white hair flying behind her like a witch's, bicycled to their cottage each day after that to massage Husen's shrivelled leg. For ten days he continued to carry a cane and hobbled about. Then on the fifteenth day, he discovered he could walk normally again and that the muscles were once more becoming firm and strong. One day Karlina's husband came from Djakarta. "Already good, Husen?" he asked. Husen told him about the old *dukun* who had cured him.

"Tjarti's father died suddenly, you know. It was terrible. He had swelling and sores all over his body, his face as well. He is mercifully dead."

Husen said nothing, remembering Suleiman's words.

"Husen," his brother-in-law hastened on, "I came here to tell you your little girl is very sick. Influenza."

They returned to Djakarta on the first bus. When they reached the store, Husen told Karlina he was going to see Taminah. Their baby was very ill. Karlina was furious he had come back from the village. "Why did that woman leave you? Why do you go back to her now? Why? Are you going back to *betjak* driving? Stop driving a *betjak*, Husen. All these years you have been nothing but a *betjak* driver. Make something of your life now that you have one again." Husen did not understand Karlina's anger, which was to last for years, so that in the end he would give up seeing her altogether.

Now he said levelly, "Karlina, I want to see my baby."

"Oh, you're not looking for the baby. You're looking for the mother. I do not like you go back to her. Why? When you are sick she left you to die. Why do you go back to her now?"

Husen arried at Taminah's parents' house to find Misri, his baby daughter, had died of fever a few hours earlier. He carried the infant to the cemetery, buried it and went back and told Taminah he was divorcing her. For two years he did not return to Bongkaren; he let himself go, parking his *betjak* outside the Hotel Indonesia, driving around passengers and gambling, drinking and satisfying his lust with whomever he could find. One was a *djoged* dancer from a theatrical troupe, and then there was a girl who sold rice in the Djatinegara market; finally there were prostitutes. Whenever there was a Tjirebon *pesta* or wild drinking party in the slums, Husen was sure to be there, kissing and whirling around with the dancing girls, performing drunken feats of daring, even once swimming in a crocodile-infested river. "Husen, quickly get out!" his friends called but he shouted back at them, "You don't spare one hair off my head, Crocodile you! You must eat all of me!" He would drink himself to sleep or vomit and return to drink more. He spent more and more of his money for *visang,* fiery Javanese whiskey; sometimes he would stay up all night at two or three *pestas* a week, or sleepily nod until dawn over a game of dice, or slip off to Planet or Tandjung Priok, where the whores were packed into cubicles by the hundreds and a man could lose himself and never come out.

In this way Husen was oblivious to the great political upheavals that were shaking Indonesia and the abortive Communist coup that would climax in an orgy of killing, claiming anywhere from a third of a million to a million lives. On the fatal night of September 30, 1965, when the late President Sukarno drove up to the Hotel Indonesia to fetch his Japanese wife from the rooftop nightclub as his generals were being slain in their homes by Communist terrorists not half-a-mile away, Husen was getting drunk on *visang* at a stall behind the hotel. He learned of the coup five days after it had failed from a passenger riding in his *betjak*. Soon afterward, on a visit home, he saw a crowd of young men gathered in the street in Djatibarang; later he heard they were Moslem youths out killing suspected Communists. Twenty were said to have been beheaded in Bojon village, just south of Karanggetas across the Tjimanouk River. Husen assumed they were guilty persons but he did not know for certain. Other party members, he learned, were taken to camps near Indramaju, given food, and put to work building irrigation canals; some said they got a kilo of rice each day. Later they came back to Bojong and resumed their lives; the killings, revenge murders, and *jehad* or holy struggle died away. Husen told his father a *betjak* man in Djakarta was lucky because everyone assumed he was dull-headed; passengers seldom spoke of politics. "I will only look for money in these troubled times," he told his father. "Not to this side or that side." As a permissive, lapsed Moslem, it never occurred to him he was in any way involved.

And then, in the summer, a page turned in Husen's life. It happened one evening in Pasar Senen, the teeming, noisy, central marketplace which seems the very heart of Djakarta. Husen stopped his *betjak* to buy a bowl of chicken soup at a street stall. A young girl handed it to him and for a moment their eyes met, stayed and then she laughed with embarrassment. It was a happy sound. He came back every night until she said, "You must like chicken soup. You've had nothing else for ten days."

He asked others who she was and learned she came from Karanggetas village, just across the river from Pilangsari. He knew her family. She was staying with an aunt in Djakarta. Although only fifteen, she had been briefly married. He was told she had asked for the divorce after discovering her husband was seeing other women. Husen found the former husband, a handsome youth of nineteen, and asked him, "Was she your wife who sells soup in Pasar Senen?" Told yes, Husen asked, "Are you finished with her?" When the answer was again yes, Husen asked the girl a few nights later, "I heard you were married already. Are you finished with that boy?" She only laughed and Husen, watching her, felt the breath of life storm through him for the first time in years and he felt happy and confused and thought to himself, "I don't know. . . . Maybe Allah has fixed. I am twelve years older. I don't know. Because I love this woman." He thought and thought and finally to Karniti he put just three words.

"Do you want?" They were married in the village that September.

Between eight and nine o'clock in the morning. It had rained in the night but now the sun shone and each flooded rice field was an irridescent golden mirror with its shimmering face to the sky; hundreds of fields stretched eastward from the Tjirebon Road and the mango and banana orchards of Tjibanteng Garden. In this mirror were reflected Husen and his younger brother, Tarja—muscular, stripped to their waists, glistening with sweat and ankle-deep in muddy water, bent over, swinging their sharp-bladed *patjul* hoes to open up the bunds between the paddies. Not far away, their father, a black conical sunshade on his head, guided a wooden plow drawn by two borrowed fawn-colored cows. Along the garden pathway, the lavender blossoms of morning glories, the *kangkung welanda,* were just beginning to fold up in the sun; they still sparkled with dew. The voices of women doing their laundry drifted up from the banks of the sluggish brown Tjimanouk River; Tjiremai Mountain, wreathed in cloud, was just visible in the faint blue distance.

Husen worked hard; there was still a morning freshness and not a hint of the oppressive, smothering heat which would force the men to stop at noon. To Husen, the whole landscape seemed to breathe with new life after the squalor and rush of the city, and he listened intently to the croaking of an angry frog, the faint whistle of the train to Surabaja and the song of birds from Tjibanteng Garden: the coo-coo of the *derek* bird, the nervous twittering of the *tjitji* sparrows, the low-pitched croon of mourning doves. There was the stir of a breeze from the Java Sea, six miles to the south. It carried the voice of a girl, somewhere far away, just a snatch of song. A *betjak* came along the road to town, bells jingling, gong clanging. Long chains of copper-skinned women in sarongs went by, their heads laden with baskets of rice, vegetables and fruit. There was the tinkle of a pony cart's bell, a procession of silent bicyclists and a few solitary farmers with their hoes and *perangs,* or bolo knives, on their shoulders.

Some little buffalo boys came along the garden path, aimlessly prodding with green switches eight enormous black water buffalo. Most of the boys wore tattered, shapeless, men's felt hats, but one had on a cone of red-painted bamboo and resembled a walking mushroom. The buffalo had no pasture for grazing—land being too scarce in Java—and they roamed the lanes between the fields and riverside gardens all day, munching on grass and weeds, and followed by a horde of small boys. As he worked, Husen listened to their idle chatter.

"I took these baby birds out of a *glatik's* nest."

"Be careful. They're alive. Don't crush them in your pocket."

"That one is dead already. Throw it in the bushes."

"You can make ants fight together. Take a black one and a red one."

"The black is outnumbered. The reds all gang up on him. They bite his back. Look at him. Very sick he is."

"Let me pull out his feelers."

Husen noticed Tarja was angrily watching the children, pausing in his work until they ran off to chase some yellow dragonflies. Tarja was twenty-seven and strong as an ox, but he had the simple mind of a child and had not married nor ever left the village. He became agitated when any living thing was tormented or treated cruelly, and to distract him Husen called, "Listen, Tarja, how angry that frog sounds. He is praying for rain." When Tarja began working again, Husen flirted with some giggling girls who had come to weed the next paddy. He offered to help them if they let him work in their midst, and when one of the girls accepted the others rained mock blows on her in protest.

Just then a rickety old truck came up the road from Djatibarang. It was piled high with tarpaulins, canvas scenery, trunks and electrical apparatus, and some thirty young men and girls were clinging to the top. Husen waved, recognizing the local *sandiwara* theatrical troupe. It was composed of farmers, soldiers, petty officials and pretty girls from the surrounding towns and villages, who performed at weddings, births, circumcisions and harvest celebrations. Usually the plays began at nine in the evening and went on until dawn, and since the forty or so dramas in the troupe's repertoire were familiar to cast and audience alike there were few rehearsals and a sponsor could choose the play he wanted just before curtain time.

Such a performance, given at one's home, was always preceded by a *slametan,* the core ritual of Javanese society. This was a short ceremonial meal of tea, roasted chicken, fish and rice, attended by men, at which the village *modin* or priest led a prayer from the Koran; the host thanked everyone for coming to his celebration, and told them they were witness to the purity of his intentions. To Husen and his fellow villagers, to be present at a *slametan* was obligatory since it symbolized the mystic unity of friends, neighbors, spirits, relatives and dead ancestors. As a traditional *abangan* peasant, which meant his Islamic faith was soaked in the older dyes of Hindu, Buddhist and animist belief, Husen felt such ceremonies relieved tension, uncertainty and conflict. For a time, he said, he became *slamet,* a state he described as *"Gak ana apa apa,"* or "believing nothing is going to happen to anyone."

In his youth, Husen, like most Javanese villagers, had performed in the *sandiwara,* not in a leading role but always as a soldier who did the *pentjak,* a half-dance, half-fight in which two men struck each other with hands, feet, and knives, but withdrew the blows at the last possible moment so they did not land. While the troupe's orchestra beat drums and the audience clapped with excitement, the two fighters would throw each other to the ground, the victim cooperating in exact rhythm with the attacker and leaping around in formal menacing poses. Husen loved it. The shouting and grimacing and thrusting always seemed as if at any moment they would break into actual combat, but they never did.

He found the same magic in the traditional dances that were performed as curtain raisers for the *sandiwara* plays. Usually a gorgeously dressed young girl, with the painted moustache and gilded paper helmet of a Hindu god, would begin by fluttering her hands downward and then suddenly turning and twisting them as if they were detached from her body. Every move was intricate—a pointed flipping of a sash with long-nailed tapering fingers, a kick of the sarong train, the bend of the hands back almost to the wrists, the movement of the head horizontally along the plane of the shoulders. With every movement, the troupe's *gamelan* orchestra would strike out a series of clear tones, following one another in a flowing rhythm. Now there would be a limpid boom from a big gong, then the furious beat of a double-ended drum, finally the loud bamboo sound of the full percussion orchestra.

The plays themselves were melodramatic, improvised versions of episodes from Java's history, many of them relating the conversion of the Javanese to Islam, with Hindu holy men and nobles portrayed as buffoons and crazed tyrants. Often an actor in the role of a Sufi or gentle Moslem missionary delivered a long Islamic religious sermon. Some of the plays were pure entertainment, like the story of a virtuous heroine cruelly mistreated by her stepmother, the wicked queen of Bangawangi, until she is rescued by a handsome prince. Sometimes children in the audience became so excited they booed and hissed and pelted the stage with stones, forcing the actors to improvise a quick change of scene.

Since the female roles were played by men, husky local farmers and soldiers garishly done out in wigs, lipstick and padded costumes and speaking in falsetto, the dramas also had the titillating air of the illicit and forbidden. Often the leading "lady" was a *bantji* or transvestite, who would flirt backstage with the village farmboys. Husen and his friends often teased these *bantjis,* waving their thumbs between two fingers toward them in the universal obscene gesture, or pushing their bodies roughly against them in a kind of horseplay they would never engage in with an actual girl.

But the chief attraction of the *sandiwara* dramas was slapstick comedy, usually performed by one or two older professional actors, who never seemed to fail to bring down the house with their pratfalls, mock battles, mournful recitals of the misery of a poor man's lot or graphic, illustrated jokes about bodily functions.

Like most Javanese, Husen was a born actor. As a small boy he had loved to pretend he was a *dalang,* the puppeteer of the *wajang kulit,* or Javanese shadow play. He would improvise little theatres out of bamboo, make the puppets of Hindu gods and nobles and Javanese clown-servants out of mango leaves, and act out the scenario of a *wajang* play for the other little boys of Pilangsari.

"Okay," he would begin, holding up each of his mango-leaf puppets. "This is Judistira, one of the five Pendawa Kings, and over here is Dorna, from the Astina Kingdom. Judistira is a king of Pendawa. Stay in Java. He has four brothers: Bima, Ardjuna, Nakula and Sadewa. Before, both kingdoms were friends. But now they are fighting because Pendawa is poor and Astina is rich. Now Judistira is very *alus,* very kind. If somebody say with him, 'Judistira, I kill you,' he say, 'Okay, please go ahead.' If somebody say, 'Judistira, I take your wife'—but he have no wife—he say, 'Please.' He has white blood not red blood. Now, Bima, his brother, is hot-blooded, many fighting. He sleeps standing up with his fists doubled. He has many wife and stabs people with his very long thumbnail. Ardjuna, the third brother, he's very slow, very cold. He likes girls the best and is the nicest looking man in the whole world, with many, many wives. If nice girl, beautiful girl, okay, he is like to make love to her, even in the Astina Kingdom which is the enemy. The other two Pendawa kings are twins, Nakula and Sadewa."

"What about Semar, 'Sen?"

Here, with the great Javanese low clown, the boy was on surer ground. "On the inside, his *batin,* he is very nice but his *lahir,* outside life, is not good. If look at Semar, is very bad, very fat, very ugly with a black face. Now, before, this earth was empty and Togog, he was the first man out. But Togog sees the earth is empty and so he goes inside again. And Semar is out from the earth. Then Togog called to Semar, 'Hello, little brother, you are second after me.' 'No,' says Semar, 'I am the first.' 'You only think so because the earth is empty,' says Togog. 'I am out first, take a look and go back. So you are little brother from me.'"

"Hey, what about Adam and Eve?" The boys all learned at the mosque the story of the creation. Husen would laugh and say he didn't know; then after thinking a moment: "Adam and Eve, earth and sky, left and right, east and west, man and woman, all two-by-two. The meaning is peoples must marry. Sometimes queer, *bantji*. But all else is two-by-two. Only Allah is one. That is why Semar has only one tooth. He is god but his children are very naughty. Semar says, 'Oh, you must going to work in the garden.' But Semar's children—Gareng and Petruk and Bagong, many going to answer the call of nature." Then he would chuckle infectiously and all the boys would join in.

In those days, what Husen liked best was to stage a comedy, with Semar and his children fighting a giant, bumping into each other, or burning Dorna—the Astina king's treacherous court adviser—with the cigar Petruk always carried. He also made jokes with plays on words that sounded the same in the Javanese and Sundanese languages but, as all the boys knew, had different meanings. This was easy since the words for "kiss," "sit" and "water" in Javanese meant "drink," "go home" and "feces" in Sundanese. Since Javanese was spoken in the village and Sundanese was familiar as the language of Djakarta and western Java, Husen's sallies never failed to keep the children laughing, no matter how often he repeated them.

There were always *wajang* performances in Pilangsari and the surrounding villages. After the rice harvest and in prosperous times, there might be two or three in a single week. As a boy, in the evenings, Husen would hear the haunting bamboo melody of a *gamelan* orchestra come drifting across the Tjimanouk River or from a far-off treeline, and he would slip away from home, hurrying through the darkness with mounting anticipation as the music grew louder and louder. In the paved courtyard of some wealthy peasant's farmstead, he would dart past the glowing orange lights where women sat at tiny stalls selling cakes and tea and cigarettes, throwing a long black shadow behind him as he moved toward the arc of half-light from the *dalang*'s coconut oil lamp. Sometimes Husen would pause behind the big white screen set up between the pillars of a portico and watch the puppeteer unpack his performers, sticking the puppets into a fibrous banana trunk. Perhaps the *dalang* would have arranged them already and be sitting crosslegged, head bowed, in an attitude of prayer. This meant the performance was about to begin.

Usually Husen was late, and he would run at once to the front of the screen where the grown men, proud and tall in their black Moslem caps and sarongs, made their way into a favored pavilion or to rows of comfortable low chairs where tables with tea and bananas and ashtrays were set before them. Like water seeking its own level, Husen and the other small boys would scramble to the front of the men, falling upon each other like pups in a heap and drowsing off and even going to sleep during the long court debates and philosophical discussions, until it was time for the battles and the clowns to come on. But sometimes Husen would sit wide-eyed and match everything, and gradually, as the years wore on, the *wajang* came to seem to him, as it does to all Javanese, a truly sacred drama. A king wrestled with demons, a holy man combated evil spirits. The bodies of the puppets, buffalo leather painted in gaudy gold, reds, blues, yellows, greens and blacks, came to seem, hidden as they were on the other side of the screen, an illusion, and their shadows, which he watched as they seemed to tremble and breathe with life in the *dalang*'s hands, the reflection of that illusion. And somehow, wholly unconsciously, the boy absorbed the belief that soul, shadow, spirit and ghost are one, that the soul and God are one. And, although nominally a Moslem in this way, the Hindu beliefs penetrated deep into his being and his true religion was formed. Most of the stories came from the Hindu epic, the *Mahabharata,* the struggle between cousins, the five Pendawa kings and the one hundred Korawas, which culminated in the great war of kinsmen, the Bratajuda; it was an endless struggle portrayed in the *wajang,* since the final battle was never shown. The struggle was less between good and evil, than between *alus* and *kasar* feelings, or between detached, effortless self-control and base animal passions. The dramas were extremely subtle, and in time transformed simple peasants into the complex mystics and believers in magic and human tolerance that are the Javanese. All of the characters took on symbolic importance:

Judistira was man's inability to act if drained by kindness and compassion, he who believes that *tout comprendre c'est tout pardonner* and is praiseworthy but pallid; Bima, his brother, was both human vitality and the dangers of passionate commitment; Ardjuna, the ability to sustain action by stifling compassion, the force of cool capability and merciless justice. These were the nobles. But the heart of the *wajang* and the soul of Java itself, was Semar, the old servant-clown; he had great wisdom and kindness but a fat, awkward body, an ugly, black face, and was full of crude talk and action, such as breaking wind to chase away his children or throwing feces at opponents. But to Husen and all Javanese, Semar was the father of all men and actually a god in all-too-human form. Although physically repulsive, he was believed to be the kind, all-knowing guardian spirit of all the Javanese from their first appearance until the end of time.

As he grew older, Husen never tired of the *wajang,* and now, in his thirties, he liked to rent for a few rupiah an illustrated *play* in the Djatibarang market and read aloud from it at night to his family. He would sit for hours at the wooden table in his father's cottage, holding the book close to the coconut oil lamp as his mother and father, Tarja, his little brother Warjono, and Karniti would sit hushed, listening. Karniti, especially, enjoyed these evenings; these were her happiest moments in the village, because Husen stayed home with her. As he read, Husen acted out all the roles, his voice rising to a high squeak or falling to a deep rumble, as when he acted out the part of a giant or demon. No one in the family ever seemed to tire of hearing Husen read the *wajang* legends. The clownish Semar and his comical children and the elegant Pendawa kings were forever fighting giants, ogres and the evil Korawa kings, Dorna was always hatching his ingeniously treacherous plots and the good characters kept killing the bad over and over.

Why was this? To Husen it seemed natural since the giants and ogres were like human passions and lusts; they kept arising again and again and one had to keep fighting them off with such good impulses as Judistira's compassion, Bima's vitality, Ardjuna's sense of justice and Semar's magic powers and common sense. No one could defeat his opponents once and for all, any more than he could defeat too much rain, a flood or a drought. They kept coming back and you had to keep struggling against them, an endless, indecisive battle. If there was a key to Husen's mentality, this was it.

The most popular *wajang* story in Pilangsari was not drawn from Hindu mythology but sprang from Tjirebon's soil itself. It told of the unrequited love of a bewitched, leprous and evil-smelling prince, Budug Basuh, for a beautiful young girl who throws herself on the *kris* or twisted dagger of the gods rather than marry him. The first green shoots of rice on earth rise from her grave and today she is known as Dewi Sri, the goddess of rice and fertility. The grieving Budug Basuh kills himself, and the gods order his coffin to be carried to the Ganges. On the way, its bearers cannot restrain their curiosity when they hear strange noises inside, and although forbidden to, they open the coffin. Out swarm all the rice-eating animals and insects which down through history have plagued the Javanese peasants.

Once, when Husen's youngest brother, Warjono, asked him if the legend were true, Husen replied, "About half-half, maybe a little more." But there was no doubt in the mind of his mother. All her married life she had left a plate of rice, sauce, tea and an upturned mirror under the family rice bin each evening so that Dewi Sri could come in the night and take her nourishment.

One morning, after several days of heavy rainfall, Husen was working in a paddy near Tjibanteng Garden, when the buffalo boys came running and shouting, "Uncle! Uncle! Come quick! There is a *tjulik!* We're afraid!" Husen ran to the river. Seated someways down the bank was a young man in a white shirt; he did not look like a demon who carried small boys away in a sack—still he was a stranger.

"Please, Uncle! Get the *tjulik!* He brings a net!" the buffalo boys urged him in an excited chorus. Husen called harshly, "Hey! Who is that?" When the youth merely looked at him with astonishment, Husen approached him. "Where you come from?" he asked accusingly. "I never see with you before."

To his surprise, the other smiled and explained he was a student of agriculture sent by the government to work in Pilangsari; he said he was waiting to fish and had brought a net, but the water seemed too high and the current too strong after the rains. Husen laughed and apologized for his rough manner. He told the stranger the buffalo boys had thought he was a *tjulik* and were afraid.

The youth's eyes twinkled with amusement. "Do you believe in *tjuliks* then?" he asked in his educated city voice.

[255

Husen chuckled in embarrassment. "Because, you know, now, how many years ago, it was like that. Maybe a ghost said, 'I want that boy's head. I want the heads of forty boys.' So maybe that man, the one a ghost bewitches, he becomes a *tjulik*. And he must steal little boys and cut their heads off. Maybe he drinks their blood and carries them away in a sack."

To Husen's dismay the stranger laughed. "Until now," the former went on stubbornly. "In the village. Sometimes a boy disappears. All. Not only head. Maybe bad men take them away in a truck." When the other only kept smiling, he hastened on, "I read in the paper some days ago in Tandjung Priok a man kidnapped a little boy, killed him and drank his blood. He told the police a ghost forced him to do it."

The stranger introduced himself as Abubaker Djauhari, B.Sc. He refused a *kretek,* so Husen, feeling awkward, lit one himself and sat down on the bank beside him. "Jump in!" he called playfully to the buffalo boys, who had moved to the edge of the river bank and were kicking clods of dirt into the rain-swollen river to hear the "plop!" sound they made in the water. Abu, as he told Husen to call him, shook his head and said, "That is the soil loss due to human activity. It is the erosion." Husen did not know what to make of this and shouted gleefully at a friend on the opposite bank who was looking with dismay at some inundated tomato plants, "Hey, where is your garden? Under the river?"

Abu commented dryly, "They must protect those vegetable plots with contour plowing and terrace gardening and must make greening movement activity. To make soil and water conservation and prevent soil erosion. But there is a plan to deepen the Tjimanouk River so it will not flood all the time."

"Yah?" Husen was interested.

"Now three-fourths of the water flows to the sea. After the rice harvest, they will dredge the canal into Pilangsari until the rains come."

The buffaloes wandered too close to the riverbank and the boys drove them back with cries. "Hsssss, *kija, kija,* go, go! Yak eee yak eee yak djrrer-r-r-r-r!"

"Maybe you like to ride?" Husen joked. "Please, sit on the buffalo."

"This is grazing process," said Abu, who was oblivious to all frivolity. "Because there is no special grazing place in this village. Is that your ricefield over there? It needs weeding."

"*Eeeyah,*" Husen shrugged. "We haven't money." He brightened to wave at a girl passing on the road; she wore a bright red skirt, a yellow blouse and heavy makeup.

"Hello," said Abu. "I think that is taxi girl. Is negative social problem in village." When Husen started to laugh, the other gave him a reproving look. Feeling foolish, Husen kicked a few clods of earth into the river. "That is negative soil crosion activity," the student reminded him. He asked to see Husen's fields and as they left the garden, Abu told Husen, "All farmers in Pilangsari need money for clean weeding like you do. Now they spend more than they take in, especially for *sandwara* dramas and *wajang kulit*. It is the irrational tradition of the village. Now the government has issued a special warning about it. Not so many *wajang* plays. They will make every *wajang* get permission and make the procedure difficult."

"Why do you come here?"

"It is population density and food problem, is interest of my life." Abu told Husen he was finding Pilangsari's economy very mysterious. "If it is from harvest to harvest and you make calculations, there is not enough money coming in for the people to live on. But everyone survives. If you make calculations about the output and input, it is minus. It is not open here; there is no effort to be open. It is mysterious." When Abu asked about Husen's life and learned he drove a *betjak* in Djakarta, he told him, "I want to help people like you. This urbanization, looking for a job in the city because in the rural community there is much unemployment, is very bad. But we must go slowly. I am afraid of the antiseptic society as in Sweden."

When Husen returned home that evening and found his father planting papaya trees he objected they were being put too close together. "Near like that is not good. I go to work and separate them. We must cut some out."

"No, no, son," his father said in alarm. "These flowers are good and the fruit will be sweet."

"No, father. Abu says to plant them two meters apart. Abu says

[257

if you plant papaya you must make a hole first and put fertilizer from the compost pile."

"Who is Abu?" his father asked in all innocence.

Since he had turned sixty, Husen's father had become increasingly introspective; he rarely went to the fields any more, but left them to Tarja and Husen and stayed home pottering around his house and garden. A practicing Moslem or *santri,* he rose at four o'clock each morning to say the first of the five prayers of the day, then paced around the dark garden until daybreak. His wife would appear then, hurrying to the pond to splash cold water on her face and gather up dry grass and stalks to heat the morning tea. Normally, after some rice was warmed, the father joined the family for rice, chillies, bean curd and a glass of clear, sweetened coffee. But now, for the past month, he had remained in the garden, fasting in hopes that Allah would be generous and save his rice crop from a plague of insects; his last two crops had failed and the *lumbung* or enormous basket bin of plaited bamboo in the kitchen, was now three-quarters empty. Sometimes at dawn, he would follow the dyke tracks to his fields. The plants were growing tall and the heavy loads were yellowing, but some were white and stiff at the grainhead, a sign green leaf hoppers had eaten the stems. The earth was cracked and dry between the plants, and he could also see where mice had taken their toll. In one of the seven plots of paddy he had bought piecemeal over the years almost all the rice was white and dead, chewed away at the root. The father would gravely shake his head. It was as if a curse had fallen over Pilangsari since the introduction of the new dwarf rice in Java a few years before.

Husen's father did not read newspapers and seldom heard the radio, so he was not aware the Djakarta government was staking its very existence on success in adopting modern farm technology and the new "miracle" rice. A countrywide extension program, staffed by two thousand professionals and reinforced by several thousand more agricultural students like Abu, had been formed to help educate peasants to grow more food with the new seed, more fertilizer, better control of insects and diseases, better irrigation and what was officially called "improved cultural practices."

A high priority government program, to contract with big foreign corporations to supply a package of the new seed, fertilizer, insecticide and technical assistance to entire villages, had meant real hardship for Pilangsari. Its one-hundred-eighty hectares of riceland and fifteen hectares of garden lay on the wrong bank of the Tjima-nouk River; lacking enough water, as its main canal had fallen into disrepair, Pilangsari was not included in the program. But the new rice, growing dense and luxuriant in the villages across the Tjima-nouk, had proved a spectacular breeding ground for insects. Lands under the program were protected to some degree by aerial spraying and insecticide; the farmers in Pilangsari, growing their traditional rice in the traditional way, suffered because the insects came across the river. They spoke darkly of the new rice being cursed by the gods; the first crop had brought stem borers, the second rats, the third cutworms, the fourth army worms, the fifth green leaf hoppers and so on.

Aerial spraying was a further curse as it sometimes drifted across on the wind and killed the blossoms on Pilangsari's mango trees. Some villagers angrily claimed insects thrived on the spray, while it killed birds, dogs and chickens. Abu, faced with the villagers' suspicions and fears and such tangible evidence of unexpected backlash from modern technology, wrote his ministry, "The contractors or scientists must discover why these things are happening. Because of the insect plague many farmers cannot pay back their crop loans." Despite such local setbacks, the new rice was not abandoned. Population pressures were so great, with their rice requirement growing by a third of a million tons a year, that willy-nilly the central government had to increase food output and prevent any further downslide in living standards, without worrying too much about the social consequences. This had led to a remarkable upsurge in national food production, from nine million to eleven million tons in the first four years after the "miracle" rice was introduced; the hope was to stop having to import rice and to produce about fifteen million tons by the mid-1970s.

A few days after their first encounter, Husen brought Abu home to meet his father. The latter, wearing his usual *pitji* or black velvet hat, greeted the student politely, but with feigned lack of interest went into the garden to split some bamboo stakes. Not to be put off, Abu followed him and watched for a time silently as the old man split the bamboo from top to bottom with his *perang;* the student saw he barely had the strength to work it past the knotty joints. Seeing Abu intended to stay, the father finally began to talk. "This land in front of the house is used only for seeding. It is our best land."

Abu smiled. "The experts tell us to use 100 kilos of fertilizer per hectare. If you used so much on this land, the rice would fall down. It is rich land."

The father was pleased. "I scatter on it the leaves of the *jowar* tree. And compost from my garden. That is my fertilizer. It is the way of nature."

"Yes, about half a normal dose of urea would be enough here. Do you get much rice per hectare?"

"About 2,000 kilos. We lack water. Look at the earth, how dry it is already."

"Do you ever spray? You have a lot of green leaf hoppers, it seems."

"I just tried it once. I borrowed a sprayer from the district agriculture office. It killed the rats but it also killed my chickens. A dog ate the rats and he died too."

"How much land do you have?"

"Riceland? One hectare. But not in one place. Seven places. Here, there. I am only a poor peasant."

"Do your children supply you with other income?"

No."

Abu realized the old man was very defensive and proud. Tarja had told him Husen sent at least a thousand rupiah each month from Djakarta, and two other sons lesser amounts. He asked the same question a different way. "You just live off the land?"

"Yah." For some time the father seemed preoccupied with his work. Abu persisted. "How do you protect your rice from insects?"

"When the army worm attacked, my paddy was safe. I have no army worm in my fields. My friends all did. But Allah blessed me. My friends would say, 'Your rice has ripened. Why don't you cut it?' I told them, 'Let it ripen more.' They all failed but I didn't. I fasted and prayed and Allah blessed me."

"What about the new rice?"

"I never tried because of lack of capital. It seems that if I spend money for the new rice I need results. I think, better with the old rice. Less risk."

"Do you think you know how to use it?"

"I am a poor man. I have no capital. If old rice, you don't need much. I have watched men in other villages who tried to grow the new rice without enough capital; they failed. My income comes only from rice and my mango orchard. Now it's not so bad if the crop fails, for the investment is low. I must always pay taxes, 1,944 rupiah last year for the 'territorial development assessment.' " [Four hundred and ten rupiah equal one dollar.]

"Do you double crop?"

"Only if I am sure of water. I was the first in Pilangsari to try . . . five years ago."

"Who gave you information?"

"No one. No information at all. I just tried. We always had the first crop. I tried two because it was raining and the paddy was full of water and I thought, why don't I plant it? Maybe the water will be enough until the paddy grows. I didn't think it would succeed but it did. But now we have trouble from the government. They cut off our water last year so they could use it in the villages across the river to grow the new rice. So we didn't get our water. They cut off the flow in the canal. So we failed twice. Once from insects and once from lack of water. The first crop did not completely fail, but the second was a total loss. This new rice over there is like a curse upon us."

"Did you ever try to borrow from a bank? The government is starting up a rural credit program for farmers."

"No, never. It is like those money lenders who buy your crop cheap and then hold the grain and speculate with it. I have no dealings with them."

"You wouldn't mortgage your land at a bank?"

The old man was emphatic. "No. Never. Never mortgage the land."

"Where do you get capital?"

"Just my land, my garden. My mango trees. Selling a little rice. Sometimes I have to borrow from my friends. I give them the fruit of my mango trees as interest. My friends do the same for me."

"Why don't you borrow from the government?"

"The interest is too high. Sometimes my friends and I lend each other money without interest, no interest at all. Or we lend without interest to our relatives. If Allah blesses us, we won't starve. If my rice fails, I can still eat manioc or maize."

"Have you ever calculated your expenses and income?"

"No, never. Because I never take credit. So I think it is not necessary for me. . . . I just watch my fields and try to improve them. I got a prize years ago without asking. I planted some maize seeds and a government official came and they gave me a sarong. You can imagine a poor Javanese who never had a sarong until then. We were forbidden to wear them by the *prijaji* nobles in the old days, and I got one for a prize!"

Abu rose as if to go. "This land is good enough so you need not use a full dose of fertilizer. If you want to try urea, fifty kilos is enough along with the *jowar* leaves."

The father rose quickly to his feet. "Only fifty kilos? Tell me how to use it."

Abu gave him careful directions on how to prepare the seedbed, how to apply half the urea during the first weeding and the rest at the second weeding. "Only for this soil. Every field is different."

Husen joined them as they moved out to look at the nearest paddy. Abu spotted a field of the new rice not far away and the father said it belonged to one Rustam, the most prosperous farmer in Pilangsari, who had just introduced it into the village.

"How is he doing?"

"Let us wait and see," the old man said.

Husen, hoping Abu had been persuasive, now spoke up. "Look, father, the next time I come from Djakarta, I'll stay here a long time. I want to buy some fertilizer in Djatibarang and do like Abu says. I want to try. Now I go back to Djakarta and find some money. But after you cut this paddy, father, I want to try planting some new rice. Abu will show me how. I want to try."

The father would not commit himself. "You must be careful about money, Husen," he cautioned. "You spend very easily."

"Maybe if we can grow the new rice I can stay in the village."

"Better you are a farmer here, Husen," the father said, weakening. "You are strong and not old and tired like me and can make many, many plantings in the garden."

"Yah, father, and maybe I even might try to build a little shop along the road. Karniti wants and I like to try."

The father looked quickly from Husen's face to Abu's, and that night paced for a long time in the garden. Back in the rented village room where he lived in genteel poverty, Abu thumbed through a dog-eared copy of an American textbook, *Getting Agriculture Mov-*

ing by Arthur T. Mosher. Ever since he had come to Pilangsari, especially when he became discouraged and depressed, it had been his bible and manifesto.

It opened:

> To increase the agricultural production of a country is a complex task. It is frequently a baffling task as well. . . . It is baffling because the spirit of a people is involved also. Techniques are not enough. . . .

He flipped through the pages, past his favorite passage with its cheering certainty:

> Enthusiasm and determination are the engine; skills and knowledge are the tools; occupations and citizenship are the opportunities. . . .

He found what he was looking for:

> Farmers want to be treated as human beings, as intelligent and responsible persons. They can accept help and advice from others only to the extent that doing so does not violate their own self-respect.

By the small oil lamp at his desk, Abu made some calculations. The economics of the new rice were simple: For every hectare of riceland, a farmer had to spend 2,600 rupiah for 100 kilos of urea, 900 for 35 kilos of phosphate, and 2,200 for two liters of insecticide and 100 kilos of rat killer, or 5,700 rupiah altogether. Husen's father averaged a crop yield of only 2,000 kilos of paddy, of which the family ate 80 percent. This left him with a cash income per crop of only 8,000 to 10,000 rupiah. Farmers using the modern methods were getting yields just across the river of 3,000 to 5,000 kilos per hectare, a few as many as 9,000. Abu concluded that with the new rice and proper inputs Husen's father could support and feed sixteen people on his land instead of only five as at present.

At the end of *Getting Agriculture Moving,* Dr. Mosher had asked the reader to list "things you can do to increase the rate of agricultural development in your country." Abu had written:

> I can give the farmers information so that if the government gives them the credit and water they need they will know what to do and can grow the new rice.

Now he added:

> So there is enough employment in the village and there does not have to be urbanization so people must leave their homes and go to the city.

But Husen's father was not converted. When the rice harvest began, Abu was dismayed one morning to find Husen and his brothers sitting idle while hired laborers cut their rice. "It is the *tjeblokan* system," Husen explained. "It is our custom that those who plant the rice cut it; at planting time I was in Djakarta." Abu observed that the father's five hired workers, when they weighed their share to take home, took the best one-sixth of the crop. He told Husen, "No wonder your father is poor."

Husen was soon to return to Djakarta; one afternoon Abu asked him to accompany him to a *wajang kulit* performance in Bojong village across the river. The host, one of the former Communists there who had survived the 1966 massacre, had achieved the local production record of 9,200 kilos per hectare of paddy and had been given a government prize; he was giving his neighbors a shadow play to celebrate. After the performance, as rice had once more sprung from Dewi Sri's grave, and Budug Basuh's coffin had again unleashed trouble into the world, their host took Abu and Husen to see his rice; they found when they reached the field someone had vindictively severed about twenty plants from their stems with a *perang*. The former Communist reacted with a frozen smile and said he had no idea who had done it. "Maybe jealous," he said. Some days later Abu reported the good farmer could not obtain harvesters, and his prize crop was overripe and shattering. His fellow villagers had told him he would have to wait until all the other fields were cut.

Even the *wajang* puppeteer or *dalang* revealed his hostility to change when Abu tried to persuade him to inject some support for modern rice technology into his dialogue. Abu cited the former Communist's crop and said the record yield came because he used urea, phosphate and insecticide in the right amounts. "Couldn't you have Dewi Sri or Budug Basuh say just a few words about the new rice?" The *dalang,* an old man the same generation as Husen's father, refused. "It was the wind," he told Abu. "It blew down from the forests on Tjiremai Mountain and carried all the insects from that man's fields to his neighbors. Now everyone must suffer for his success."

In the green luminescence of the pond, Karniti was bathing and softly singing in her bell-like voice. From the river came the cries of children, "Put me on your shoulders, Uncle Husen!" "Run, here he comes, run!" An old woman came along the path, carrying a bundle of green bananas on her head. Somewhere from the bamboo thicket came the cry of the *prekutut* bird, which always called shrilly at sunset, "Prekut-tut-tut!"

Husen, dripping wet and wrapped in a faded sarong, came and flung himself down on the bamboo bench.

"Back from the river already, Husen?" his wife called cheerfully. Karniti emerged from the pale green water, a soaked *batik* clinging to her wet, golden body, and began to shake out her long black hair.

"Hey, Kar, what was that over in Karanggetas last night? I saw some girls dancing there. Somebody said a man could pay ten roops and dance inside the same sarong with a girl. I think that is a dirty thing. The police should chase them away. In Djakarta, okay. But the village is not Djakarta. What is that over in Karanggetas?"

"Oh, for kissing. That was only for kissing, I hear." Karniti shook her hair more vigorously in the fading sunlight. "Please, if you like, you can go."

Husen rolled over on his back impatiently. "Why if I like to go should I tell you? If I like kissing those girls I not tell you about it. I am just go myself." Husen lay on his back with his hands behind his head, watching the sky grow dim. In the morning, he and Karniti would return to Djakarta; after some argument, he had persuaded her to come with him. He day-dreamed, half listening to some children who came to play with his little brother, Warjono, who was acting out a story from the *wajang kulit* with puppets of mango leaves, just as he himself had done twenty years before: a typhoon, in the form of a hideous giant, carried away Dewi Sri and was pursued by all the gods. But no, the typhoon was really her rejected lover, Budug Basuh, in gruesome reincarnation as a black tusked boar, and once more, he tried to seize the rice goddess. All the gods of heaven failed to stop him until, at last, wise, repulsive little Semar produced a magic flying dagger and Budug Basuh was slain once more. Karniti called—she had mislaid ten rupiah she thought she left on the table, and the children teased the simple Tarja and said he took it. "No, no, oh, everybody suspects me today," wailed Tarja, and his tormenters started to chant, "Oh, Tarja, stealing money. . . . Oh, Tarja, confess, confess, confess!"

Husen stirred from his reveries as Tarja chased the boys into the garden and they scattered with hoots of laughter. Karniti appeared in the doorway and Husen laughed and said, "If no children, not so happy." He instantly regretted his words, seeing her face.

The bus to Djakarta was overcrowded and Husen and Karniti had to sit in back near the engine. Perhaps it was the gas fumes, but they had not ridden an hour before Karniti turned very pale, beads of perspiration appeared on her forehead and she had to get off the bus at the first stop and vomit. Husen wanted to turn back. He felt guilty. That morning when they went to leave, Karniti had found she had left their marriage license at her parents' house across the river; it would have delayed their departure had she not located another document proving their marriage. Husen bowed in the traditional solemn farewell to his parents, kneeling before them and letting their hands slide slowly through his hands as was the·Javanese custom; but all the while his mind was filled with annoyance at her. Now Karniti insisted on going ahead to Djakarta. She had left their rooms with two young girls, relatives she did not trust. She told Husen, "Maybe my cousins have been having men there. It is better we go to Djakarta. It is a long time already."

Husen was ashamed of his earlier anger, and then the thought came to him that she might be pregnant again; at this his heart swelled and something seemed to thicken in his throat. He reached over and held Karniti's hand tightly.

"Why, Husen? Oh, maybe you were remembering our son. He was here in my arms the last time we took the bus to Djakarta."

"I hope with God our boy is happy, Kar. Now he stay over there in Heaven. Until now I think all the time about our boy. *Mendoa kepada Allah.* Pray with God." But in his heart, he prayed that she would give him another son.

Husen felt depressed, as a *betjak* carried them out of Banteng bus station; he was sorry they had returned to the city, and wished fifty or sixty thousand rupiah would drop from heaven so they could return to Pilangsari and never come back. On the highroad of Djalan Thamrin and along the dirt roads beside it, crowds of people were starting to move among the street stalls; there was the sound of talk and laughter in the evening air. Husen looked at the *betjaks* and young people. He felt better; he would soon be moving in his plain rough life among the crowd. Before long they reached the outskirts of the city. Here there were broad overgrown fields alternating with bamboo shantytowns; then came Kebajoran Baru with its big solid bungalows standing in their tree-shaded compounds. It was the wealthiest and most aristocratic suburb in the city; the houses were set back from the streets and in the gardens there were beds of merrigolds, roses and bright red kana flowers and every kind of tropical tree: the white-blossomed cambodia, the fiery red flamboyant, the whispering green *tjamara;* there were thickets of bamboo, and pink, lavender and orange bougainvillea hanging from the rooftops. The houses were protected by high wire fences and uniformed guards stood at most of the open gates. Sometimes in the evening, Husen and Karniti would go for a stroll and look into the bright-lit windows and see the chandeliers and pictures, the book shelves and the television sets, the servants hurrying to and fro.

At last the *betjak* rolled down into the hollow to the market on Sinabung Street. Only the glimpses of teeming alleyways in openings between the shops hinted at the sprawling shantytown of densely-packed wooden and bamboo huts that spread year by year more deeply into the low, steamy swamp behind. Too low to catch the cooling breezes from the Java Sea and sometimes flooded waist-deep in the monsoon rains, the hollow remained an enclave of poverty as the modern suburb grew up around it. Many of the residents of Kebajoran Baru were not aware of its existence; their servants did their shopping for them in the Sinabung Market, which catered to both the rich and the poor. Here there were tailor shops, bakers, barbers and carpenters. For a pittance one could buy either a snack or subsistence: a piece of fried mutton on a skewer, coconut and lentil porridge, soda, coffee, tea, iced beer, rice, boiled eggs, fried chicken, sweet cakes, roasted peanuts, scrimp cakes, peanut crisps and vegetable soup. The grocery shops sold mostly to the poor; they were stocked with all their daily needs: dried fish, lentils, beans, dried peas, potatoes, onions, eggs, noodles, rice, ketchup, coconut oil, kerosene, matches, tea, soap, mosquito repellent, cigarettes, apples, bananas, papayas, combs, handkerchiefs, toothbrushes, toothpaste or charcoal in tins, perfume, paper, cheap ballpoint pens, notebooks, sugar, flour, ropes, lamps, knives and candles. Some of the vendors had movable bamboo pole shops they carried about on their shoulders; one brush salesman sold enough to fill a storeroom: brooms, wicker laundry baskets, tin tubs, long-handled brushes, shoebrushes, whisk brooms, hairbrushes and every other imaginable kind of brush. Usually there would be cheap sales, hawkers' voices amplified by loudspeakers, crying, "I don't sell anything. I just give you prizes. Who wants to try?"

Husen and Karniti had found rooms in Simprug, as the settlement in the hollow was known, a few months before. For Husen it meant pedaling the *betjak* an extra three miles, often late at night and without a fare, back and forth to the Hotel Indonesia on Djalan Thamrin. But he wanted Karniti to have a safer, pleasanter place to live than the denser, filthier slums nearer in.

Now the Sinabung Market was full of life and movement. The eating-stalls and beer-stands were noisy. If someone who did not belong in Simprug but lived in the shady suburb around it had driven past the market now, he would have noticed nothing but dirty, poor, and sullen-seeming people; but Husen, who had lived in such slums for fifteen years, was constantly recognizing a face in the crowd: a friend or another *betjak* driver, or someone from the village. A dark, deep, evil-smelling alleyway led between two shops, from which came the sound of men coughing inside. Leaving the *betjak,* Husen and Karniti carried their cardboard suitcases and went in. They crossed a rickety wooden bridge over a deep canal; there was still the same loathesome smell as in the alleyway, and two men were squatting, their pants pulled down, over the canal from a high wooden stilt platform. The couple climbed down a slippery staircase carved from mud and entered their own lane, which snaked through tightly-packed huts of bamboo, salvaged wood or beaten tin cans. The skinny chickens picking in the dirt; the greasy, swinging lanterns; the stench; the piles of garbage where rats scurried as they passed; the rags hanging from washlines; the haggard women in the doorways; the men smelling of sweat, varnish, tar, according to their occupations; the multitudes of naked, barefoot children wtih sores on their heads—all these had become familiar to them long ago. Their own doorway had been painted blue by Husen in a pathetic attempt at decoration. It faced an open space, and if one looked beyond a garbage pit and makeshift bathhouse which always stank of stale urine, one could see a stretch of open, if malarial, green marsh and the tall graceful lines of palm trees against the city skyline. When Husen opened the big padlock and pushed the door open, Karniti's fears were realized. Beer bottles and newspapers were scattered about, a chair was overturned and there was a peculiar rancid, sour smell; it semed to envelop them on all sides. Husen at once opened the three small windows onto the lane, fetched water from the pump, and Karniti, without even changing clothes, set about scrubbing the cement floors, wiping off the lone table and three low rattan chairs and spreading a clean white cloth over the table. In a remarkably short time she had transformed the little room into something comfortable and cheery by hanging a silk print of an Arabian desert scene on the wall and preparing a glass of clear, sweet coffee and a plate of cookies for Husen. Their living space had been divided into three cubicles for privacy: the living-room, a hall-way and a small bedroom. Here was a big bamboo bed, a primus stove, some pots and pans and dishes, a few drinking glasses, a kerosene lamp, a water pail, and a cupboard for their clothes. Karniti carefully unpacked Husen's only white shirt, his other pair of trousers, the six tight shorts he wore when driving the *betjak,* and his green windbreaker; then she turned to her own *batiks,* blouses, jackets and underwear, and a small case with their toothbrushes and her mascara, powder, lipstick and perfume.

When she came back into the living room, Husen was sipping his coffee and reading an old newspaper. He smiled at her. "You are a nice wife, Kar."

She was pleased to be in a place of their own again and free of his parents' criticism. She laughed. "Maybe you want to take a second wife. Keep me to cook and clean the house."

He reached out and slapped her bottom. "Maybe I want ten wives." His smile died. "No, Kar, I don't want to marry another wife. I have you. Two-by-two, that's the best way in life."

A very thin woman, far gone in pregnancy, with wispy hair and a worn yellow face, stuck her head in the door. She was wearing a faded batik and a grimy, grey blouse, and had a cooking spoon in her hand. It was Bibi, a distant relative of Karniti, whose husband owned their shack; they lived in the other side. "Karniti!" she cried in a hollow voice. "So you come back from the village already. How long will you stay this time?" Her head disappeared for a second and they heard her screech to her husband, "Kasum! They're back!"

"I don't know, Bibi," Karniti told her "aunt", "maybe long time."

"Very good there? Many *wajang* and drama there, Husen?"

"Not much now. Before, at harvest time, many."

[269

"You know I have family not far from Pilangsari. My sister is in Djatibarang."

"You should go back when the mango season comes. Many *wajangs* then."

Bibi heaved a sigh. "I almost never leave the *kampong* any more. Why should I? I can buy everything I need there. You know, Husen, once I was a maid for some rich people and got around. But now I can't find a job." After a brief silence during which nothing could be heard but Husen blowing and sipping on his coffee, she sighed again. "More and more people are moving in here all the time, and they come from all parts of the country, especially on the south side over by the road. It's getting very crowded here and dangerous to go about at night. Not like the old days." A man joined her in the doorway. He was flatchested and bony with narrow shoulders and sunken temples; his eyes were small and anxious with dark rings around them. It was Bibi's husband, Kasum. A kernel of rice clung to his chin and he smelt of beer.

"Hey, Husen!" he clasped their hands. "I see you pasted newspaper on your walls already. Those girls you left here went a few days ago. They said they were afraid here. Ghosts. Say, if you want to paint these walls in color, don't buy Alkarim. I can get you some imported stuff cheap. It comes on very good and doesn't chip off. One can is only 1,300 roops. My friend has a couple of cans he'll sell you. If you buy in a store it's 1,700 roops a can." Kasum, like all the construction laborers who lived in Simprug, was always trying to make ends meet by selling materials he pilfered from work.

"No, that's too much," Husen told him. "I don't want to spend the money. Never mind. I'll use Alkarim if I paint. If I have money."

"Like it is now is fine," Bibi said. "Maybe you want to make it white?"

"White is best," Karniti said. "It makes the lamplight brighter. It's good." A chubby child of about three, with hair that stood up like a hedgehog's, appeared behind Bibi, tugging at her skirt. "I want to eat, mama."

"Waiting short time." Bibi turned to her husband. "Shall we take this boy and go home?" Husen and Karniti were glad to be left alone; they both were fighting the desire to flee back to the village, to escape these people and their air of being totally defeated by the city. Husen went back to his newspaper as Karniti began to prepare a meal in the other room. From time to time he would call to her. "Oh, a robber was shot near the Ramayana Hotel. . . . Oh, a student killed his friend. He will get three years in the black house. They were friends of a professor at the Agriculture Academy at Bogor. An old Dutchman. Homosex. He hired one to do it. Fifty thousand roops to kill his boyfriend. . . . Oh, a Japanese got stabbed in a *betjak* on Djalan Thamrin. You know, Kar, when I see some men who look like robbers I smile and shout 'Hello!' and I think they won't rob or hurt me. That is my tactics. Fifteen years a *betjak* man in Djakarta and I never got robbed."

"Yah," Karniti called from her work, "maybe someday you smile and shout and they stab you anyway. You must be careful, Husen. Not going to everywhere." He heard the clink of pots and then she spoke again.

"Abu asked me about Tarwi. He likes her."

"Tarwi!" Husen hooted at mention of a young girl who lived next door to his father in Pilangsari. "She have five husband already and is only eighteen." Husen laughed. "Be careful, old Abu! *Awas!* You will be number six."

He could hear Karniti washing out pans. "Her father is rich," she called.

Husen remembered his last conversation with Abu in the village. "Your father does only the primitive agriculture," the student had told him. "He only opens the soil and drops the seed. What you need is a mixed economy, maybe have a shop on the road and sell things. Is good for farmer, the mixed economy. Your earth is good. All you need to do is improve the soil texture and soil structure. The land is good."

"Abu looks thin," Karniti said. "Maybe his food is not good, there in the village."

"He should take vitamins. He should exercise and get strong."

In truth, Husen felt Abu was growing discouraged. He had told Husen, "Sometimes the government leaves sprayers, fertilizer and insecticide in the village but because of mismanagement the help doesn't get to the farmers. There is too little cooperation and too much mismanagement. If the government gives five sprayers, the people only get four. . . . But I must speak about the technical side only. If I told others about the *korruptsi* here, Husen, it is possible I will not get rice or a place to live. I could become *persona non grata*."

"Abu is right," he called to Karniti. "If sell the land is finish for the farmer. If have not land, garden, life in the village is very difficult. Kar, maybe if I can get capital to open a small shop for you, okay, very good. We stay in village. Maybe buy mangoes or bananas and sell in Djatibarang. If you buy many mangoes from the farmers —maybe you have four people with 100,000 roops each or 400,000 altogether—you can sell in Djakarta and make good money, Kar. Kar?"

He listened. She was talking to someone else, the wife of a policeman next door, through the back wall.

"Already back from the village, Kar? How do you feel?"

"Have you seen the Djakarta Fair, Titin?"

"Yah, the other night. My husband is angry. He was asking everywhere for me. I went with my sister. First time out of the house in five months. He's afraid to let me go out because he thinks there might be a fire here."

The two women lowered their voices and Husen could only hear snatches of their words. "Oh, he looks like his father. . . ." "He never smiles. . . ." "I think the baby's shirt. . . ." He listened to Karniti's happy, infectious laughter. "I know the woman who sells them. . . ." "Walking all day. . . ." They started giggling.

The walls were so thin you could hear all the neighbors if you listened. Now Husen could hear Bibi saying, "In our family the man is number one."

Another woman's voice answered, "That's all right. I don't mind if the man is kind to me."

Karniti and Titin stopped talking and Husen could hear the voice of Titin's husband. He was scolding a baby in a gruff, low tone. "You don't be cross, my girl."

"Never mind." Titin's voice, sharp-edged. "She's only a baby."

"Where's matches?"

"On the table."

"Yah, yah. Titin, get me cigarette from the table."

"Get it yourself. My hands are wet."

The policeman raised his voice. "Quickly! Get cigarettes!"

"Please, wait a minute then. Okay, here is."

"Where's my sarong?"

"Over on the chair where you left it."

Bibi again. "That's bad. The baby wet his blanket already." Bibi sneezed. "I'm catching a terrible cold."

"Maybe we'll all get influenza again."

"Don't say it." There was a pause and then Bibi stuck her head in Husen's door. "Where's Kar?"

"Making rice."

"Husen, my friend's husband has three sacks of cement. You want to buy some?"

"No, because I haven't money for cement."

"Very cheap. Maybe he gives one sack for a hundred roops."

"*Tida apa apa.* Never mind. I haven't money."

"If you have to buy in a shop, it will be seven hundred."

Husen buried his nose in his newspaper and she went away. Karniti came out and sat in the doorway. "Waiting some time," she told Husen, "Titin wants me to watch her baby a minute." In a moment Titin, a pretty girl in her late twenties appeared, carrying a small boy. "Here, Kar, hold him a minute. I want to go to the shop and buy bananas."

Karniti cradled the child in her arms, rocking back and forth gently and whispering to it in a hushed voice. "Are you a nice boy? When you are big, you mustn't be cross. Oh, you are very clean. Just like my little boy before."

The policeman came, a broadfaced, muscular man. "Is that my boy with you, Karniti? Where is Titin?"

"I don't know. She went to buy bananas."

"It's a long time already."

"Maybe she is going to find her girl friend," Karniti told him. Titin's husband was very jealous. "Because her friend's house is just behind the banana stall. She'll be right back."

"Here. I'll take my baby. You looked tired."

"No, never mind." Karniti cuddled the child closer to her. The policeman saw Husen. "Back from the village, Husen?"

Husen came out on the stoop and sat down beside his wife, putting his arm around her shoulder. "Yah. Very nice your son. Our boy was like this. White, like Holland people. With a long nose. But he was too hot . . . like influenza."

Bibi appeared in her doorway. "If your little baby had only lived, Kar. He was so pretty. He could be playing with this little one soon."

[273

"When did you get back?" the policeman asked.

"Just now . . . okay, very happy to be back in Djakarta. Well, how is the policeman's life?"

"Ah . . . you're better off being a *betjak* man. You are only looking for passengers. When you have money you can go home."

"Yah, it is different for the policeman. But every month, you can always find rice, much money; you can eat fish and good food."

"Yah, sure, but I must stay all the night in the station and if I want like you, going to everywhere, I cannot. Okay, let's go, baby." He took the child from Karniti. "Husen, please come to my house soon. Now better I go looking for Titin."

"Thanks, I'll come later on."

Karniti rose and started inside, but stopped and leaned against the doorway; her face had become very pale and there was perspiration on her forehead.

"Kar, what is?" Her eyes looked sunken. She told him, "Husen, it is better you serve yourself food tonight. I want to lie down."

"You are ill?"

"You must be hungry. Can you serve yourself? I feel a little feverish. Maybe I'll take a bath and be all right."

"Don't take a bath; because it's dangerous if you have fever. You should not get wet. I'll bring some water from the pump and you can wash off here. Do you like that I bring some 'Tiger Balm' medicine from the shop?"

"No, not like."

"Please take a pill, an aspirin with some hot tea."

"No, no. I just want to rest." She went in and lay down upon the bed. Husen busied himself frying an omelette and cutting up some chillis for *nasi goreng*. When it was ready he mixed it with the rice and brought a plateful to Karniti. She turned away as if the smell of food sickened her.

"You not like to eat, Kar?"

"No, no."

"But, please, Kar, you must eat rice. Just plain rice."

"No. Please, you buy some ice. That's all I want."

"You! That is dangerous. You cannot only have ice. Please, if you like, you must drink much hot tea." He went to boil some water on the primus stove, telling her, "Kar, you rest. I want going to drive the *betjak*."

"Please, don't go."

"I must, Kar. We have no money to eat tomorrow." He went out to the doorstep, not knowing what to do. Bibi was sitting there; she must have heard them for she told Husen, "If you're going to everywhere, Husen, Karniti is afraid. Maybe you'll have trouble in the street, maybe an accident. She doesn't know. She doesn't look well, Husen. Why didn't she stay in the village?"

"She vomited this morning on the bus."

"Ah, maybe she has a baby inside her. Send her to the *dukun* tomorrow, Husen." Bibi heaved a long sigh and got up. "Somebody told me my boy got into a fight and he doesn't come home. If Kasum comes, tell him I went out looking for my boy." Husen decided not to go to work that night; he still had a few rupiah.

On a stoop down the alleyway some boys were playing a guitar and Husen joined them; he asked to see it and, after strumming a few chords sang a melancholy Tjirebon ditty:

> Thousands of stars in the sky
> But the moon shines unconquerably
> Thousands of girls of beauty
> But my love for you is unconquerable. . . .

He stopped after half a minute and started again, his voice sliding up and down the scale from bass to high falsetto. He sang passionately and with longing and the boys smiled and accompanied him in soft voices:

> Adiguru is a king of the universe
> Narada crowns himself with a basket
> Don't hurry into a divorce, my love,
> Beware the loneliness that follows in the night. . . .

With a laugh, Husen sang in English songs learned in his schooldays in Indramaju:

> Oh, I went down south for to see my Sal
> Singing Pollywollydoodle all the day
> Oh, my Sally Ann was a friendly gal
> Singing Pollywollydoodle all the day. . . .
>
> Dashing through the snow
> In a one-horse open sleigh
> Over the fields we go. . . .

"What's a one-horse open sleigh, 'Sen?"

He chuckled. "I am not know. Maybe somethings and so on."

"Hey, 'Sen!"

It was Muri, a neighbor who worked as a blacksmith and practiced sorcery. Evidently, he came straight from work; his face looked dark and grimy, on one cheek was a smudge of soot. His hands were black and his bare shoulders shone with oil and grease. He was a man of forty with black curly hair, ox-like shoulders, and a look of great physical strength. His eyes were half-closed; he was always staying up all night, believing that unless one fasted and denied the body sleep one could not understand magic and the occult. Husen had never tried it; he did not even observe the Moslem month of fasting, Ramadan, when it is forbidden to believers to eat between dawn and dusk. Abu, back in the village, had fasted for five days once to test his "work effectiveness" but found he kept dropping off to sleep in the daytime. Muri took sorcery seriously. He had left his wife and children in the village, and once, through the bamboo walls of his room, Husen had heard him chanting in a strange, low voice:

> As the head of the buffalo hangs down,
> Stiff as a seashell,
> May Sujono lower his head as my servant,
> Bow down as if he were the slave of my penis.

Now Muri wanted to speak to Husen alone; they returned to Husen's house and Muri shut the door and windows. He took from his pocket a small black stone idol, shaped as a man sitting in prayer, but worn into an almost unrecognizable lump from constant fingering. Husen knew this was Muri's *djimat,* a magic talisman the blacksmith claimed to have found one night on far-off Dieng Mountain, whose jungles were inhabited by men who wore only black shirts, black pants and black capes. Muri had told Husen that when he first found it the stone erupted in a fountain of sparks, and when he turned his lamplight on it, the light slowly went out, the last flicker falling upon the little idol.

A grin now appeared on Muri's grimy, violent face and he told Husen, "Last night my *djimat* had a fight with another ghost. My friends called me—I was outside—and said, 'Muri, Muri, come here! We hear drums beating inside your room!' I unlocked the door and went inside but the room was dark and empty and silent. I came out again and we waited. There it was! 'Tomtom te tomtom, tom te tom te tom, tomtom, tomtom, tomtom. . . .' 'What is that, Muri?' my friends asked. I went inside and the room was empty. I came out again and shut the door and we heard the sound of the drums again. Now my friends said, 'Muri, get your *djimat* outside our house. We're afraid to sleep in the house while it is here. Perhaps it is fighting with some *setan* or ghost.' So, Husen, maybe you want to borrow my *djimat* for tonight and I can leave it here."

"What for?" Husen laughed. "If I hear the drums I'll take your stone and I'll break it with a hammer. If your stone is really a *setan* or a ghost, I'll die."

Muri grinned, handing the stone to Husen with his black hands. "Okay, please try."

Husen took the little idol and put it on the floor, squatting over it with a hammer. He raised his arm. "Okay, I'm ready." Muri saw he would really try to break it. He snatched it up again. "No, no, Husen, please. I'll have trouble to find another one like that."

"*Wah,* Muri. I'm not afraid of all your demons and *setans* and ghosts. I'm not afraid of a stone. Okay, leave it here tonight. If it has magic, maybe I'll be like you. Old but strong. Every day going to work but not sleep. At night going to everywhere."

Muri shrugged his powerful shoulders. "Okay, Husen. Titin's father wants to play cards. C'mon and we'll play some rummy."

"No. Karniti is sick. You go play cards. I am very tired if I have to wait for you all the time in rummy. I like to play quick."

"Oh, don't worry, Kar," Muri called toward the bedroom. "Never mind. We won't play for money."

Karniti's voice sounded weak and drowsy. "Yah, Muri, but it is difficult. Once Husen takes the cards in his hands, he doesn't like to come home."

Bibi's husband, Kasum, stuck his head in the door. "C'mon, brother Husen. Please, we are three men already. How can we play if you don't come? My uncle, he will get angry if you don't play."

Husen went back to Karniti's bed. "Wait a short time, Kar. I'll make you some more hot tea. I want to play cards a short time. Just across the lane at the house of Titin's father. We'll be out front and you can call." Looking into his face, Karniti smiled. She knew he would play for hours. Standing over her bed, Husen saw from her face, and especially from her eyes, how exhausted and sleepy she was.

Better she sleep. He hurried to join the others. "Take Muri's stone with you," she called after him. "I'm afraid of it." But he did not catch her words and left it lying on the table in the front room: he also left the door ajar.

The card game lasted until one 'clock. For some time Karniti lay there with her eyes open, listening to the players' voices before she drifted into sleep.

"If somebody has the eight of spades. . . ."

"Up to how much?"

"One thousand."

"Who dealt this?"

"Loser deals."

The voice of Titin's father, old, husky: "Please, Muri. If Muri keeps shuffling those cards all night, I'll cut his ear off. You must be careful with Muri. He has supernatural powers. Sometimes he has four eyes. Two for his cards and two for yours."

Husen's voice. "Oh, Muri, scratch my back. Something bit me and I can't reach it. No, not there, down lower." A hoot of laughter. Husen broke wind, a favorite joke of his.

"Stand behind Muri, uncle. He is such a fast dealer, he'll get tired soon. If you have no money, you can massage his shoulders."

Muri: *"Bohong,* Husen. *Kurang adjar, sialan.* Shaddup, 'Sen. Go to hell."

"I think you will take to sunup to shuffle."

"Wah! A triple three, and I have two fours and two fives, both clubs. Husen, you're crazy! *Sialan!* Yah, I'm waiting for you next time. I know you're clever."

"If I play all the time with you, I wach my cards every minute, you bastard. Okay, deal."

"Maybe it is I have magic."

"I understand about you and your magic. Deal." Time passed. . . . Karniti stirred. She heard no voices. She must have slept. The oil lamp had burnt low. There was nothing to be seen in the room but darkness. She heard a rustle in the lane, nothing more. Instinctively, she reached out on the bed for Husen; he was not there.

Suddenly, amid the stillness, Karniti sat bolt upright, pricked up her ears and strained with her eyes at some invisible object in the darkness. She sensed someone approaching but could hear no footsteps. Where was Husen? A minute went by in silence. But now she heard footsteps; someone was approaching in haste out in the lane. She called out, "Husen!" But beyond the glow of the lamp by her bed there was nothing to be seen. She remembered the stone idol and shivered at the thought it might be in the house with her. At last the footsteps sounded quite close, and someone coughed; the flickering light by her side seemed to withdraw, and, as if a veil had fallen from her eyes, Karniti suddenly saw before her the figure of a man. "Husen," she gasped. "You frightened me."

Either it was that the lamp glowed brightly, or that she was so anxious to see this man's face, that what she saw of him first of all was not his face nor his clothes but his smile. It was the most hideous smile that she had ever seen; a twisted black gap of open mouth; a wet, black moustache; tiny bubbles shone on the thick, sensual lips. She had an instant impression of height, long arms and long legs; he was dressed all in black. He lowered his head and thrust his fiery face close to her own; she caught the hot fumes of his breath; it whistled in his throat as he panted. He was trembling and when his hand ran down her body the flesh was hot like a hand in fever. She was cold with panic and a sickening dizziness, bordering on nausea, swept over her. In the flickering light, she saw his eyes now, filmy, feverish, dilated. She opened her mouth, but from her throat came only a hoarse hollow gasp. The more she strained her throat and breast, the more hollow grew her breathing. He bent closer and his eyes grew sharp and narrow. She felt his hot, moist hand moving down her shoulder and shuddered convulsively and tried to squirm away. He seized her wrists and slammed her back hard against the bed. The pain grew sharp and she saw his mouth open again, coming down upon her own and he was upon her, crushing her under his heavy weight and she drew back wildly, jolting her head to the side and was able to scream. . . .

Husen, returning from the canal, was at the water pump splashing cold water on his face when he heard a succession of moans and thought Karniti must be having a nightmare. He had just reached for a rag to dry himself when he heard such a scream as he had never heard; no one would have thought so small a girl as Karniti could have uttered such a scream. A silence fell over the lane as he ran to the door and burst into the house. Karniti was sitting up, dazed with terror, staring into the darkness.

"Where?" Husen shouted. He seized the nearest thing, a broom, and flayed it around the dark corners of the room.

"He's gone, he's gone, he's gone," she repeated, witless with panic.

"Already gone? If go away, why you so afraid, Kar? I am not afraid with ghosts." And then he saw her face and ran to the bed and she tumbled into his arms; sweat glistened on her forehead; violent sobs shook her body. Husen held her close; no mere ghost could have frightened his wife so badly. And then he remembered the *djimat*. He was thinking in confusion of what to do when someone began pounding on the door. He could hear excited voices in the lane. Muri, followed by their other neighbors, crowded into the dark hallway, wanting to know what had happened.

But Karniti was still speechless with fright. "He . . . he . . . a man in black. . . ." She stared into the darkness as if disbelieving the intruder was gone. "I can see; there's nothing there," Husen said, holding up the lamp. In the gloom, the light flickered across the anxious faces. Shadows danced over the walls and everyone crowded closer toward the halo of light. "Perhaps it was a dream," Husen ventured.

"No." Muri's deep voice boomed out. "I also saw him. But I did not know he came from your house. He ran past me. A very big man dressed in black." He paused, his grimy face shining like a demon's in the eerie light. "It was a *setan*. I should not have left my *djimat* here tonight."

"Are you sure?" Husen's voice was disbelieving. "It was a ghost? Not a man?"

There was a commotion in the crowded hallway; Bibi pushed her way in. With a moan she ran to Karniti, gasped and clasped her hands in a thrill of excitement. "A *setan*, a *setan*! You poor, poor child!" she brought out breathlessly. She turned toward the rest of them and said in a sobbing voice, shaking her fists, "Those poor girls, Karniti's cousins, ran away from this place one night while they were in the village. The *setans* came and tried to embrace them too!" Bibi clutched Karniti's hands again, moaning inarticulately as though she were paralyzed; she pressed her yellow forehead to Karniti's long black hair and seemed as though she were in a swoon. "Why, why?" she cried in her thin voice.

"Why is she carrying on so?" thought Husen, with shame and annoyance. He told Bibi. "I don't know. My wife, she sees the *setan*. I come back, I cannot see. I don't know. Muri, he says he sees too."

"Say something from the Koran, Husen," Bibi advised him breathlessly. "Dispel the evil spirit around us; it is too cold in here. I can feel it now." Husen muttered a few phrases in Arabic; the neighbors joined in with low voices. Bibi, moaning and sighing, wrapped her arms around Karniti and gently rocked her as one would a child. "There, there, Kar. Better you come and sleep in my room. Get out of this place!"

"No, no," Karniti sobbed. "I want to stay with Husen."

"Never mind, Bibi," Husen said with annoyance. "The ghost won't come again."

"Before also, your cousins like you also," Bibi crooned to Karniti. "They saw *setans* in the night and ran away from here. They came and slept in my house. They were so afraid like you." She turned on Husen, looking at him wrathfully. "Where were you?" she hissed. "Play cards all night, going to everywhere, leaving your wife alone! There, there, Kar. So all right. If you can already get up, come, we go to my house."

"*Wah!* You don't be afraid, Kar," Husen said sternly, moving Bibi aside. "*Setans* don't eat people. Where is the *setan* that eats people? No."

He hastened the neighbors out of the house, telling Muri, "Better you take away your stone; better you take it back to your place, Muri." When all were gone, Husen took the lamp and went about the rooms, holding it in the dark corners. He even crushed an ant he saw crawling up the wall to be on the safe side. Then he kneeled by the bed, gazing at his young wife in mournful perplexity; then his eyes, too, began to water, and he laid his face against her arm and without words it was clear he was ashamed to have left her. Finally he spoke, "I thought you were good, Kar. That's why I went to play cards. Oh, Kar, I am sorry. Your parents are in the village. In all the world, I have only you to look after me and you have only me to look after you."

Karniti smiled weakly. Husen looked at her and thought, what if it was a man and not a ghost? She was only nineteen; beautiful, soft and shy. Had some stranger tried. . . . No. The idea of it was too horrible. Her face now looked calm; he saw how tired and exhausted she was. She spoke, her words barely above a whisper.

"Come to bed, Husen. Why do you just sit there? I'm all right now. Go to sleep." He lay down beside her without undressing. "I'll just be here, Kar. If any *setans* come, I'll be right here. . . . I remember how it was in Bongkaren that time, Kar. With no one to help me. I wanted to die, Kar."

He had never told her before and she opened her eyes and looked into her husband's worried face. "Husen. . . ."

"Go to sleep, now. Everything's going to be all right. I am right here beside you."

"Husen . . . I think I have baby now in myself. I want to go to the *dukun* tomorrow." Her voice was calm. He looked at his wife and she looked back at him. "It is three months already, Husen. Her lovely black hair was wet with fever and spread out on the pillow. Her eyes were sunken in shadows, but beyond this she was as she always was. To Husen, she was unbearably touching, lying there. His heart rushed out to her and he said, not knowing what else there was that could be said, "*Alhamdullillah,* God be praised! I hope God gives us happy."

"Yah, I am also."

"Kar, if this time I have a little success in finding money in Djakarta, if not too bad this time, then we save everything and go back to the village. I want to escape this place, Kar."

"Yah, maybe in the village . . . the air is good. . . ."

"If Abu helps me, I want to know the new ways and the different things about planting. I want to try, Kar. I want to build you a *warung* by the side of the road, just a small shop where you can sell some little things like you want, maybe a little tea, cakes, coffee, rice. Not big. Just a little one at first and. . . . And when our son is big enough. . . ."

She squeezed his fingers. "I was so afraid, Husen. I reached out for you and you were not there. . . ."

She slept. Husen in his bewilderment, remorse, confusion and happiness, talked on. "I will ask my father to give me a little land by the road, and I want to carry earth from Tjibanteng Garden and sand from the river to make the ground higher. . . . Maybe plant some banana, papaya. . . . Yah, and get some red stone from my uncle in Kliwed and cut down some *djati* trees. . . . Maybe three rooms is enough, one for the shop, a small kitchen and a bedroom for us until our son is bigger. . . . Because I am tired, Kar. Seventeen years in Djakarta; a long time already. I think better we go home . . . leave this place. . . ." In the morning when she awoke, refreshed and the fear of the night gone, she found Husen still lying there in his clothes, a hammer clenched in his hand.

Twilight at the Hotel Indonesia. A clear, pleasant evening. Deep blue sky, a fresh breeze from the Java Sea. Europeans strolled on the amber-lit verandas. In the shadows of the street outside, *betjak* men squatted on the pavement, eating or gambling. A tall man came down the driveway, passing several other *betjaks* to climb into Husen's. He half turned in the seat and said softly, "Better your *betjak.*" The man fished a cigar out of his pocket and lit it; he smelled of alcohol and eau de cologne. Husen glimpsed a bald, silver-fringed head and plump pink face; the passenger's dark suit was of expensive silk.

"Maybe you want going to bar, okay?"

"No, not to a bar. Just drive around."

"What do you like, Mister?" When the man gave no reply, Husen moved the *betjak* down the highroad of Djalan Thamrin, past Sarinah store and turned into Kebon Sirih, a broad avenue leading to many bars and restaurants. As they passed under the shadows of the tamarind trees, Husen felt the man's hand rest on his thigh. "This . . . your leg is very strong," he said softly. Husen chuckled with embarrassment. "Okay, mister. Of course I am long time driver of *betjak.* You like boy, *tuan?*"

"Yes."

"Do you like with me?"

"Yes."

"If you like with me, *tuan,* I am not like. Because I have wife." Husen thought of Karniti, alone in their rooms in Simprug. He did not want to lose the fare. He did something he had not done before. "I have friend, *tuan,* if you like boy. His name is Rodon. He is very smart and strong. He's a *betjak* driver at the hotel."

"Where is he?"

"Over there in Senen market, *tuan.* Over there I can look for my friend. He is many times in Pasar Senen, in a small restaurant there."

The man agreed. When they reached the central marketplace, with its thousands of people, the blinding glare of endless naked electric bulbs and the noise of traffic and amplified music, the man told Husen to go and find his friend while he waited at a beer-stall. Husen pedaled around Pasar Senen for an hour without success; it was after eleven when he returned to find his passenger drinking beer with a young, long-haired Javanese boy who appeared to be a student. There were six empty beer bottles on the table. The two squeezed into the seat of Husen's *betjak;* the foreigner told Husen to go to Surapati Park. It was not far away but the tree-lined streets were dark and empty as they neared the park. The foreigner, with a nervous giggle that sounded unpleasant, took off his jacket and spread it over his lap. Husen asked the boy in Javanese, "Do you want to go with this gentleman? Are you sure?

The boy twisted back in the seat to say something; Husen saw he was afraid. His mouth was slack but he was trying to smile with it, as if to appease the foreigner. The older man laughed and jerked the boy's head to the front before he could speak. The boy again started to struggle, telling Husen, "Oh, let's go to another place. I'm afraid here." Husen said in English, "Better find another place, *tuan*. You can rent a room in Pedjompogan."

This seemed to satisfy the man who straightened up and Husen pedaled quickly to brightly-lit Djalan Thamrin, passing the Hotel Indonesia once again. He had to dismount to push the *betjak* up a bridge behind the hotel; neither the man nor the student dismounted and Husen realized how old and tired he was becoming. Husen was wondering what to do next when he saw Rodon's *betjak;* he called to the other *betjak* driver, who came to the curb to meet them. Rodon was a common fellow, yellow and thickset and black of hair and eye and clother in ragged blue *betjak* garments but he had a handsome face above his bearded lips and Husen knew he sometimes went with *bantjis.*

"Who's this?" the foreigner asked.

"Rodon, my friend."

"Ah, this one is better."

Husen spoke to Rodon in Javanese. "Well, what do you think? Do you want to go with this white man?" The other said nothing but motioned to the foreigner to follow him. The foreigner handed the student his coat and told him, "You wait here. I'll come back for you." He disappeared with Rodon into a dark passageway. The boy at once handed Husen the coat and fled down the street, disappearing in the crowd.

The next afternoon as Husen waited in his *betjak* outside the hotel, a bellhop brought him a note written in English. It said, "Last night I lost $40 in American money and twenty thousand rupiah. Help me to recover this money or I shall notify the police." The bellhop described the foreign *tuan* who had sent him; it was the same man as the night before. Husen found Rodon and asked him, "Did you take the money?" When his friend said no, Husen told him, "We'd better go find who took it. If you didn't, I think the *tuan* means me." They hired another *betjak* and searched Pasar Senen for the student; the beer vendor said he lived in Kali Barutim, a nearby slum. "Do you know how much money he got last night?" Husen asked the vendor, trying to conceal his anxiety. "That *tuan* really liked him."

"No, except he had two pieces of green foreign money with 'twenty' on them."

They found the boy in Kali Barutim; his house was in a squalid lane not far from the market. "Hey! How are you?" Husen called with a grin when they saw him. "Remember me?"

"Yah, you took us around in your *betjak* last night."

"You shouldn't have run away," Rodon told him. "That *tuan* is rich. He gave me ten thousand roops and two shirts and a pair of trousers. Now he wants to see you. He wants you to come to the hotel." The boy seemed to swallow the lies.

"Why?"

"He's going to Tokyo tomorrow morning. He wants you to come to the hotel."

The boy began to protest as soon as they got in their *betjak,* Husen and Rodon squeezing in on either side of him. He tried to get out, complaining, "I don't want to go."

"I think you better," Husen said, firmly holding him in the *betjak.* "We came all the way here to tell you. You can get a lot of money from that *tuan.*" As they neared the hotel, the boy confessed to them. "Please let me go! I'm not a student. I am a poor man. I sell cigarettes in Pasar Senen. Okay, I took the money. I'll split it with you."

Together they went into the hotel. To Husen's surprise, the foreigner had a large suite of rooms; it must have cost thirty thousand rupiah a day or more. The man, pink-faced, sweating and with eyes of slate, was waiting for them; he wore a red silk bathrobe, and his bare legs were white and hairy. "Where's the money?" he asked.

The boy gave him what he had. He was whimpering. "I sold the dollars for eight thousand rupiah."

"Impossible! If you changed the dollars you should have got fifteen thousand. Give it all back or I'll call the police." The boy was too terrified to speak; they went out and with the help of Husen and Rodon he was able to borrow seven thousand rupiah from a Chinese money lender at seventeen percent interest; he told them it would take him many months to pay it back.

It was a danger all the *betjak* men faced; that one of their foreign passengers would accuse them of theft after a drunken night out on the city. Once, after Husen had taken a foreigner to a house of prostitution in Planet near Pasar Senen, he was told by the hotel's security police someone had stolen the man's wedding ring. Husen feared arrest but told himself, "Remember the proverb, 'An innocent man knows no fright.'" Husen found the girl, a plump, good-natured Sundanese and, again under the pretext the foreign *tuan* wanted to see her, brought her back to the hotel. To his surprise, she showed no fear of the foreigner and the security men. The *tuan*, a stout, grey-haired American, at first said it was the wrong girl.

She laughed in his face. "You forget me already?"

When the security men asked her about the ring, she said, "No, Pak, I didn't steal nothing. I was given the ring by this *tuan*." She giggled with embarrassment. "He said he was in love with me. He said he wanted me never to forget him. He was happy, happy. But the ring was white, not gold. I thought, who wants a ring like that? So I sold it to my boyfriend for two hundred roops. Why? Is it valuable?"

The ring was platinum and Husen, the two security men and the girl had to search the city for her boyfriend. Once it was found, the security men apologized. "This was a foolish *tuan* to give his ring away and want it back again. But we have to worry about our jobs too."

The American was so pleased to get the ring back he gave Husen a six thousand rupiah reward which Husen divided with the security men. Then the foreigner invited them all to stay on for a drink, including the girl and her boyfriend, telling them, "Forgive me, everybody. If I hadn't gotten this ring back I couldn't go back to my wife. I dunno. Maybe she'd even divorce me."

"Hello, mister! Where are you going?"

Another night at the Hotel Indonesia. A chubby, grinning Japanese settled into Husen's *betjak*.

"You like 'round the town'?" Husen asked cheerily. *"Aruku kah . . . sampo sampo?* Maybe you like going to casino? Bar? Senen market? To see the shadow play? Very good, Javanese shadow play."

"Oh, thank you. Just a round. I want to see Djakarta."

"How are you tonight, sir?" Husen pedaled out into the circle and across to Deponegoro Street where many big villas and foreign embassies were.

"Oh, you can speak English very well."

"No, sir, just a leetle. You like going for 'round'? No casino? Night club?"

"Just around the hotel. Because it is late."

Husen pointed to the dark skeleton of an unfinished skyscraper. "This is Wisma Nusantara. Japanese construction."

"Oh, Japanese construction. Ah so!"

It was a cool, pleasant evening and there was not much traffic on Deponegoro Street. From out of the shadows beneath the tamarind trees, a woman's voice called invitingly, "Hello, mister! Where are you going?"

"Oh, stop, stop," said Husen's passenger. "I want to talk to that girl there." He smirked. "Very nice, the young girl."

The figure of a beautiful woman emerged from the shadows. The little Japanese saw the coal-black eyes, lustrous hair, full red lips, nostrils breathing passion.

"Ah-h-h-h-h so-o-o-o-o-o-o-ooooo!"

"No, *tuan*," Husen hissed in his ear. "That is not girl, that is queer." He recognized, underneath the disguise, the face of Yan, a poor peasant from Babadan village, not far from Pilangsari.

"No, no, no, no, no! Stop! Stop at once!" the Japanese sputtered with indignation.

"No, no, *tuan,* that is queer!"

The Japanese whirled round in his seat, and opened and shut his mouth, looking furious. Husen pulled over to the curb. Yan approached, giggling in a high falsetto voice. "Hi-hi, hi-hi; such a handsome. . . ." He ran his fingers up and down the sleeve of the passenger.

"Hello there. . . . hee, hee, hee, hee. . . . Do you have a room, miss?"

"Oh, yes, *tuan*. Just behind the Kartika Plaza in Baturadja Street."

"Is it far?" The Japanese giggled nervously.

"No, it's very near." Yan squeezed into the *betjak* seat beside him. "C'mon, please, let's go."

Husen started to pedal. The Japanese shifted about his seat as if he were on needles, moving his elbows as if he were trying to keep his balance; he gaped at Yan like someone suffocating and leaned over to breathe on Yan's neck. "Ooooo! Don't do like that!" Yan gave the Japanese a limp slap. The man's breathing became labored as he tried to embrace Yan again and then suddenly he sat up with a jolt and cried indignantly, "Hey, you're not a girl! You're a man! Stop this *betjak*! Please get out!" His voice rose to a squeal. "Get out! Get out!"

"Please give me money," Yan said in a twangy low voice.

"Hah! You must be a girl to get money from me. Now get out! Get out!" Husen stopped the *betjak*. The Japanese spun around, sputtering indignantly but Husen's face was frozen into a mask of neutrality.

"Look, mister, you already brought me too far." Yan stabbed the Japanese in the ribs with his finger. "And not pay. Maybe I lost a customer back there. Give me two hundred roops."

Relieved it was not more, the Japanese hastily counted out some notes and thrust them into Yan's outstretched hand. Once paid, Yan jumped out of the *betjak* and, without another word, vanished once more into the darkness.

"Take me back to the hotel!" the Japanese cried, his voice cracking.

"Okay, right or not?" said Husen triumphantly. "That is not girl. What I tell to you?"

"Yes, yes. Just take me back at once!"

When Husen related the episode to the other drivers at the *betjak* stand, everyone laughed. One said that some of the *bantjis* wore foam rubber vaginas and turned the lights out so their foreign *tuans* never did discover they were really men. Another told how a *bantji* on Baturadja Street had left his up on the roof to dry and a cat came along and carried it down into the crowded market. Just then Husen saw Yan crossing Djalan Thamrin in back of the hotel and he pedaled off toward him, telling the other *betjak* men, "I am go speak to the *bantjis*. I very much like joking with queer."

Yan was sitting with two other *bantjis*, Ringit and Moomoo, on a low wall behind the hotel swimming pool; a thick bamboo hedge concealed them from the hotel gardens. "Hey, Yan!" Husen called as he pulled up beside them. "Now my Japanese *tuan* won't come outside again for a week!" He parked the *betjak* and sat down beside them. In their makeup, false eyelashes and wigs, it was hard to tell one *bantji* from another or even guess what they really looked like. Most of them came from Djogdjakarta, but some were Sundanese from the capital city itself. Some were educated—students or even married professional men who earned more money in the evening as transvestites. Most of them, like Yan, were poor village youths who worked in their fields part of the year and seasonally migrated to the city in search of jobs. Some turned to this way of life in desperation, others to avoid the strenuous physical labor of coolie work or driving a *betjak*. The *bantjis* were to be found in certain sections of the city each night, even along the leafy boulevards of Kebajoran Baru. The biggest concentration was around the Hotel Indonesia, giving rise to the popular belief most of their clientele was foreign tourists. They were a not uncommon sight in the city, and the governor of Djakarta, a tolerant Javanese, had given them their own concession at the Djakarta Fair, where they gave musical and dance performances. Like the *kangkung welanda,* they bloomed only at night; one almost never saw a *bantji* before sundown.

"Are you looking for money?" Husen asked them cheerily. "Give me fifty roops and I'll go and bring some foreign *tuan*."

"I know you, 'Sen," Yan said in his own twangy voice. "We give the fifty roops and when I ask you where the *tuan* is you say 'Oh, he's sleeping now.' " Husen chuckled. He had played that trick before.

"Not yet find money, 'Sen," Moomoo complained.

"If I am looking for you, 'Sen, I not see. You are not stopping here a long time now. I always watch you. All the time you stay with other *betjaks* in front of the hotel. You look happy. Joking with friends." Ringit, like most *bantjis* when they talked, kept looking around the street, as if he expected someone he knew to appear at any moment.

"Why you sit here, no stand under the bridge of Dukuhatas?" Husen asked. "It is late already, maybe eleven o'clock."

"If I am seeing you, you look very happy," Ringit went on. "I know about you, 'Sen. You are nice boy. You are sometimes many joking with your friends. You never look angry."

Moomoo put his arm around Husen. "May I kiss you?" he joked. Husen laughed and dodged away.

"Why? You are boy? Why you want to kiss me? You are *sama sama* me. If you are girl, okay, I kiss. But you have beard. Your chin is *kasar*, rough." He poked Moomoo in the lap. "Oh, you have big one!"

"Ngentot lu," Moomoo cursed him in a bored manner.

"If I haven't husband already, I like living with you, 'Sen," Ringit said in his peevish voice.

"You have husband?" Husen gave a hoot of laughter. "Please, also get married with me. So I not have to drive *betjak*. Buy me pants, buy me shirt, buy me watch. You looking for the money and I stay in house waiting for you. But if not enough money, I not like."

"Have you been in school, Husen?" Moomoo asked.

"My school is in front of the Hotel Indonesia, speaking with my passengers."

"Why can you speak English?"

"Because much practice. You must listen closely with both ears when the foreigner speaks," he told them seriously. "And you must also read, sometimes you must read in the English book. And you must borrow book from your friend, if your friend is a student."

"If you haven't house, 'Sen, please sleep with me," said Moomoo, who like most of the *bantjis* was illiterate and not interested in learning. "We have a house now in Kebon Katjang," he said, naming a squalid slum where many prostitutes and *bantjis* lived.

"Hey, Yan," Husen asked. "Where did you buy that wig?"

"In a shop."

"You have much money to do like that. Oh, but why do you dress like that? You are a man. Better you looking for job like a man. Selling somethings. Come drive a *betjak*."

"I am a girl," Yan grinned. "Why you not think me a girl like your Japanese friend?"

"Okay, if see far away, you look like a girl, okay. But open your shirt and pull up that *batik*. If you not *sama sama* me, I be sure you are a girl." He gave another hoot of laughter. Yan flounced down the sidewalk in mock indignation. "Sometimes you don't speak many with Husen. He is crazy boy, this Husen." Yan left his purse behind and Husen snatched it up, opened it, found the two hundred rupiah from the Japanese and took out a fifty rupiah note. He put back the purse before the others noticed. "Waiting short time," he told them. "I want to buy cigarette. *Kretek*. One packet." He purchased ten Bentoul *kreteks* from a vendor down the sidewalk and came back, offering each of the *bantjis* one. As they lit up and clouds of clove-spice smoke rose around them, Husen asked Yan if he had any money. Yan said only the two hundred rupiah from the Japanese.

"Please, I want to look at this money. Where is?" Husen said suspiciously, snatching up the purse again and running away a short distance to open it. "Your handbag is like a woman's," he told Yan, who jumped about, trying to grab it back from him. "Powder, mirror, lipstick, comb and black for the eyes. Oh, you are like a girl to bring like this." He gave the purse back. "Hey, Yan, better look your money. I want to borrow."

"I have only two hundred, 'Sen."

"Sure? Is enough or not? Better you look to see."

"Oh, 'Sen! *Sialon lo!* You bedbug! Is only a hundred fifty!" Yan lunged at Husen but he jumped to the side, laughing. "You smoke your *kreteks,* not mine." Just then four Dutch sailors in white bell-bottoms came around the corner from the hotel. With high-pitched squeals of "Hello, mister! Where are you going?" the three bantjis ran to intercept them. Yan turned back for a moment to curse Husen in an undertone. "Okay, 'Sen, you bastard. But watch out the next time you see me. I'll reach into your pocket and take your money." Husen laughed and threw Yan the rest of the packet of *kreteks.* "Maybe you find something else in my pocket."

Mr. Wyatt was Husen's favorite kind of passenger. He had introduced himself as a visiting Australian engineer with only one night to spend in Djakarta who wanted to see the sights and buy some souvenirs for his children. Husen pedaled first to Merdeka Square, the seven-hundred-acre park in the center of the city. Here Husen showed his passenger the huge phallic pillar of Italian marble with its golden flame—forty kilos of pure gold costing a third of a million dollars. Then to the glittering, white, floodlit Merdeka Palace where the president's office was; then to the vast, shadowy ruins of the still-unfinished "biggest mosque in the world"; to the West Irian Monument topped by its bronze giant breaking his colonialist chains, and back to the bright colored lights of Djalan Thamrin again. Sukarno's legacy to Djakarta might have been a useless pile of hollow and half-finished monuments, but they made a perfect setting for guided tours in a *betjak*. This was Husen's specialty.

Mr. Wyatt seemed less concerned with the grandiose splendors than the number of open manholes they skirted by. "Are you sure you know where you're going?" he kept asking Husen. "You might fall down into one of those big manholes. Some are open and uncovered."

"Neverr-r-r-r mind," Husen answered serenely, trilling his r's with a sing-song flourish. "Must go slowly."

Wyatt jokingly asked if Husen could fix him up with a girl. He was surprised to be rebuffed. "No, no, I cannot. I think not good, *tuan*."

"Why?"

"Because I am people. People sell people, I not like." He had not forgotten the episode with Rodon. "Because I am ashamed. If you want girl you must take taxi to Club 69."

"No, I was just joking."

"Never mind. If driver *betjak* speak, speak, not get tired."

Husen pedaled through Menteng, a tree-shaded residential district near the hotel. As they turned into Tjikini Raya, Wyatt asked to see the central marketplace, Pasar Senen. "Who founded Djakarta?" he asked as they rode along. The Australian was beginning to enjoy himself. Once a passenger got used to Husen's labored breathing and overcame the feeling of being a sitting target for every approaching car, a *betjak* ride was agreeable. One was carried along just fast enough for the air to seem cool; it was possible to lean comfortably back and look at the stars without being bitten by insects.

"I don't know," Husen answered. "Before, it's name was Batavia. In 1602 the Dutch came here."

"I wonder what it looked like in 1602."

"Oh, was only village."

"How many miles from one side to the other now?"

"Maybe seventy—seventy-five kilometers. This name is Kramat Raya Street."

"Not many signs in English here."

"No. We are coming to Senen market." The big open square was full of life and movement. The eating-stands and beer-stalls were crowded and noisy. Vendors shouted, *betjaks* clanged their gongs, there was a steady beep-beep of car horns. The crowds looked dirty, poor, sullen and unfriendly. Wyatt felt groping hands on his sleeve. He jerked his arm back involuntarily; a group of pink-powdered prostitutes moved on, their coarse laughter scattering over the air. Somewhere near, a hoarse voice swore obscenely, then burst into a roar of unpleasant laughter. They could hardly move forward; the way ahead was jammed with *betjaks,* the drivers clanging their bells impatiently and shouting abuse. . . . The thousands of light bulbs was dazzling. Across the square some men were shouting excitedly. Wyatt felt uneasy.

"They're open until very late at night," he told Husen.

"Only in night time only," Husen answered cheerily. "In daytime not."

"Let's go a bit further and see if we can cross over and go back. Get out of this crowd." Husen maneuvered the *betjak* to the edge of the road; Wyatt glimpsed a large black hole slide past just inches from the *betjak* wheels.

"Ah-h-h. . . . That was a hole in the street. A big manhole! I thought we were going down that hole. It was a manhole and the manhole cover was missing." Husen seemed unconcerned; he was craning his head from one side to the other, trying to see why traffic was stalled. Wyatt raised his voice in irritation. "That hole we nearly went down into. How many weeks has that hole been there?"

Husen grinned back at him serenely. "Oh, long time already."

"Why doesn't somebody fix it?"

"I don't know. Maybe if I know I could close that hole myself. Dangerous, that is." The traffic slowly began to inch forward; with relief Wyatt saw they were returning to Kramat Raya Street. In a moment they would leave this congestion behind them. He noticed some people were running down the wide boulevard. Others were scrambling to get on a bus. Now a crowd was running and two men were ahead of it as if they were being chased. "What's that?" Wyatt asked Husen. Husen, too, had just noticed the commotion. "Maybe that is pickpocket. From the market. Thieves, maybe thieves. The people are chasing them."

"They look excited. If they catch the pickpockets it will be terrible for them." Wyatt thought there seemed to be a great many people chasing the pickpockets. Then he looked around; everyone near them was running, running away from Pasar Senen. At that moment, inexplicably, all the lights in the market went out and the firing began.

It happened so suddenly that for a moment Wyatt was stunned. The square was plunged into almost total darkness, people were running and someone was shooting at them. For a half a second, he just sat there hearing the rifle fire; then he heard the crack a bullet makes if it comes close and the next moment he had jumped from the *betjak*, shouting to Husen, "Run! This is dangerous! Take cover!"

"Better we go back," cried Husen in confusion, trying to wheel the *betjak* around. The firing increased in volume; they could hear it rake a building above them and Husen dragged the *betjak* behind a cigarette stand. He turned to Wyatt but could not see his passenger in the darkness. *"Tuan! Tuan!"*

Wyatt dove for cover. In the darkness he sensed a great many people were running, crouching, crawling, falling to the pavement. He heard Husen cry quite near him, *"Tuan!* Where are you? Let's go! Those men! They've got spears and knives!" Jesus, thought Wyatt. A revolution! The crowd now seemed possessed; there were shouted oaths, screams, howls. He could no longer hear Husen. He tried to push in the direction of his voice, but others were crowding to get past him and the way was impassable. The heat of the pushing, tightly packed bodies was suffocating; people seemed to have gone mad, trying to escape the rifle fire. Wyatt thought, I'm a white man. He can make it back; I've got to get out of here. He started running, he didn't know where, but it was away from the crowd and the rifle fire. Now that he had lost Husen his only thought was to get as far away as he could from the market place as soon as possible.

Then he'd try to reach the hotel. He heard cries from houses on both sides of the street he had entered; he ran about fifty paces and stopped short, freezing in his tracks. Surging toward him were perhaps twenty or thirty men carrying spears and knives; they were stripped to the waist and their bodies gleamed in the dimness; he couldn't see their faces but they were howling like beasts, he had never heard such inhuman cries. For a moment the fury he faced overpowered him; the scene seemed to shimmer, the distorted faces to dissolve in a haze. The men hesitated when they reached him, their bolo knives raised to swing and then to his amazement they ran past him toward the market place. . . .

Husen had pedaled his passenger into Pasar Senen without knowing that nine men had been stabbed to death in a fight between Ambonese and Padang islanders the night before. The riot had been sparked by a seemingly insignificant incident: An Ambonese teenager, a member of a gang known as the "Alamo boys," bought a single *kretek* cigarette from a Padang street vendor. He paid only five rupiah instead of the full price of eight. The Padang, from west Sumatra, demanded three more rupiah but the Ambon youth, already high on hashish, instead hit him savagely across the face. Other Padangs rushed to the defense of the vendor, but a policeman intervened and broke up the struggle.

It might have ended there had not a feud for control of prostitution in Planet, the city's main center of vice just behind Senen Market, been smouldering for some time between a gang of Padangs and the Negro Ambons. The Padang leader, having been warned that some of the Ambons had threatened to set Planet on fire, appealed to the leaders of the Alamo gang to arrange a settlement and avoid further violence. The Ambonese gang, whose members lived in a stockaded community on Kwini Street, just off Pasar Senen, sent a deputation of four Ambons, all heavily-built construction coolies. An agreement was reached over several bottles of Javanese whiskey; on the way back to Kwini Street, one of the now-drunken Ambonese coolies told the others, "You come behind and I'll go first to see those Padang sons-of-bitches don't jump us. You can't trust a Padang." He was overheard and in the darkness of Kwini Street he was jumped, dragged into an alley, beaten and knifed. When the other three Ambons found him he was dead. As soon as the body was carried back to the Alamo gang's headquarters, the Ambons cried for vengeance. They took a solemn vow to burn down Planet—its bamboo shanties and abandoned freight cars were highly inflammable and jammed with prostitutes and dope addicts—and a force started moving down to the market. They were intercepted by a company of Indonesian army soldiers who argued that if they burned down Planet the Padangs would retaliate and set Kwini Street on fire; the entire inner core of Djakarta would be in flames. Turning back in Pasar Senen the Ambons seemed pacified, but suddenly they ran amok, running through the market place with their oil cans and kerosene, starting fires and stabbing and knifing merchants and idlers alike—anyone who looked like a Padang. Like crazed beasts, they struck out at everything in front of them, and eight men were killed and dozens more hospitalized. The next night, the Alamo gang vowed to resume the attack; an attempt was made to scale the walls of Planet, since all the entryways were heavily guarded by military troops. Hand-to-hand fighting had just broken out on the steps of the city's new municipal market building as Husen arrived in Pasar Senen pulling Wyatt in his *betjak*. The Djakarta police chief gave orders to fire above the heads of the nightly crowd in the huge market square to disperse everyone. He also ordered all the lights switched out. What Wyatt had done unwittingly, was to turn and run into Kwini Street, straight toward the barricades of the Alamo gang. . . .

For a second it had seemed to Wyatt he would be cut to pieces. When the men seethed past him—they were mostly bushy-haired Negroes—he saw a *betjak* by the side of the road and ran to it, jumping in and shouting to the driver, to hurry, hurry, get out of there. "Go! Go!" he shouted. The driver, aware the Ambonese barricade was just ahead, stared at the crazy foreigner in confusion. Wyatt was about to get out and run again when an Ambon on a motorcycle roared up and shouted at him, *"Tjepat! Tjepat! Hurry!"* He thought it meant jump on so he took a seat behind the cyclist. With a roar of exhaust, they sped into an alleyway; Wyatt had no idea where they were headed as the machine twisted and turned down one narrow lane after another. "Two hundred roops?" the driver asked him several times and Wyatt repeated again and again, "Yes, yes. Just take me to the Hotel Indonesia." They had not gone far before Wyatt saw with relief that people were strolling or sitting in cafes; Djalan Thamrin looked normal. When they reached the hotel, he pulled out his billfold but the Ambon grinned and pushed his money away. "No, no, *tuan*," his rescuer said. "But can you give me your address? I am very like to have pen friend with people from another people's country."

Back in Pasar Senen, Husen had crouched behind a cigarette stand with another *betjak* man. "Wah! Where is mister?" he said, telling his companion, "Okay, better I wait here short time. Because my *tuan* I not find. Better you go quick to Hero's Monument. If he runs that way you can stop him." He gave the man Wyatt's description. "I want looking for him in Pasar Senen. Maybe dangerous. He don't know this place. Maybe he fall in manhole." Ignoring the still sporadic rifle fire overhead in his concern to find Wyatt, Husen ran at a crouch from manhole to manhole, calling into each dark shaft. When a tall young thug with a spear suddenly loomed above him, Husen forgot his fright and sputtered indignantly, "No! No! I am trying to find my friend from Australia. He is maybe fall inside." A soldier, too, collared Husen but when he heard a foreigner was involved he joined Husen in peering down all the manholes and drainage ditches until word came Wyatt was safely back at the hotel.

Alarmed by the rising tempo of violence in the city, Husen resolved to take some precaution. Robberies of *betjak* drivers on their way home late at night were on the rise. One night a Batak tried to steal the *betjak* of a driver from the hotel. When the driver pushed the *betjak* into a canal, the Batak stabbed him and threw his body in after the *betjak*.

This made up Husen's mind. He went to a *dukun* and asked for *susuk,* an ancient Javanese practice of having small slivers of gold or diamond inserted just under the skin to give one magic protective powers. Husen told the sorcerer, "I want to be safe from a knife." The *dukun* inserted twelve diamond slivers for two thousand rupiah. During a weekend visit to Pilangsari soon afterward, Husen's father noticed two of the slivers, inserted near the outer corner of each eye; the rest were on less visible parts of his body. "I'm afraid in Djakarta," Husen told his father. So many 'cross boys' and gangsters now, and they might kill me."

His father was aghast. "If you are a Moslem, son, you have fallen down on your religion. *Susuk* is forbidden."

"I wanted to try only. Whether sure or not."

"You must have them removed at once, Husen. If you are a Moslem and you practice *susuk,* you will die a slow, agonizing death." Husen had the slivers removed, regretting he had gone home without first putting the powers of the magic to the test. After that he relied more than ever on smiling and being friendly toward strangers in Djakarta.

Husen had reason to be afraid; Djakarta had one of the highest crime rates in the world. As violence increased, its upper classes asked themselves why. Some sympathetically held that poor villagers, coming to the city, unable to find work and perhaps with sick or hungry wives and children, could become so desperate and despairing they would sever their ethical links with the village and take to crime. More hostile observers blamed Djakarta's criminals on childhood experience, pyschic debility or even derangement.

Although most of the ctiy's poor were uprooted Javanese peasants, they committed only a small proportion of the city's crimes. Instead, Djakarta's jails were filled with the more aggressive and less cultured outer islanders: Bataks from Sumatra, Makassars from Sulawesi, Ambons, Dyaks and Mindanaoese. None of these shared the traditional tenets of Javanese culture that had filtered down to the peasantry over centuries from the old *prijaji* or Javanese court traditions: the air must have no tension; to rush is indignified; to preserve one's calm and poise and remain soft-spoken, smiling and polite in all circumstances is to be desired; truth is less to be valued than avoiding pain and giving joy. One might have thought the hectic tempo of modern Djakarta would rip such values into shreds, but this does not seem to have happened. Java was a small island, and most Javanese did not seem to suffer serious alienation in the city as long as they went home to their villages often enough. Husen had never seen a movie in Djakarta, preferring the *sandiwara* dramas and shadow plays of Tjirebon. As he would say, "I am a villager; wherever I go, I must respect the ways of my village."

Not all Javanese survived the effects of urbanization; a few of Husen's friends among the *betjak* drivers became alienated from both the city and the village they left behind. Typically, one of these, Tjasta, whose shopkeeping family in Pilangsari was more prosperous than Husen's, and who was of the same age and had come to Djakarta to drive a *betjak* at almost the same time, had gone astray when he was only eighteen after a friend dared him to steal a watch. Caught, kicked, beaten and trampled by soldiers who ordered him to identify any accomplices, Tjasta in terror singled out an innocent bystander and later was meted out a stiff two-and-a-half year sentence for giving false evidence.

A pale, sorrowful youth, he was gang-raped one night in Djakarta's big Tjipinang prison by older Negro convicts from Makassar, who forced him to inhale heroin smoke until he sank into wild hallucinations. For the next two days they forcibly tattooed his arms with such legends as "Adventure of Love," "The Spirit is Neutral; the Blood is Hot" and "Sacrifice to Love," along with the picture of a naked girl, a death's head and other, more cryptic marks, all of which he still bore. Released from prison after two years he drifted in and out of common-law marriages and jobs, working for a time as a construction coolie, a stevedore at the port, and a *betjak* man; in time he became addicted to hashish, and sometimes engaged in pimping or petty thievery to support his habit. He rarely returned to the village, and only then to borrow money, usually lying to his parents that his *betjak* had been stolen or that he had to pay gambling debts or go to jail. In time his father refused him another rupiah, and when he no longer came home his elderly mother would complain to the neighbors, "Tjasta never comes to see us any more; he doesn't like life in the village." Now, plying his *betjak* from the stand at the Hotel Indonesia as did Husen, he wore only a black singlet and black shorts; and with his coarse black hair falling over his eyes, a bristling black moustache and the empty stare of the hashish smoker, he looked so threatening many foreigners quickly passed by his *betjak;* Husen had once heard an American lady remark, "That man looks like a killer."

Most of Djakarta's *betjak* men were villagers in temporary sojourn like Husen, but there were enough culturally uprooted Tjastas, with their shattered values and disintegrated lives, to make the streets of Djakarta dangerous at night. Sometimes a band of five or six armed with *perangs* might in some dark lane set upon a lone pedestrian or *betjak* passenger, who would be lucky to escape with merely losing his valuables.

There were also times when even the usually law-abiding *betjak* men formed into leaderless mobs. This happened when they felt some intolerable grievance; for instance, if a driver was brutally treated by a policeman, thousands might come to his assistance and tear apart a police station. Once, when a truck from a visiting Indian circus struck a *betjak* and sped away, within a few hours five thousand drivers were pelting its tents with rocks. After students got into fights with *betjak* drivers, usually over the fare, the drivers had been known to wage pitched battles against student hostels at the universities. Again, when an Ambonese gangster had tried to pull a girl from a *betjak* in Pasar Senen and the driver, defending her, was knifed, *betjaks* poured in from all over the city, and before the army quelled the rioting scores of men were wounded and two *betjak* drivers were stabbed to death.

Late at night. Husen was taking two soldiers in his *betjak* to Bongkaren, where he had lived with his first wife. They wanted girls. He stopped in front of a shack where red paper pasted over coconut oil lamps cast an orange halo on the rubbish-strewn road. The soldiers had started to pay him when a small boy darted up from the darkness.

He held out a bony little hand to the soldiers, until he saw Husen. The child's face was pale and pinched with malnutrition; a threadbare shirt hung loose from his frail body. Husen glanced hurriedly at the soldiers and then whispered to the child, "Rus! What are you doing here? Don't be out at night. Run home. If I find money I'll come back."

"I need money now." The boy's voice was unexpectedly harsh and guttural. One of the soldiers grunted impatiently. Husen twisted his face into a grin, "Say hello to the uncles."

The boy ignored him. "No, *na*," he said, using the rough form of address of Djakarta street gangs, "give me money now!" One of the soldiers handed him a rupiah note; the child snatched it and was gone before Husen could speak again.

"Who's the kid?" the soldier asked.

Husen mumbled absently, as he stared off into the dark street, "My son. . . ."

The next day Husen went back to Bongkaren to find Rustani. He took fifteen hundred rupiah with him and stopped in Tanahabang market to buy a boy's shirt for five hundred. Seen in the noonday sunlight, Husen realized, Bongkaren was the worst slum in the city; there was an air of tension, of grim defeat, about the place. It lay between a fetid brown canal and an abandoned railway yard; its rows of bamboo and beaten-tin shanties were built among empty freight cars where vagrants lived. There were no trees for shade; it was festeringly hot. A whirling hot wind chased and scattered flying bits of dry rubbish along the rusted railway tracks in front of him. It lifted the swarms of flies from the tops of rubbish heaps that seemed to lie everywhere. In the leprous ruins of a leaning old train stop shelter some vagrants were living in filthy squalor; old charcoal baskets, still grimy with black dust, served as walls, worn-out mats gleaned from garbage dumps made do as floors. The roofs of these small boxes were made from blackened and rusted old tin cans, patched together with bits of cardboard. As he passed one of these, a woman crawled out, sobbing and pulling at her dirty, matted hair. "You made me a whore!" she shrieked. "Now, look, look!" Like a maniac, she thrust her arms in the face of a small, barefoot man who stood dumbly watching her. Her arms were covered with sores and rashes, hideous in the bright sunshine. The man pulled his belt from his torn pants. Quivering with rage, he began lashing the woman hysterically. She screamed as the blows struck her face, giving an animal cry and snatching at the belt. He pulled it back with a jerk and it shot through her fingers, ripping at the skin. No one paid any attention. Husen hurried on. Old women with dazed expressions wandered back and forth, carrying water containers, and cooking pots, their bare feet treading on the filth and garbage. Underneath the freightcars, girls were sitting on the ground, picking lice out of each other's hair. With relief, Husen, having crossed the railway tracks, approached a row of bigger, more solidly-built shanties. He entered a narrow alleyway and had to walk carefully, as the mud was slippery under foot. The path turned and twisted several times, and then Husen stopped before a small food-stall. There was a larger room behind and a doorway leading into a bedroom; he could glimpse a large bed covered with a mosquito net, there was a hint of relative prosperity about the shack.

A wizened, yellow old man jumped up and rushed to greet Husen, tightly clasping his hands and chuckling, "*Asallam muallai-kum,* praise be to Allah, my son-in-law. It has been a long time. How are you now?"

"Well and good. And you?"

"We are also."

"Where is my son, Rustani?"

A middle-aged woman appeared in the inner doorway and advanced toward them. "I don't know," she said in a hollow voice, without greeting Husen. "I want to look for him." Her eyes were vacant and dull. She called down the alley, "Rus! Rus! Your father has come!"

The child came running and snatched the shirt from Husen's hands. "I am inside school now and could use this," he said possessively.

"Rus," Husen said gently, squatting down and drawing the child toward him. "I was wrong not to come sooner. But now I buy this shirt for you." He looked at the boy's face and stood up quickly. "How much money for inside the school?"

"Five hundred," said the mother. "I only give two hundred fifty so far."

"Where is your husband?"

"I don't know. Maybe he drives the *betjak*. Long time now he does not come home. Ten days already."

From inside the bedroom came the cry of a baby. She went inside and brought out a tiny, whimpering child with red-rimmed, rheumy eyes and a wet, feverish-looking face. She held the baby to Husen. "Please hold my girl. I want to heat water for coffee." As she drew close, Husen saw how badly Taminah had aged. She was barely thirty and all of the softness of youth was gone; now she was thin as a serpent with a long, pale face. Her long eyelashes were all that remained of her beauty; her nose was thin and sharp, her chin was thin and sharp; the whole expression of her face was of sharpness and stinginess. Only the serious, self-centered look was as he remembered it.

As she prepared coffee she complained that Rustani would no longer mind her; he insisted on swimming in the filthy canal with other boys and became angry when she called him, and often did not come home in the evening.

"Never mind, Taminah," Husen reassured her. "He is still a boy. If a boy is a little wild it means he will be clever at his lessons."

She complained that Rustani needed to be circumcized and that Husen seldom visited his son. They were badly short of money even though Husen's sister, Karlina, sometimes gave Rustani a little. Her husband stayed away from home for weeks at a time, smoking hashish and gambling. If she criticized him, he beat her. Only Allah knew what would happen in the future.

Husen said the circumcision ceremony would have to be in Pilangsari and would cost more than four thousand rupiah; they would have to wait some time before he could afford the cost of the *slametan*. A breath of life crossed Taminah's face. "What about me and my mother, Husen? Will you bring us to Pilangsari to see Rustani cut?"

He looked at her sharp, ruined face. "Better you and your mother . . . better you come if you want to." Taminah served the coffee and took back her baby girl, telling Husen it was sick, but she could not afford to take her to the doctor. He gave her the thousand rupiah note he had left. Husen drank the coffee hurriedly, anxious to go. He told his son, "Rus, you don't be cross with your mother. You do what she says. If you want to go with me and stay in village with your grandmother, I think better."

"No, no," the boy said. "Better you help me buy book, give money for food and so on, so I not have to beg in the street. I want to learn in the Moslem school. If I am with you I am afraid of your wife. Maybe if I stay with you, she is angry with me."

"No, Rus, she will not be angry; she is very kind."

"No, better I stay here. You must many times visit me." Husen rose to go, taking his son's hand; suddenly the boy embraced his legs, clinging to them so that Husen had to gently pry him away. At this hint of rejection, the child's hostility seemed to return and he said nothing more but stared stonily at Husen. When Husen left, Taminah came out into the lane watching him go, leaning against the doorway until he was out of sight. That night in Simprug, Husen could not sleep. For a long time he lay restlessly by Karniti's side, thinking of Taminah, what she once was and what she had become. He did not feel pity, just a hollow sense of futility and emptiness.

Day by day amidst the wealth of the city, Husen and his friends lived in the wide base of poverty upon which it was laid. They pedaled their *betjaks,* strained their legs and backs until the muscles stood out like ropes, ate hungrily of their unnourishing food, slept out their brief nights, cursed their lot and hoped for a better future. And all the time the numbers of poor grew and grew and the leaders of the city feared what would happen if ever there were not enough food to feed their hunger. Finally, the governor of the city, a military general, declared the capital would henceforward be "a closed city to new jobless settlers." It was the most drastic action that had been taken in any great urban center to stem the flow of peasant immigrants; at a press conference the governor said that the flood of incoming poor had reached such proportions it was "endangering the safety and order of life in the capital."

"What about all the coolies and *betjak* men who are already here?" a journalist asked.

"No, not them," the governor replied. "But this does apply to their little brothers."

Publicly, rumors were circulated of sudden sweeps, identity checks, detention camps, forced evictions, and whole shantytowns being forcibly emptied, set fire to, and razed during the night. Privately, the governor knew he could only try to reduce the flow of migration into the city, not stop it. How could anyone be denied entry to his own country's capital city? But officially the governor had a sort of license to end terrorism, and he announced that anyone found by the police without proof of job and residence would be sent out of the city by "the cheapest possible transport." Soon truckloads of people were driven hundreds of miles away and just dumped. He also decreed that all street vendors must cease operations. He declared to the press, "Vending in public places not only violates the existing laws, but also demonstrates indifference toward the interests of others, which should not happen among civilized people. Without serious enforcement against the street vendors, we can predict that the streets of Djakarta, within two or three years, will be filled with rubbish and jammed with vendors."

Soon afterward Husen's youngest brother, Warjono, managed to catch a ride on a freight train, and came to the city for the first time to try his luck. Soon he found a job with a street vendor, selling ices near the city's big sports stadium. He had been given a "way letter" from the village chief to visit the city for a month, a letter he was to easily renew each time he visited Pilangsari, since the local authorities too wanted to get rid of surplus people. When the thirteen-year-old Warjono told his friends he could earn one or two hundred rupiahs a day selling ices, one returned with him to Djakarta. The next month two more came. And then another, and another, and another and another.

iv / Husen

Makin lama, makin tunduk—
—*an old Javanese folk saying, meaning, "the
older the man, the more bowed down with hum-
bleness and wisdom." It is also an allusion to rice,
which, the more it matures and ripens for harvest,
the heavier hangs the grainhead.*

"When I was a young man, I felt life was going up, up. Now it
has begun to go down." Karniti listened to her husband's words.
"Ah," she said tranquilly, "I know what is your thought. You want
to go home to the village." Husen took the package of soiled notes
from under the bamboo matting on their bed and counted it again,
as he had done over and over again so many times. "Forty thousand.
. . . Is enough, Kar?" "Maybe not enough, Husen. Waiting some
time." The days passed. Husen's growing knowledge of English
earned him better payments and such generous tips that Tjasta told
the other *betjak* men at the hotel, "Husen has a *djimat*." Husen
laughed at the idea a magic talisman had given him supernatural
powers. "My eyes, my ears, my tongue," he told his friend "that's my
djimat."

Finally his little hoard of rupiah notes grew to fifty thousand, the
most money he had ever been able to save at one time. He knew he
should spend some of it on his son's circumcision ceremony; the boy
was already seven. But the years of straining at loads too heavy for
him was beginning to set deep wrinkles in the flesh of his forehead
and about his eyes; veins stood out on his muscular legs; and sometimes when he tried to push a full load of passengers up an incline or
over a bridge, his breath came only in short gasps and he felt dizzy
and faint. When he complained about this to the other *betjak* men
they laughed and he himself would chuckle with them. But on the
nights he sat waiting for passengers at the hotel, he would long and
long for the village. His father might fast and pray to Allah for
rain and sun in proportion so that the rice seed would sprout in the
land and the stalk bear grain. But with the new rice and irrigation
it would not matter if the heavens rained in season; with hard work
and Abu's help perhaps he could become prosperous enough to stay
in Pilangsari forever.

Then suddenly one night in Simprug it seemed to Husen that he
could not stay one more day in this wretched *kampong,* nor could he
strain another night, his body bent forward pressing down on the
pedals, driving his passengers through the rutted streets. Each dark

corner of the city, each rutted dirt road, each muddy lane puddled with the monsoon, had become his enemy; every shadow held the thief's knife, and each cough the whistle of disease.

"Tomorrow," he cried out to Karniti, "tomorrow we go back to the village!"

He left the *betjak* at the owner's stand; they packed up their few possessions, paid Bibi a thousand rupiah to end their lease, and they were gone. Except for Bibi and Kasum and Muri, they said goodbye to no one.

Husen's father gave him a small plot of land by the road, ten meters by ten, to build a house and shop, the *warung* Karniti had wanted so long. A small *gajam* tree provided shade until Husen could plant more. He with his loyal friend Djuned and Tarja worked alone for some days, digging drainage ditches, raising the level of the earth, jogging back and forth to the banks of the Tjimanouk with baskets of clay, hiring a boat to bring sand from the other side of the river, felling six of his father's best *djati* trees in Tjibanteng Garden, having them sawn into lumber, buying red bricks in Kliwed and bringing them back by *betjak,* and finally hiring a crew of carpenters. The house and *warung* were built as Husen planned them; brick foundations, waist high, topped with bamboo walls; an *atap* roof; a small kitchen with an open hearth and brick washing platform behind; a large front room for the *shop,* with a big open window to serve customers; a narrow front porch with a long bench; and a bedroom for himself and Karniti. Time enough later to add a room for their son.

One day, as they were working on the roof, a truck with a loud-speaker came by, announcing that work would soon begin to widen the road through the village; it was to be made into a paved highway for a new bypass around the seaport of Tjirebon, linking one end of the island of Java with the other. "Old people and children must be careful," a man on a loudspeaker called. "They cannot play in the street. Because many trucks will bring stone for the new highway. If you do not heed this warning and children die by accident, there is nothing to be done." After that as many as fifty trucks roared through each day, back and forth, round the clock, coating the sides of the road with dust and filling the villagers with hopes of economic prosperity. Soon afterward, news followed that the water in the village canal would be cut off for six months. The government would dredge it and build new stone and cement locks; the coming year Pilangsari would have enough irrigation water for the first time in half-a-century.

When the *warung* was finished, Husen and Karniti started sleeping there. Djuned warned them this was dangerous; one should hold a *slametan* or ceremonial feast and celebration first. But Husen had no money left for a shadow play performance; he ignored such fears. As Karniti's pregnancy advanced, she grew listless and drowsy and slept most of the day. In the closed world of the village, his parents accused her of laziness; one day when Karniti felt unable to cook for the carpenters their hot boiled rice, Husen's old mother appeared in the *warung,* her small, sharp black eyes stinging the young girl with their contempt. "What a slothful wife you are!" the old lady cried with irritation. "Serving the workmen such poor stuff." Faint and nauseated, Karniti fled in tears to her parent's home across the river, and would not return to Husen for three days.

Then her health revived and Karniti's old happy disposition was back. She busied herself with the *warung,* adorning its big glass counter jars of cakes, candies and cigarettes with bright yellow paper. Every morning she went early to the Djatibarang market to buy supplies. From mid-morning she kept ready a kettle of boiling water for hot tea and coffee, a kettle of soup, freshly-cooked rice, a big basket of mangoes and papayas and pink lolly drinks with plenty of ice. After the dreary idleness of Simprug, Karniti thrived on activity; she gossiped and joked with all the customers, sang softly to herself as she bent over the hearth, happier now that the baby was soon coming than Husen had ever seen her. Let his parents complain and find fault, she would soon justify herself with a son. Then what would they say?

Day by day, the *warung* began to thrive. Coming from the fields, Husen would find truck drivers from the highway project were beginning to stop; he would watch them eat heartily and would apologize, "It is poor food—my wife knows only the cooking of the village." But he was proud of the dishes she served, knowing she had learned in Simprug from women who worked as cooks for the rich how to combine sugar, spices and vinegar into succulent sauces. Husen looked forward to the day the canal and highway work would be done. Every evening he entertained men who gathered at the *warung* with his anecdotes about Djakarta, his folktales and slapstick comedies; sometimes he read *wajang kulit* scenarios, gleefully acting out all the parts; or he would borrow a guitar and sing melancholy Tjirebon sea ballads. He was content; soon it would be Ramadan, the Moslem month of abstention from dawn to sunset, which, though little observed in the village except by a few strict believers like his father, was still the cause of an outburst of joy at its end, at Lebaran, the Javanese New Year. Husen was also impatient for the return of Abu, who had gone home for Ramadan, so they could talk about farming. Next crop he would plant the new rice.

For some reason, the rains withheld themselves. Day after day the sun shone with new and careless brilliance. At first no one worried. Men coming from Djakarta said the monsoon had never been heavier there, pouring down day and night so that many low places —Simprug, Bongkaren, the shantytowns behind the hotel—stood under water. The smaller streets and alleys were a morass of mud. Even *betjaks* could hardly move, and the hardships of the poor had increased with the rains. But in Pilangsari, the earth remained parched and thirsty. From dawn to dawn there was not a cloud in the perfect blue sky and even when the stars appeared at night the ground seemed dewless and dry. Although Husen and Tarja cultivated them desperately, the fields dried and cracked; the young rice stalks, which had sprung up healthily in the August showers, now ceased to grow and stood stunted at first under the hot sun, and at last dwindled and yellowed into a barren harvest. Only across the river in Bojong village, whose canal had not needed repair and where the Tjimanouk's waters flowed in freely, were there great squares of jade in the dull brown landscape. Husen saw that the former Communist would reap another rich harvest with his new dwarf rice; he envied his full rice bin and grew angry when he heard that some of the men of Bojong, prospering on the misfortune of others, were buying up mangoes cheaply and selling them in the city for high profits. Husen vowed that somewhere he would find the money to buy the new seeds and fertilizer and pesticides, even if he had to go back to driving a *betjak*.

Husen's father, who had reaped less than 1,000 kilograms the previous harvest, when his fasting failed to drive away the insects, now got nothing. A dull green patch of cucumbers was the only color on the dead earth of his fields. Now Husen and the village men carried water from the Tjimanouk to their last remaining crops, heavy steel buckets slung upon bamboo poles across their shoulders. But though a furrow grew upon Husen's flesh and calluses formed there, no rain came and the cucumbers died too.

At last the water in the pond near his father's cottage dried into cakes of clay; even the water in the well and the river sank low. There were reports of a cholera epidemic near Indramaju; then they heard some forty persons had died in villages to the south. The toll continued to rise, fifty and then more than a hundred. One day a government nurse came to Pilangsari to give inoculations; the *dukuns* said the injections caused one to fall ill and affected one's mind, so many of the villagers hid in their houses until she went away. And then Djuned, so husky, young and healthy, complained of diarrhea one night when he and Husen went to swim in the river. He was dead by sunrise. After that a shudder of panic swept the village and everyone rushed to Djatibarang for inoculations.

Week after week passed and still no rain. Ramadan came, and in the evening wandering bands of village boys with drums would come across the fields from the far treelines, from the villages across the river. *"Tomtom te tomtom, tom te tom te tom, tomtom, tomtom, tomtom. . . ."* The throb of the drums would echo along the Tjima-nouk and re-echo from the dry, burnt treetops. The mangoes ripened, withered and were stunted; Husen's father got only three thousand rupiah for his entire yield, half the usual amount. Some days clouds would gather in the sky, small light clouds, and Husen and his father and brother, Tarja, would turn their faces to the sky, judging closely this cloud and that and speculating whether any rain would come of it. And Husen would shake his head and say, "The wind takes away," and sure enough, a bitter wind would come from the mountains and blow the clouds off. So the sky remained empty and yellow with rising dust, and a pale sun rose each morning, moved across the heaven and set each night, and there was not a drop of rain.

The day came when his father called Husen and told him to look in the family rice bin. When Husen saw how empty it was, with only small heaps of stalk paddy at the bottom, he thought, "This is serious now. How shall we eat?" He waited for his father to speak and the old man said there was only enough rice for himself, his wife and Tarja for three months; and the next harvest was still seven months away. He told Husen he would have to find his own rice for himself and Karniti. Karniti went across the river to Bojong where rice was plentiful and started buying it at the inflated price of twenty-five rupiah a day, spending more than they made from the *warung*. There were fewer customers now—none of the villagers had money for tea or coffee or cakes—and Husen told her one night, "I must go back to the city. How else can we find money to eat?" She answered, "Wait some time. Until the baby is born. Then we will see." The entire family was reduced to eating only a small portion of rice once a day; it was hardest on Tarja, who did most of the heavy physical labor for their father, and one day Husen caught him stuffing Karniti's rice for the *warung* into his mouth in hasty fistfuls, but he said nothing to anyone else. Seeing Karniti heavy with their child, he forced her to take his share of their rice, feeling as he watched her lips move and swallow, that at least his son was being fed. Husen himself lived on the coarse fibers of tapioca root when it could be found, and he grew haggard and thin. Both of them were silent and fearful, watching the craving of the village children and seeing their empty bellies grow distended.

Husen's father summoned him again and said, "Because I am old and already tired, whoever of my children wants to plant my land— if Allah wills that the rain returns—please, my land is yours. Because I am so old now. I am only fit to eat. I will give you half of what rice you grow."

Husen saw his mother's eyes fill with tears; she told his father, "Better like that if you are tired, my husband. Better you try your children now." They both knew he was admitting defeat. As the days passed, the sky darkened and from time to time there would be outbursts of deafening thunder, with flashes of lightning cutting through heavy, billowing clouds, but still no rain.

And then it came. A few drops at first one morning, then Husen heard a steady patter on the roof; when he ran into the street a great cloudburst came down, great straight sheets of rain pouring, pouring down. He heard cries of joy from the other houses; children ran into the road cavorting about, hopping from one foot to the other, shedding their clothes and turning their open mouths to the sky, as if to catch a drink.

Karniti was at the market in Djatibarang and she came home in an open *betjak,* wet and dripping, but with a serene smile of happiness. Now it would be good again. They could grow vegetables in the rich volcanic soil until the time came to plant rice.

But she must have caught a chill. Since early morning she had been experiencing sudden dull pains in her stomach; now they became sharper, and when she reached home she was feverish. She hid it from Husen, fearing his concern and his temper, and busied herself preparing coffee, soup, rice and sugar cakes. By noon she was icy and shivering and had no appetite. She told Husen in a weak, dry voice, "I am not happy for eat." He took little notice until an hour later he heard her utter a sharp cry from the kitchen. The pains stabbing through her stomach had become acute, stupefying; when he reached her she was panting and clutching at the doorway for support, her breath coming in gasps.

Within an hour Husen was almost numb with panic. He had long since carried her to bed. Now as she lay there, her pale face dry and flaky with fever, exhausted with pain, choking for breath, her eyes shut and her magnificent black hair twisted all over the pillow, he knew he would have to get help. Her eyes flickered open and then shut again; they were inflamed and watering; her forehead was burning hot to his touch. The rains poured down all around them, whipping against the thin bamboo walls. There was no doctor for miles around. Desperate, Husen whispered to her that he would fetch the *dukun,* the old crone who had once nursed him back to health; despite her toothless gums, bent body and spidery fingers, Husen still had more faith in her than in the other village midwives. Karniti gasped and her breast heaved as she tried to speak; he could barely make out the words. . . . "No. . . . stay. . . ." He saw the terror in her eyes then and she was finally able to tell him about the stomach pains and to ask him to wrap a towel around her waist. When he did he saw for the first time the pool of blackish-colored blood that was slowly spreading over the bed. . . .

And that afternoon, before he could summon help, as she lay consumed by fever and pain, and Husen held her hands and whispered over and over, *"La illa haillah . . . la illa haillah. . . ."* their son was born too soon.

As she sank back into unconsciousness, Husen washed away the blood, brought clean bedding and wrapped the handful of bone and skin and blood in an old newspaper. Then he carried the blood-soaked package through the rain and across the fields to the hut of the old *dukun.*

He opened the package before her and asked her what it was.

"It's a little boy," the *dukun* said.

"No, it's blood," he said.

"It's a baby."

"No, it's blood."

"Husen . . . Husen . . . it's a baby."

He borrowed a hoe and took the package and buried it deep in the garden by the river. Then he hurried home, not feeling the rain on his face, not seeing the swollen river, not caring about the dead thing behind but only about the living girl.

Her eyes were closed and her face the color of ashes and he lay down beside her and put his arms around her and put his cheek next to her cheek and the sobs shook his body. When she opened her eyes and her eyes asked him the question, he sobbed, "That was no baby . . . only blood."

A few days after Lebaran, the joyous celebration of the Javanese new year, Husen's parents forced him to divorce his young wife. A woman doctor in Djatibarang had said she could have more children, but the old village *dukun* decreed otherwise and his father threatened to disown him and send him off the land if he did not. The parents quickly arranged his remarriage, to a plump, healthy girl from Kliwed village, whom he left after three months. Floods damaged the next rice crop, the *warung* failed, and Husen was obliged to return to the city and drive a *betjak* once more. One evening a year later he encountered Karniti in Pasar Senen. She was selling rice at an all-night stall. He scarcely recognized her. She was heavily made up, her cheeks rouged to the eyes, her eyebrows and eyelashes thick with mascara, and her mouth scarlet with lipstick. He told her to go back to the village, and tried to give her train fare. She refused. He told her he loved her and would go on loving her until the day he died, and then he went away and did not see her again.